Marketing for CPAs, Accountants, and Tax Professionals

HAWORTH Marketing Resources
Innovations in Practice & Professional Services
William J. Winston, Senior Editor

New, Recent, and Forthcoming Titles:

Marketing for CPAs, Accountants, and Tax Professionals

William J. Winston
Editor

The Haworth Press
New York • London

The Haworth Press, Inc., 10 Alice Street, Binghamton, NY 13904-1580

Library of Congress Cataloging-in-Publication Data

Winston, William J.
    Marketing for CPAs, accountants, and tax professionals / William J. Winston.
    p.   cm.
  Includes bibliographical references and index.
  ISBN 1-56024-873-4 (pbk. : alk. paper)
    1. Accounting–Marketing. 2. Tax consultants–Marketing. 3. Tax planning–Marketing. I. Title.
HF5657.W54   1994
657'.068'–dc20
                                                        93-41763
                                                          CIP

CONTENTS

PART TWO: PERSPECTIVES ON MARKETING

PART THREE: ADVERTISING

PART FOUR: MARKETING TOOLS AND STRATEGIES

ABOUT THE EDITOR

William J. Winston is a Management and Marketing Consultant based in Albany/Berkeley, California, specializing in providing advisory services to a variety of professional services. He concentrates on the governance, strategic and marketing planning, customer/client service, and applied training needs of professional service organizations. He possesses over 17 years of consulting experience.

In addition, for a decade he was Dean and Professor of Management at Golden Gate University in San Francisco, California.

Mr. Winston's instructional areas were in graduate-level economic analysis for health organizations and marketing planning and strategy development for health organizations. In addition, he has been actively involved in developing and lecturing in marketing seminars and workshops for health professionals. In fact, the graduate course that was instructed by Mr. Winston in health marketing was one of the first ever offered in the country for practitioners. Many marketing and economic papers and speeches are given for health and medical organizations each year.

Mr. Winston is also the Senior Editor in marketing for The Haworth Press, Inc. He edits four national journals, *Health Marketing Quarterly, Journal of Professional Services Marketing, Journal of Hospital Marketing,* and *Journal of Customer Service in Marketing and Management.* Books edited or written by Mr. Winston include *Marketing for Long-Term and Senior Care Services; Innovations in Hospital Marketing; Marketing Ambulatory Care Services; Marketing Strategies for Human and Social Service Agencies; How to Write a Marketing Plan for Health Organizations; Advertising Handbook for Health Care Services;* and *Marketing for Attorneys and Law Firms.*

Formerly, Mr. Winston was Managing Associate of Professional Services Marketing Group and President of Winston & Associates, economic and marketing consulting firms. His graduate education in health administration and planning was completed at The Johns Hopkins University and his doctoral work is in business management. He has been named Marketing Educator of the Year nationally and is involved in multiple professional associations.

CONTRIBUTORS

(All authors are listed with organizations with which they were affiliated at the time their article was published in the *Journal of Professional Services Marketing.*)

Paul W. Allen is affiliated with the School of Business, Mississippi State University, Meridian, MS.

Danny R. Arnold is affiliated with the School of Business, Mississippi State University, Meridian, MS.

Nora Ganim Barnes is affiliated with the Department of Marketing, University of Massachusetts–Dartmouth, North Dartmouth, MA.

Mohamed E. Bayou is affiliated with the Department of Accounting, University of Michigan–Dearborn, Dearborn, MI.

Michael H. Brown is affiliated with the School of Business, University of Mississippi, University, MS.

Gene E. Burton is affiliated with the School of Business and Administrative Sciences, California State University, Fresno, CA.

William K. Carter is affiliated with the Department of Accounting, McIntire School of Commerce, University of Virginia, Charlottesville, VA.

James R. Dalkin is a Certified Public Accountant in Arlington, VA.

Ellen Day is affiliated with the Department of Marketing, University of Georgia, Athens, GA.

Luther L. Denton is affiliated with the Department of Marketing, University of Georgia, Athens, GA.

A. Diamantopoulos is affiliated with the Department of Management and Statistics, University of Wales, Swansea, United Kingdom.

Paul Dunn is affiliated with the College of Business Administration, Northeast Louisiana University, Monroe, LA.

Dennis J. Elbert is affiliated with the Department of Marketing, University of North Dakota, Grand Forks, ND.

Brien Ellis is affiliated with the Department of Marketing, University of Kentucky, Lexington, KY.

Carl S. Farinacci is affiliated with the Department of Accounting, Clarion University of Pennsylvania, Clarion, PA.

Jeffery M. Ferguson is affiliated with the Department of Marketing, University of Colorado, Colorado Springs, CO.

Troy A. Festervand is affiliated with the Department of Marketing, University of Mississippi, University, MS.

Sherman Folland is affiliated with the Department of Economics, Oakland University, Rochester, MI.

Ralph M. Gaedeke is affiliated with the Department of Marketing, California State University, Sacramento, CA.

Barbara C. Garland is affiliated with the Department of Marketing, Clarion University of Pennsylvania, Clarion, PA.

Thomas A. Gavin is affiliated with the Department of Accounting, University of Tennessee at Chattanooga, Chattanooga, TN.

John W. Gillett is affiliated with the Department of Accounting and Business, University of North Dakota, Grand Forks, ND.

Jim Grant is affiliated with the Department of Marketing, University of South Alabama, Mobile, AL.

Jerome A. Hickner is a Certified Public Accountant, Lafayette, IN.

Lexis F. Higgins is affiliated with the Department of Marketing, University of Colorado, Colorado Springs, CO.

Arthur A. Hiltner is affiliated with the Department of Accounting, University of North Dakota, Grand Forks, ND.

Robert E. Hite is affiliated with the Department of Marketing, Kansas State University, Manhattan, KS.

Thomas G. Hodge is affiliated with the School of Business, University of Mississippi, University, MS.

Earl D. Honeycutt, Jr. is affiliated with the Department of Marketing, The Cameron School of Business, The University of North Carolina at Wilmington, Wilmington, NC.

Robert E. Jordan is affiliated with the Department of Accounting, University of Mississippi, University, MS.

Helen Ann LaFrancois is affiliated with the Department of Accounting, University of Massachusetts–Dartmouth, North Dartmouth, MA.

Abdul Aziz Abdul Latif is affiliated with the Universiti Utara Malaysia, Malaysia.

John H. Lindgren, Jr. is affiliated with the Department of Marketing, McIntire School of Commerce, University of Virginia, Charlottesville, VA.

David L. Loudon is affiliated with the Department of Management and Marketing, Northeast Louisiana University, Monroe, LA.

James R. Lumpkin is affiliated with the Department of Marketing, University of Mississippi, University, MS.

John A. Marts is affiliated with the Department of Accounting, The Cameron School of Business, The University of North Carolina at Wilmington, Wilmington, NC.

C. William McConkey is affiliated with the Department of Marketing, Northeast Louisiana University, Monroe, LA.

Jeannie S. Mosher is a Business Consultant in Lexington, KY.

Abdul Latif Shaikh Mohamed al-Murisi is affiliated with the Universiti Utara Malaysia, Malaysia.

S. O'Donohoe is affiliated with the School of Management, University of Edinburgh, Scotland.

Eric Panitz is affiliated with the Department of Marketing, University of Detroit Mercy, Detroit, MI.

Eileen Peacock is affiliated with the Department of Accounting, Oakland University, Rochester, MI.

Sandra Pelfrey is affiliated with the Department of Accounting, Oakland University, Rochester, MI.

N. Petersen is affiliated with Young Craig & Co., CPA, California.

Ralph A. Pope is affiliated with the Department of Finance, Illinois State University, Normal, IL.

Antonio L. Que is affiliated with the Department of Accounting, Clarion University of Pennsylvania, Clarion, PA.

Carmen C. Reagan is affiliated with the Department of Marketing, University of Tennessee, Chattanooga, TN.

R. Eric Reidenbach is affiliated with the Department of Marketing, University of Southern Mississippi, Hattiesburg, MS.

Robert H. Sanborn is affiliated with the Department of Accounting, University of Virginia, Charlottesville, VA.

Sandra L. Schmidt is affiliated with the Department of Marketing, University of Virginia, Charlottesville, VA.

Norman O. Schultz is affiliated with the Department of Accounting and Taxation, Colorado State University, Fort Collins, CO.

Madhav N. Segal is affiliated with the Department of Marketing, Southern Illinois University at Edwardsville, Edwardsville, IL.

L. Murphy Smith is affiliated with the Department of Accounting, Texas A & M University, College Station, TX.

Robert E. Stevens is affiliated with the Department of Marketing, Northeast Louisiana University, Monroe, LA.

James H. Thompson is affiliated with the Department of Accounting, University of Mississippi, University, MS.

Dennis H. Tootelian is affiliated with the Department of Marketing, California State University, Sacramento, CA.

Scott J. Vitell is affiliated with the Department of Marketing, The University of Mississippi, University, MS.

Thomas C. H. Wong is affiliated with the School of Business, Griffith University, Australia.

Oliver H. M. Yau is affiliated with the Department of Marketing, University of Southern Queensland, Australia.

Introduction and Overview

Welcome to the wonderful world of marketing! This book consists of articles which have appeared in the *Journal of Professional Services Marketing* as applied to marketing accounting-related services and organizations. It is intended to be a reference reader for the accounting professional who is in private practice. The book is divided into four sections and reflects applications to the generic marketing process, perspectives on marketing, advertising, and various marketing tools. It is hoped the reader will find the articles useful for enhancing their existing marketing endeavors. The Editor wishes to thank all of the authors who wrote and contributed such excellent articles for *JPSM*.

INTRODUCTION TO PART ONE:
MARKETING PROCESS

Marketing has become more widely accepted and utilized by the accounting profession during the last decade. Just as other professions have used marketing applications and strategies, accounting has followed suit. Most of this is due to the fast-changing marketplace for accounting services. The marketplace has changed significantly. Some of these changes include:

a. More accountants and related services than ever in practice;
b. Profit squeeze on existing practices;
c. Rising overhead expenses;
d. More educated accounting consumer/client;
e. Greater competition to obtain clients as well as retain existing ones;
f. Clients being more willing to change accounting professionals than before;
g. Greater questioning about cost-effectiveness of services;

1

    h. Emphasis on accountability and liability for accounting services;

    i. Changing role of accountants to expand input into strategy and managerial issues; and

    j. Expanding regulatory constraints on accountancy.

Overall, this highly competitive marketplace has created greater risk but has nurtured opportunity and creativity. Accounting firms have responded by:

    a. Being more selective in staff hiring and promotional activities;

    b. Developing improved cost and quality control systems;

    c. Emphasizing client attraction and retention; and

    d. Paying attention to client/customer service, quality, and value.

Today's accounting firm has accepted marketing more as a regular part of practice management and enhancement activities and systems.

    The top ten roles and uses for marketing in accounting firms include:

    a. Informing clients about services;

    b. Educating the community about specific issues impacting them;

    c. Attracting new clients;

    d. Retaining existing clients;

    e. Identifying potential clients;

    f. Keeping up-to-date on marketplace changes;

    g. Nurturing professional networks;

    h. Part of overall strategic planning process;

    i. Enhancing customer service and quality; and

    j. Enhancing the professional image of the firm.

Based on these goals, the main purposes of marketing in accounting firms are informational, educational, practice-development, planning, service enhancement, networking, and image-building.

    The first section of the book provides six articles that discuss various aspects of the overall marketing process and status in accounting firms.

The first article by John W. Gillett, Arthur A. Hiltner, and Dennis J. Elbert explores the use of marketing by accountants within the areas of advertising, competitive bidding, and direct solicitation. The results of their survey were derived from a sample of over 700 CPAs to gather evidence as to their utilization of the marketing mix within their respective practices.

The second article by John H. Lindgren, Jr. and William K. Carter provides an excellent follow-up to the first article by demonstrating the step-by-step approach to marketing planning as applied to accounting firms and banks as a comparison. This is especially important as the scope of financial services being provided by CPAs has expanded and diversified.

Earl D. Honeycutt, Jr. and John A. Marts contribute the third article and it reviews the marketing practices of 550 CPA firms nationwide regarding product (service), place, price, and promotional activities. They found newer and larger firms adopting marketing more readily and untargeted advertising and promotional activities to be the primary strategies.

A. Diamantopoulos, S. O'Donohoe, and N. Petersen look at the formalization of marketing in accounting firms in the fourth article. They examine how accounting firms have organized for marketing internally and their overall marketing system. This paper is very interesting because it examines how British accounting firms have adopted the process and organized. This gives our reader a different perspective for comparison.

Antonio L. Que, Carl S. Farinacci, and Barbara C. Garland present a study which surveys the historical changes in the profile of accounting service users. They identified that the amount of taxes and level of education influence the utilization of accounting services.

The last article in Part One by Carmen C. Reagan and Thomas A. Gavin reports on a study to determine the present service offerings and marketing activities of small accounting firms. The authors provide suggestions for altering the marketing mix to reposition new services in the minds of consumers.

INTRODUCTION TO PART TWO:
PERSPECTIVES ON MARKETING

There is nothing more important in successfully marketing today's accounting firm than:

a. Understanding the client it serves;
b. Gathering feedback from clients; and
c. Integrating this feedback and understanding into effectively enhancing client service and quality while offering value.

Section Two provides the reader with six articles which discuss various client and provider perspectives and perceptions about accounting services.

In the first article of Section Two, Nora Ganim Barnes and Helen Ann LaFrancois highlight how effectively accountants are meeting the needs of their clients. Over 400 accounting firms provided clients to be surveyed. Key characteristics of the firm are identified which can assist in enhancing quality and service.

Paul W. Allen and Danny R. Arnold provide a debate in the second article between a marketer and a CPA about the impact upon the marketing of accounting services from the AICPA-FTC agreement. Key points discussed are related to contingent fees, commissions, referral fees, solicitation, advertising, and trade names.

In the third article James R. Dalkin researches buyer behavior as it relates to the purchase of tax return preparation services. The study provides the basic research on client attitudes needed to create a successful marketing plan.

Jeffery M. Ferguson and Lexis F. Higgins report in the fourth article the results of a study that examines two important questions of marketing accounting practices: Do fees influence quality? and Does the CPA credential impact expected quality?

The fifth article by Thomas C. H. Wong, Oliver H. M. Yau, Abdul Latif Shaikh Mohamed Al-Murisi, and Abdul Aziz Abdul Latif compares how CPA firms perceive the concepts of advertising and marketing in the profession as situated in Malaysia and Hong Kong. There were key differences in perspectives which again, as in section one, provide the reader with some international comparison.

The last article in Part Two by Ellen Day, Luther L. Denton, and

Jerome A. Hickner reflects the increasing competitive marketplace for small accounting firms. This article found that there are two primary determinants of success for the small CPA firm: a quality image and referral networks. Strategies are suggested that can be developed based on these two attributes.

INTRODUCTION TO PART THREE: ADVERTISING

Advertising by accountants has definitely become more common today. Part Three provides six articles related to various aspects of advertising by accountants.

In the first article in Part Three, Robert E. Stevens, C. William McConkey, David L. Loudon, and Paul Dunn complete a national study of accountants' attitudes toward advertising. It appears from their findings that younger accountants are more favorable toward advertising. Seminars, yellow pages, and brochures are identified as three of the most effective advertising methods. There also appears to be some apprehension as related to the potential cost-effectiveness of advertising their services.

Robert E. Hite and Norman O. Schultz survey 500 accounting firms on their practical use of advertising in the second article. It is interesting that their findings as to the most common advertising techniques include (a) attending social events, (b) contributing to charity activities, (c) newsletters, (d) seminars, (e) press releases, (f) articles, and (g) media tours. The preferential forms of media placement for advertising include newspapers, specialty ads, direct mail, and select industry and business journals.

Jim Grant discusses the aspects of deceptive advertising in the third article. His paper addresses how effective accountants felt the efforts have been in eliminating deceptive and misleading advertising by accountants. This relates to select AICPA guidelines on attempting to police deceptive advertising by their membership. Very little direct deception was found, but rather value judgments by the accountants surveyed influenced their perceptions.

The fourth article by Sherman Folland, Eileen Peacock, and Sandra Pelfrey investigates accountants' attitudes toward advertising and the relationship of these attitudes to advertising practice.

Besides younger accountants appearing to be more favorable to advertising, female accountants appear to be less favorable than males toward it.

In the fifth article, James H. Thompson, L. Murphy Smith, and Robert E. Jordan also delve into the changes in advertising by accountants. The paper analyzes advertising by the Big Eight CPA firms in 12 selected professional journals. They found that the incidence of advertising by the Big Eight is on the rise and will continue to expand, especially in specialty niche marketing and for select product lines such as software. Targeting is becoming more refined and is being used primarily for building awareness.

The last article in Part Three is presented by Gene E. Burton. His survey identifies that consumers continue to have a more positive perception of advertising by accountants than the professionals themselves. He explores this scenario as applied to accountants, lawyers, and physicians.

INTRODUCTION TO PART FOUR: MARKETING TOOLS AND STRATEGIES

Part Four offers the reader nine articles which discuss various marketing tools for today's accounting firm. For example, the first article by Troy A. Festervand, Scott J. Vitell, and R. Eric Reidenbach provides a nuts and bolts approach to developing marketing strategies for the small accounting firm. It considers a wide range of strategies including integration, expansion, and diversification, among many others.

Thomas G. Hodge, Michael H. Brown, and James R. Lumpkin continue the discussion in the second article on marketing planning. They studied to what degree accounting firms have embraced a marketing orientation through the formal development of marketing plans and advertising campaigns. It is not too surprising that a very small percentage of the firms have developed formal written marketing plans.

The third article in Part Three by Sandra L. Schmidt and Robert H. Sanborn explores the need for a change in accounting firms to move from a product-driven to a market-oriented profession and direction. This paper also offers a thorough description of consumer-oriented financial statements.

Brien Ellis and Jeannie S. Mosher extend the traditional four 'Ps' of marketing to six 'Ps' including people and presentation in the fourth article. Their direction is to have the accounting firm develop a more specific and effective market position. Over 100 CPA firms were surveyed to identify their current market positions and recommendations are made for improving these positioning strategies.

The fifth article by Dennis H. Tootelian and Ralph M. Gaedeke explores the tax segment of the accounting profession as to the extent to which the interests of the client are represented relative to those of the profession. In addition, they look at how much variability there is in representation by service providers.

Quality will be the most important marketing strategy during the next ten years. The sixth article by Lexis F. Higgins and Jeffery M. Ferguson attempts to establish specific methods for the accountant to evaluate how their clients perceive value in the services rendered. In addition, the marketing audit is described as to how it can influence service quality.

Madhav N. Segal investigates the important area of pricing strategy for accounting firms in the seventh article. The study utilizes a multivariate approach to describe and quantify the fee structure of public accounting.

The eighth article is presented by Eric Panitz and Mohammed E. Bayou. Their study examines when CPAs use persuasion to support the growth of their firms. Their premise is that persuasion is the key construct in the promotional component of the marketing mix and is made up of two key elements, process and content. Persuasion can play a key role in retaining existing clients besides attracting new ones.

The last article in Part Four, and the book, by Ralph A. Pope presents a survey of CPA firms' participation in offering financial planning services. It investigates why they entered this market and ascertains the financial planning training of CPAs and discusses the perceptions of CPAs toward other professionals in the financial planning market.

It is obvious that the marketplace for accountants will become even more competitive in the future. This dictates that they need to become more knowledgeable about marketing and what it can do for them. However, marketing is not a savior but one managerial tool which must be integrated with finance, planning, human resource management, and general management. The effectiveness of marketing is totally dependent upon (a) the level of understanding the firm possesses about marketing, (b) their commitment to making it work effectively, (c) their ability to integrate it into the culture of the organization, and (d) giving it the financial, human resource, and moral support it requires for long-term success.

William J. Winston
Editor

PART ONE:
MARKETING PROCESS

Chapter 1

Marketing: Are Accountants Responding to the Challenge of Change?

John W. Gillett
Arthur A. Hiltner
Dennis J. Elbert

The past two decades have seen significant change for the public accounting profession. The loosening of the restraints on marketing has allowed accountants to use advertising, competitive bidding, and direct solicitation. This loosening, when coupled with a worldwide emphasis on customer service, has forced accountants to view their profession as a service-oriented business (Shenkman 1989). As a result, marketing by accountants has seen slow but steady growth (Marts, Honeycutt, and Kenan 1989). In the early stages of change within the accounting profession, not all of the range of available marketing activities were considered appropriate. Marketing was typically viewed only as advertising (Bloom 1977), and often delivered less than the expected results. Today, however, most of the accounting literature has taken a more positive broad-based approach to marketing (Beauchemnin 1989). The traditional marketing mix framework of the Four Ps, Product, Price, Promotion, and Place (Kotler 1991) is more commonly discussed in the accounting literature.

Marketing literature indicated that the four Ps have been expanded on numerous occasions to include many different components (MacGrath 1986), and as many as sixteen Ps have been in-

This chapter was first published in *Journal of Professional Services Marketing*, Vol. 8(2) 1993.

11

cluded. Noted marketing authority, Philip Kotler, ventured to expand the marketing framework when he cited six Ps and included both Political Power and Public Opinion with the traditional Four (Kotler 1984). This six-P version appears to have particular relevance for CPAs who are service providers to their clients. The six Ps of the marketing mix along with the items defined by the survey to fall within each category of P, are shown in Figure 1. Because of the unique aspects of marketing professional accounting services (Sinclair 1988), public opinion issues that include reputation, image, and other elements appear to be a natural expansion of the marketing mix for accountants. Additionally, Political Issues that include Community Involvement, Networking, and Memberships in Professional Associations are also viewed as typical activities utilized by accountants.

A study was conducted in order to gather evidence on the use of the marketing mix by accounting practitioners. The study used a questionnaire designed to provide evidence on which items of the marketing mix are important to CPAs.

THE SURVEY

The questionnaire used was pretested in a sample of 440 CPAs who are members of a state society of certified public accountants. The revised questionnaire used in the study was then mailed in June 1990 to a random sample of 700 CPAs selected from a national listing of AICPA members designated as partners, principles, or sole practitioners in public accounting firms. A second follow-up questionnaire was sent to non-respondents in July 1990. There were 239 responses received, a response rate of 34.1 percent.

When answering the questionnaire, the respondents were asked to designate their firm affiliation as a sole practitioner, or a member of a local, regional, or national firm. The analysis of the responses indicated that 32.9 percent were sole practitioners, 50.6 percent were with local firms, 7.2 percent were with regional firms, and 9.3 percent were associated with national firms. The location of the firms' practices was essentially divided into two major categories: those in cities with populations of less than 100,000, 35.8 percent of the respondents, and cities of 100,000 or larger with 64.2 percent.

FIGURE 1. The Six Ps of the Accounting Marketing Mix

Product

Auditing
MAS
Taxes
General Acct. Services
(incl. compilations)
Review
PFP
Meet Time Schedules
New Product Areas
Specialization

Price

Cash 'n' Carry Only
Delayed Billing
Accepting Credit Cards
Cash Discounts
Controlling Expenses
Quantity Discounts
Retainer Fees
Annual Price Reviews
Competitive Pricing

Promotion

After Sale Services
Advertising Specialty
Items
Newsletters, Brochures
Yellow Pages
Direct Mail
Personal Contact
Broadcast Advertising
Public Relations
Print Advertising

Place

Client Meeting Rooms
Office Location
Fax Machines
Parking Availability
Going to Client Office
Waiting Room
Atmosphere
Office Signage

Public Opinion

Customer Relations
Program
Client Surveys
Reputation of Firm
Seminars for Clients
Published Policy
Statements
Reward Personnel
Accomplishments
Employ Market
Research

Political Issues

Community
Involvement
Club Membership
City Gov't
Involvement
Chamber of
Commerce
Industry Contacts
Professional
Memberships
Networking

13

As noted, the majority of these respondents were from larger, more urban communities.

The analysis also revealed that over one-third (35.9 percent) of the firms had a person coordinating marketing activities for their organization. The responses further indicated that the responding CPAs had been in their current accounting position for an average of 9.4 years and worked in accounting for an average of 19.3 years. While 77.4 percent of the respondents indicated that they had taken at least one college level marketing course, the most frequent source of their marketing skills was from on-the-job training.

FINDINGS

As a part of the study, the respondents were asked to review each of the six Ps, as shown in Figure 1, and indicate which items were important for their firm. A summary of their responses is shown in Table 1. The analysis of their responses provides some insights into their opinions regarding the relative importance given to specific marketing activities within their organizations. The responses were grouped by community size, type of firm (national, regional, local), and number of partners, and the "groupings" analyzed for significant differences.

It is interesting to note that activities from all of the six Ps are considered important by the CPAs. The category of product (as shown in Table 1) had six of its nine items receiving a response rate above 60 percent. Given the strong orientation of accounting to provide a quality product this is not unexpected. However, by isolating the responses to the top ten marketing activities of all the Ps except product (as shown in Table 2), each of the remaining five Ps are represented by at least one item. This demonstrates that each of the six Ps has particular relevance for CPAs. The remaining parts of this section will discuss the responses on each of the six Ps.

Product

The first five items in Category I-Product were the traditional accounting services typically offered by CPAs. It is not surprising, therefore, that a high percentage of the respondents checked those items. However, it is interesting that over 84 percent of the respondents see Taxes or General Accounting Services (including compilations) and 60-65 percent of the firms see Auditing, Management Advisory Services, and Review as important for their firms. When the groupings were analyzed, significant differences in the responses related to Product were revealed. The analysis tended to support current accounting literature that maintains the smaller firms and individual practitioners are not doing as much auditing, reviewing, or specializing as the larger firms. The analysis further revealed that taxes, general accounting services, and personal financial planning are important to accountants regardless of the size of the community, the type of the firm, or size of firm.

Price

The category of Price was designed to gather information on two areas: setting the cost of the service and collecting the receivable. In the area of setting the cost, the three items of controlling expenses (70.5 percent), competitive pricing (71.3 percent) and annual price reviews (52.7 percent) received the largest number of responses. In the area of collecting the receivable, it is interesting to note that 8.4 percent of the respondents think that accepting credit cards is important for their firms and at the same time a relatively small percentage (11.8 percent) of the respondents use Cash 'n' Carry only. When the responses were grouped, the analysis revealed few significant differences in the category of price. However, the larger firms tended to consider quantity discounts as more important to them than their smaller counterparts. The lack of significant differences here may be tied to the service aspect of public accounting.

Promotion

In the area of promotion, almost 94 percent of the respondents think that personal contact is critical for their firms. The next highest response rates were attained by Newsletters and Brochures (67.1 percent), After Sale Services (55.3 percent), and Public Relations (49.4 percent). The items involving advertising: specialty

TABLE 1. Marketing Activities Indicated as Important for Their Firms (Percentage of CPAs Responses) N = 239

CATEGORY I–Product	%	CATEGORY II–Price	%	CATEGORY III–Promotion	%
Auditing	60.8	Cash 'n' Carry Only	11.8	After Sale Services	55.3
Management Advisory Services	63.7	Delayed Billing	36.7	Advertising Specialty Items	11.0
Taxes	95.4	Accepting Credit Cards	8.4	Newsletters, Brochures	67.1
General Acct. Services (incl. compilations)	84.0	Cash Discounts	5.5	Yellow Pages	30.8
Review	65.0	Controlling Expenses	70.5	Direct Mail	23.2
Personal Financial Planning	48.5	Quantity Discounts	5.5	Personal Contact	93.7
Meet Time Schedules	62.0	Retainer Fees	43.9	Broadcast Advertising	4.6
New Product Areas	31.6	Annual Price Reviews	52.7	Public Relations	49.4
Specialization	49.4	Competitive Pricing	71.3	Print Advertising	23.2
Other (12)		Other (8)		Other (11)	

CATEGORY IV–Place	%	CATEGORY V-P–Public Opinion	%	CATEGORY VI–Political Issues	%
Client Meeting Rooms	60.3	Customer Relations Program	39.7	Community Involvement	78.1
Office Location	78.1	Client Surveys	25.3	Club Membership	59.1
Fax Machines	55.3	Reputation of Firm	93.2	City Gov't Involvement	15.6
Parking Availability	56.1	Seminars for Clients	45.6	Chamber of Commerce	50.6
Going to Client Office	84.0	Published Policy Statements	8.4	Industry Contacts	54.0
Waiting Room Atmosphere	44.7	Reward Personnel Accomplishments	35.0	Professional Memberships	73.4
Office Signage	26.6	Employ Market Research	10.5	Networking	50.6
Other (8)		Other (4)		Other (3)	

TABLE 2. Top Ten Marketing Activities Indicated as Important for Their Firms (Excludes Product) (Percentage of CPAs Responses)

Activity	%	Category
Personal Contact	93.7	Promotion
Reputation of Firm	93.2	Public Opinion
Going to Client Office	84.0	Place
Community Involvement	78.1	Political Issues
Office Location	78.1	Place
Professional Memberships	73.4	Political Issues
Competitive Pricing	71.3	Price
Controlling Expense	70.5	Price
Newsletters, Brochures	67.1	Promotion
Client Meeting Room	60.3	Place

items, print, broadcast, and direct mail all acheived the lowest response percentages. When grouped by the type of firm, further analysis did reveal some significant differences in the respondents' opinions as to what is important for their firms. The national firms were significantly more concerned with advertising, specialty items, yellow pages, and direct mail than the local firms. The majority of respondents did not believe that those items were critical for their firms. The statistical analysis indicated that the response from local firms was not as intense as from the national firms. Another area of disagreement was Public Relations. The national firms believe that Public Relations is critical for their firm. Local firms, however, while expressing their opinion as to Public Relation's importance did have significantly less intensity in their belief.

When the data was analyzed by the number of partners in the firm the most interesting discovery was that the larger the firm, the more concern for Public Relations. When analyzed by community size, the larger population centers were more concerned with public relations.

Place

The responses in this area indicate that the firm's office location (78.1 percent) and the ability to go to a client's office (84.0 percent) are very important to these CPAs. Having a professional waiting room atmosphere, parking available, and a client meeting room were considered important by approximately one-half of the respondents. Only 26.6 percent of the respondents indicated that office signage is important. One interesting factor is that over half of the respondents (55.3 percent) indicate that a fax machine, a relatively new piece of office equipment, is important for their firms. When analyzing these responses by the groups, the only significant differences in opinions were on the items fax machines and client meeting room. These items were believed to be of less importance by the firms with the fewest number of partners.

Public Opinion

The predictable response of the reputation of the firm as important was checked by 93.2 percent of the respondents. The contrast with employing market research (10.5 percent) is noteworthy in that marketing research is often utilized to assess or monitor the image or reputation of an organization. The item with the smallest percent of respondents indicating it as important was published policy statements with only 8.4 percent viewing this item as important. It is apparent from the analysis of the responses that the larger firms are much more likely to consider customer relation programs, to offer seminars for clients, to have published policy statements, and to employ market research than their smaller counterparts.

Political Issues

The traditional areas of community involvement and professional memberships were both viewed by over 70 percent of the respondents as important for their firms. Club Membership (59.1 percent), Chamber of Commerce Involvement (50.6 percent), Networking (50.6 percent), and Industry Contacts (54.0 percent) were of moderate importance. Of note is the fact that only 15.6 percent checked

City Government Involvement as important. The statistical analysis of this area shows that the respondents from the larger firms and/or those practicing in a larger community were more likely to view industry contacts and networking as important for their firms. The analysis does show that the smaller town CPAs view city government involvement as more important for their firms.

CONCLUSION

Input regarding the value of marketing activities for accounting firms was solicited by asking respondents to complete a detailed questionnaire on an expanded marketing mix. The traditional four Ps were expanded to key in on the critical service dimensions of accounting. The expanded mix components of Public Opinion and Political Issues were added to focus on the importance of firm reputation, community involvement, and professional memberships.

The respondents' answers to the detailed marketing mix show that accountants are still very conservative in their approach to utilizing marketing tools. This is evidenced by the strong concern expressed under the area of Public Opinion as 93.2 percent of the respondents believe that the reputation of their firm is important. At the same time traditional marketing tools such as customer relations programs, client surveys, and the use of market research that aid in measuring the firm's reputation were all viewed as *much* less important. It is apparent that accountants still need to adopt a more aggressive marketing attitude. It has often been said that marketing does not start when the telephone is answered, but rather marketing makes the telephone ring. Accountants know that their reputation is their best marketing tool. Perhaps, they need to work on making that phone ring.

REFERENCES

Beauchemnin, Timothy J. (1989). "Guidelines for Mobilizing Your Firm's Marketing Efforts." *Practical Accountant*, June, pp. 86-90.

Bloom, Paul N. (1977). "Advertising in the Professions: The Critical Issues." *Journal of Marketing*, July, pp. 103-110.

Kotler, Philip (1991). *Marketing Management–Analysis, Planning, Implementation and Control*, Englewood Cliffs: Prentice Hall, Inc. 1991.

_____ (1984). "Re-Think the Marketing Concept." *Marketing News*, September 14.

MacGrath, A.J. (1986). "When Marketing Services, 4 P's are Not Enough." *Business Horizons*, May-June, p. 49.

Marts, John A., Earl D. Honeycutt, and Jane A. Kenan (1989). "How CPA Firms Market Their Services." *Journal of Accountancy*, February, pp. 111-113.

Shenkman, Martin M. (1989). "Marketing Tools for the New or Small Accounting Firm." *Journal of Accountancy*, February, pp. 60-64.

Sinclair, Roger (1988). "A Recipe for Growth." *Journal of Accountancy*, May, pp. 116-117.

Chapter 2

The Service Marketing Planning Process: A Case for Accounting Firms and Banks

John H. Lindgren, Jr.
William K. Carter

Approximately two-thirds of our private-sector work force is now employed in service industries. In the public sector, of course, virtually all workers are engaged in providing services. The service sector of the economy includes financial institutions, such as banks, brokers, and insurance companies, and professional service firms, such as medical, dental, architectural, engineering, financial counseling, and CPA firms. These firms are now devoting increasing amounts of attention to their marketing function. Today most service firms face a market that is extremely dynamic. Providers of services have realized that the changes in the markets they serve no longer allow strategies that focus on being "all things to all people." A quick look at the statistics of the 1980 census demonstrates some of the changes to which service firms must respond.

1. In 1980, 50 percent of our population was over 30 years old.
2. The number of households is increasing three times as fast as the population.

This chapter was first published in *Journal of Professional Services Marketing*, Vol. 1(3) 1986.

3. In 1950, the average household consisted of 3.37 people. In 1980, this had declined to 2.76 people per household, with over half consisting of one or two people.
4. Over 25 percent of all households are non-family oriented.
5. Over 43 percent of all married women with children under six years old are employed.
6. Currently, approximately one in five families is a single-parent family. (In 1970, this figure was about one in ten.)
7. During the past decade alone, those earnings over $25,000 a year increased from 4 percent to 35 percent, while those earnings under $10,000 a year decreased from 53 percent to 21 percent.

These trends signify a changing America. However, these demographic changes lead to other modifications in peoples' aittitudes, values, and lifestyles. These statistics represent changing markets, and today these markets are being altered more rapidly than in any other period of our history.

In the past, we have had a constant stream of change and we have reacted to it. In the 1950s when our economy was expanding at a tremendous rate, people wanted big cars, luxurious homes, and all the other trappings. Best of all–they got them! Then the 1960s came along, when people were into themselves, the "me generation." Finally, we experienced the rude economic awakening of the 1970s. Due to regulation of the banking industry, for example, the changes of the past did not call for innovative ways to market banks' products/services. Ethical prohibitions had a similar effect on marketing by CPA firms and other professional organizations. Under our present less-regulated environment, these types of firms find themselves in a highly competitive market. These changes have allowed consumers in these fields a wider choice in the marketplace, and because of the changes not only in demographics but also in value structure, we have seen two major types of consumers emerge.

The first type is the consumer looking for what he or she perceives to be most economic (cheapest) offering in the marketplace. The second type is looking for the best quality offering, even with the higher price tags of these products/services. Each type of consumer looks for different attibutes in products/services, and we have seen evidence of these two types of consumers by analyzing sales trends. For example:

1. sales trends of very cheap versus very expensive liquor;
2. sales of lower-priced automobiles or of Mercedes Benz, BMW, and luxury sports cars;
3. sales trends at Kmart and stores such as Bloomingdale's and Saks Fifth Avenue;
4. discount broker services and firms such as Merrill Lynch.

All of these trends suggest the direction strategic market planning must take for service firms. The way we react to these changes will determine whether our firms succeed or fail.

The implication for middle-range institutions is clear. These are the firms that may be squeezed out. Mid-price, mid-quality service firms need to explore technology advancement to either lower prices and become the cheapest or enhance their offerings to tap the quality market.

The implication for service firms striving to be low-price leaders is that they need to find ways to lower costs. The techniques of mass discounters' use of low overhead, low manpower commitments, and high turnover of services seem to be the proper direction, both for providers of retail services, such as retail banks, and for providers of mostly commercial services such as CPA firms.

Service firms after the quality market must consider the opposite approach, the development of enhanced services for all customers and specialized custom-tailored programs for the most profitable customers. The result of this approach will be to provide service firms with long-term customer relationships that will be profitable for both the firm and its customers.

These conditions point toward a need for integrated and continual market planning in the dynamic environment faced by service firms today. The use of continued planning allows a firm to become offensive rather than defensive in the market place. It allows for proactive behavior rather than reactive. It provides the institution with the tools and information to become an innovator that will provide strong customer alliance.

The purpose of this chapter is to detail the steps in performing a situational analysis for a service firm. In addition, a growth model will be presented for analyzing future strategies. Examples will be presented from a retail-oriented service organization (banking) and a commercially oriented organization (CPA firms).

SITUATIONAL ANALYSIS

A situational analysis is a study of those variables which help the firm develop the background material to be used in suggesting strategies for the future.

The situational analysis represents the crucial first step in the marketing planning process. It can provide the benefits of new market and service identification. The assimilation of strengths and weaknesses of the firm, its competition, the market, and external environmental factors will provide the future strategic direction of the firm. Each of the four areas of the situational analysis will be discussed to provide a framework for assessing the strategic direction of the firm.

The Firm

An analysis of the strengths and weaknesses of the firm itself provides managers with a basis for understanding those attributes of the firm that differentiate it from other organizations. Exhibit 1 gives some examples of critical questions to be answered concerning the firm.

Using the accounting profession and the banking industry as examples, a large bank or CPA firm's answers to the questions in Exhibit 1 might include the following points, among others: A single firm-wide administrative structure may have benefits in coordinating the operation and control of all the different local units, but such a structure does not allow for adaptation to local conditions. Large, full-service offices in major cities may be local market leaders, but then a single office will have to serve a large geographical area. A large bank or CPA firm also is capable of employing technical specialists whose expertise in a particular area is unsurpassed anywhere in the industry, but the firm may have great difficulty in developing generalists who can individually serve all the needs of a small client. Finally, a large bank or CPA firm is capable of providing an extremely wide range of services to its clients, but will have a difficult time trying to be a market leader in all areas simultaneously.

Many of the points listed above could apply to large banks and large CPA firms. For small firms, just the opposite might be true. The objective in answering these questions is for the firm to obtain an understanding of its present position in the marketplace that will permit its strengths and weaknesses to be incorporated in an overall marketing program.

The Competition

An understanding of the firm's competition enables managers to identify areas of comparative advantage and disadvantage in the marketplace. In addition, the periodic monitoring of competitors helps the firm to stay abreast of changes in competitor's marketing programs and to identify strategic opportunities.

Exhibit 2 provides sample questions for monitoring competitors.

For example, a small accounting firm might identify other local firms, commercial tax preparers, and nearby offices of large CPA firms as its principal competitors. For each of the competitors, the firm should identify the range of services, method of delivering those services, fee structure, and communication techniques used. Completing this step will provide the starting point for identifying competitors' strengths and weaknesses. A potential future compet-

---

EXHIBIT 1: The Firm

---

1. What are the strengths and weaknesses of the firm's organizational structure?

2. What are the strengths and weaknesses of the firm's distribution points?

3. What are the strengths and weaknesses of the firm's personnel?

4. What are the strengths and weaknesses of the firm's support facilities?

5. What are the strengths and weaknesses of the firm's present service offerings?

---

itor of both a small bank and of a small CPA firm is demonstrated by the recently established Sears Financial Centers. These centers provide tax preparation, personal financial planning, investment counseling, and a myriad of other financial services in Sears retail stores.

Combining the data on the firm and its competition will suggest areas in which the firm holds a potential advantage over its competitors in the marketplace. Equally important, the organization might identify some areas of disadvantage calling for additional allocations of resources, or possibly a decision to phase out an area of service.

The Market

Central to any intelligence system for a firm is an understanding and analysis of the needs and wants of customers and potential customers. Such an understanding will enable managers to identify current needs in the marketplace and provide direction for future offerings.

Exhibit 3 demonstrates the types of data needed for a firm to understand its customers and potential customers.

Both a small local CPA firm and a small bank might find that their customers view them as trusted, long-term advisers and problem solvers on a wide range of business and financial topics. However, many potential customers may have an opposite view. This situation presents an opportunity for a firm to capitalize on its present clientele to more effectively serve a wider range of clients.

A segment of the market presently being *least* served by the

---

EXHIBIT 2

6. Who are the principal competitors?

7. For each principal competitor, what are the components of its marketing mix (product, price, place, promotion)?

8. For each principal competitor, what are the answers to the questions in Exhibit 1?

9. What organizations represent potential future competitors?

EXHIBIT 3

---

10. What image of the firm is held by customers? By potential customers?

11. What image of the firm's competitors is held by customers? By potential customers?

12. How, why, and when do the firm's customers use its services?

13. What market segments are presently served least effectively by the industry? Most effectively?

14. What new requirements are evolving from the various market segments?

---

accounting profession might be the market for reviews (but not audits) of financial statements. Clients who are not convinced of the benefits of an audit but who want to have a CPA's name associated with their financial report in some way may be able to use the review. In contrast, a small CPA firm may find that the market segment being *most* effectively served by the accounting profession is the annual audit of huge public corporations whose sheer size effectively excludes all but the largest CPA firm from conducting such an audit.

As to the last question in Exhibit 3, a new requirement among clients of CPA firms is the need for deferred compensation plans that take advantage of IRA and Keogh regulations, and that are integrated with the client's existing payroll systems.

Answers such as these to the questions concerning customers and potential customers will lead the firm to ideas for new services it might offer and for new customers to whom it might offer its existing services. This information, combined with the earlier information on the firm's competitive advantages and disadvantages, should suggest important market segments that the firm can serve.

The External Environment

The external environment consists of areas over which the firm has least control in the short run. However, it must react to changes from these uncontrollable factors. Constant monitoring of the external environment allows the firm to adapt all the components of its marketing mix to changing conditions. Exhibit 4 identifies the areas of external environment that the firm should actively monitor.

Given the new competitive arena that financial institutions face because of deregulation, the external environment has become extremely important. Recent legislation has allowed a multitude of new products and businesses for today's banks. The developments in legislation dealing with insurance provide a very recent example of these important legal changes.

In the recent recession, for example, a CPA firm needed to recognize that changes occurred in the problems its clients faced and the services they need. Rather than seeking help in executive recruitment, clients needed advice in how to handle executive terminations. Plans for expansion into new lines of business may have changed to a desire to dispose of less profitable operations the client could no longer afford to own.

Cultural and social changes are occurring that have an impact on a CPA firm's marketing mix. There is an increased public expectation that charities and other nonprofit entities should disclose information on their financial activities. On the political and legal front, a prime example of the impact of change is provided by the passage of the Foreign Corrupt Practices Act and the many problems it created for the clients of CPA firms. The new requirements imposed on accounting systems by this Act offered great potential for CPA firms in serving their clients. In the area of ethical standards, advertising and direct solicitation of prospective clients are now socially accepted phenomena, and are recognized as such by the changes that have been made in the accounting profession's code of ethics.

EXHIBIT 4

---

15. What are the major economic developments influencing the firm?

16. What cultural and social changes are affecting the opportunities of the firm?

17. What changes in the structure of the political and legal environment are having an impact on the firm?

GROWTH MODEL

The situational analysis provides managers with a solid grip on the past and present strengths and weaknesses of the firm, its competition, the market, and the external environment. A thorough understanding of each of these factors will present management with a number of opportunities for future growth; however, because of limited resources, it is vital that managers have mechanisms for prioritizing these various opportunities. The growth vector model provides a framework for analyzing alternative future directions. The major advantage of the growth vector model is that it forces management not just to analyze new services but also to look at new markets. The evaluation of new markets will lead directly to market segmentation and to target marketing, which are the heart of a marketing plan.

The Growth Vector Model

The growth vector model is a simple 2 × 2 matrix in which alternative services and market conditions are presented. It divides services into the two categories of present services and new services. Similarly, markets are dichotomized into markets presently served and new, as yet untouched, markets. Figure 1 presents this matrix with the accompanying strategies for each cell.

Market Penetration

The most obvious way to grow is aggressively to get present customers to use more of present services. This strategy is called "cross selling" in the banking industry. A cross-selling strategy attempts to develop the firm's clientele into multi-service customers.

For banks, there are a number of programs available that focus on market penetration: service packages that combine several services for each customer, personal banker programs, seminars on financial planning, reduced loan rates or fees for high balance customers, interest rate "hotlines," and trust packages.

For CPA firms, there are similar examples of market penetration:

FIGURE 1

services present services	new services
present markets	market presentation	service development
new markets	market development	diversification

using the preparation of a client's tax returns as a first step toward providing continuing tax planning advice, bidding competitively on a small service to gain an opportunity to demonstrate the need for a larger-scale consulting engagement, and providing personal financial planning services to the individual officers and directors of a potential client company in hopes of being chosen to provide a larger scale service to the company.

All of these strategies have one thing in common–to get our present customers to utilize more of our present services. If you don't believe this strategy is a good one, just look at what happened to Arm & Hammer baking soda sales when they used it!

Service Development

The second alternative for future growth lies in the area of development of new services for present customers. While government regulation and ethical prohibitions have limited this area in the past, recent changes have resulted in a multitude of new service offerings.

By far, banks have instituted this strategy more than any other since deregulation. Some of the new service offerings by banks include sweep accounts, variable rate mortgages, in-home banking, and, now, super now accounts. The new services have been developed, for the most part, for banks' present customers.

The accounting profession had also had an expansion of its services. Specifically, CPAs now provide not just audits of financial statements, but also reviews and compilations, which are services that are technically very different from audits and which appeal to different potential clients.

While some of these services can and have been used to attract new customers (diversification strategy), the marketing mix used to implement a diversification strategy would be different. In the product marketing field Bic has utilized this strategy with great success with successive introductions of pens, razor blades, and lighters.

Market Development

Market development is probably the strategy most under-utilized by service firms. The purpose of market development is to get new customers to use the present services of the firm. The most successful banks, for example, have implemented this strategy by geographic expansion: that is, by offering present services to new customers by branching to new areas.

Market development strategy is the use of segmentation and the "packaging" of services to specific target markets. Examples of this type of strategy by a bank include: financial counseling for affluent customers, newcomer programs, expansion of ATM networks and small business/professional packages. The purpose of these types of programs is to attract new customers to our institution by combining services that each segment needs. In the accounting profession, the development of microcomputer tax software is allowing some CPA firms to profitably provide tax return preparation services to tax clients that they would not have targeted in the past, because competitive fees were too low to cover personnel costs. Computerized tax return preparation has lowered costs, for some firms, to a point where a competitive fee can now provide profits for the firm from this market.

While this strategy utilizes present services, specific needs of a particular segment might suggest new services that are needed. In this situation, the strategy would fall closer to diversification. Danskins has successfully implemented this strategy through their Danskins-is-not-just-for-dancers campaign, and Johnson & Johnson Baby Shampoo has been extremely successful in marketing to a new market, that is, to adults.

Diversification

With the deregulation of the banking industry, the most promising strategy for future growth lies in diversification. Diversification is the offering of new services to new markets. It involves the process of developing new business outside the mainstream of present business offerings.

This strategy will broaden the mission of a bank. Examples might include handling of "turn key" business systems for certain segments (becoming the accounting and control consultant for a segment) or the expansion into real estate services that would aid customers in finding, buying, financing, and maintaining their homes.

Similar developments are foreseeable in the accounting profession. The availability of microcomputers and spreadsheet software will permit a CPA firm to efficiently provide many small businesses with systems that integrate cash management, financial forecasting, and budgeting, in addition to routine accounting support such as payroll and receivables management. Routine services such as payroll can also be modified in response to market changes. For example, IRA and Keough plans can now be efficiently integrated into a small client's payroll system.

This broadened mission is totally market driven rather than service driven. Too often the focus is on expansion using the services already available rather than developing the services that a new segment needs. In the product area, Philip Morris has been extremely successful with this strategy by diversifying into sport complexes, soft drinks, and beer.

CONCLUSION

The growth vector model forces management to look at oppurtunities related to present services, new potential services, present customers, and new potential customers. Each of the four strategies has an inherent risk potential and thus a different profit potential for the firm. The balance of risk and profits and consequences for future growth strategy(s) that an institution should form are determined by the competitive situation, the cost of the strategy, and the overall growth potential of each strategy.

Chapter 3

Marketing by Professionals as Applied to CPA Firms: Room for Improvement?

Earl D. Honeycutt, Jr.
John A. Marts

INTRODUCTION

Since the lifting of the codes of ethics in the late 1970s, more and more professional firms have adopted marketing techniques. Today it is not unusual to observe advertisements in various media for physicians, accountants, and lawyers. However, as Wheatley (1983) pointed out, many of today's professionals have negative images of "marketing." This attitude can likely be traced to the fact that most professionals do not truly understand marketing. Too many professionals perceive marketing to be only advertising and promotion. And, most professionals believe they are above using any type of "hard-sell" techniques. Some are of the opinion that the ethics of their profession, even though not legally binding, demand that they not engage in overt selling techniques (Marts, Honeycutt, and Kenan 1989). But the viewpoint that marketing is simply advertising and selling is too limiting.

Professionals should realize that marketing is the process of scanning the market and determining which services are needed by the consumers found there. The professional firm then provides the

This chapter was first published in *Journal of Professional Services Marketing*, Vol. 6(1) 1990.

desired services to consumers in the appropriate form, time, place, and at an acceptable price. The formulation of long-range plans permits professionals to better deal with an unknown future. Timely reviews of marketing plans also ensure the professional firm remains aware of a changing marketplace and makes needed adjustments to the services offered. It is only after the decisions have been made about product (service), place, and price that advertising/ promotion decisions should be made (Van Doren and Smith 1987).

Many professionals believe they are above marketing, but the reality is that all professionals market, even if it is informally (Gelb, Smith, and Gelb 1988). As competition increases, professionals will continue to market; but the need to market more formally and successfully will intensify (Bloom 1984).

LITERATURE REVIEW

The use of marketing thinking and practice has been moving slowly into the professions for many years. In 1977, Kotler and Connor pointed out this trend and suggested that professionals would have to "cope" with three significant forces. These forces were:

1. Assaults on Professional Codes of Ethics.
2. Changing Expectations of Clients.
3. Increased Competition.

Kotler and Connor continued that most professionals were "ill-equipped" to cope with these forces, for the following reasons:

1. Disdain of Commercialism–Few professionals view themselves as business people. Many claim to be motivated by providing service to clients and, therefore, do not enjoy discussing fees.
2. Association Codes of Ethics–Professional bans against advertising, direct solicitation, and referral commissions were banned. These bans have been declared illegal since 1978, but their influence remains.
3. Equating Marketing with Selling–Most professionals make the mistake of viewing marketing as selling. Marketing is a much larger force than selling.

By remaining uninformed of marketing concepts and practices, professionals operate without the necessary tools to adapt to a rapidly changing environment. Kotler and Connor state that it ". . . can be fatal in a down market when competitors do" (understand marketing concepts and practices).

In a more recent article, Van Doren and Smith (1987) restate the fact that professionals must recognize their practice is a business and develop an ethical, dignified marketing plan that allows them to better position their expertise to clients. Advertising may or may not be part of the marketing plan. The authors reported that a 1985 American Bar Association survey found lawyers used various methods of making clients aware of legal services. Yellow pages were used by 74 percent of the responding lawyers, 16 percent used newspapers, 8 percent magazines, 7 percent TV, 5 percent radio, and 4 percent direct mail. Van Doren and Smith concluded that a professional services marketing plan:

> . . . clearly specifies a market position and gives the (professional) firm an objective framework which can be used to assess periodically the wisdom of maintaining that position. The time of being all things to all people is past for professionals. (p. 71)

Numerous articles have been written about the use of advertising by professionals. In an early study, Oliver and Posey (1980) examined the perceptions of national and state CPA firms about advertising. There were distinct differences between state CPA firms and national accounting firms. Most state firms did not believe consumer advertising would result in lower fees or more intelligent selection of accounting firms. Also, state firms felt advertising would result in a lower professional image. The national firms, on the other hand, did not believe advertising would have a detrimental effect on the accounting profession and felt advertising would play an important role in the future of public accounting. Both groups agreed the use of advertising by CPA firms was growing and would continue to grow.

An article by Hite and Bellizzi (1986) examined the effects on consumers of advertising by professionals. The investigators found that consumer attitudes about professional advertising were generally favorable. Consumers believed advertising would not lower professional image, could be used tastefully, and that useful information would be provided. Respondents also felt it was more proper for CPAs to advertise than lawyers or physicians. The authors suggested that professionals should reexamine their fears of advertising.

In another study that contrasted lawyers and accountants, Hite and Schultz (1987) found that public accountants' viewpoint of advertising was more conservative than industrial (private) accountants. Most CPA firms also agreed they would advertise only if other firms started to advertise. The media used and advertising objectives reported by the CPA firms are shown on Table 1. Hite and Schultz found that public relations was likely to remain the lead element in the promotional mix because most professional firms would remain relatively conservative. Finally, professionals were reminded that a well-conceived advertising program provides benefits simultaneously to clients and the accounting firm.

In a subsequent article by Hite, Schultz, and Weaver (1988), it was found that advertisement content had changed since 1979. For example: location, services provided, special talents, and degrees were now being listed at a higher rate in professional advertisements. The authors stated that accounting firms should be even more specific about how their services can benefit consumers, as well as the type of technical support to be provided.

Finally, Hite and Fraser (1988) conducted a meta-analysis and concluded that with each additional year of advertising, attitudes by professionals and consumers have become more favorable. Reservations about negative effects have decreased and expectations of consumer benefits have increased. The study implied that advertising by professionals has been neither "offensive or distasteful," but not as informative as it possibly could be.

RESEARCH OBJECTIVES

The specific objectives of this study were to determine for professionals, the following:

1. Long-range planning activities.
2. Methods used to set fees.

3. Physical distribution decisions used.
4. Methods of communication with clients.
5. Usage of advertising to attract new business.
6. Focus of advertisements.
7. Details of advertisements.
8. Success and effectiveness of advertisements.
9. Future action of firm regarding advertising.
10. Feelings of non-advertisers about advertising trend.

METHODOLOGY

Twenty-five hundred randomly selected American Institute of Certified Public Accountants (AICPA) members were mailed a questionnaire and postage paid envelope. Five-hundred fifty questionnaires were returned from the single mailing for a response rate of 22 percent. In Table 2 is information regarding years in business and annual billings of responding firms. The sample was regionally representative with returns from the following areas: Midwest (23 percent), Southeast (22 percent), Northeast (22 percent), Pacific (10 percent), Mountain (15 percent), and Southwest (8 percent).

FINDINGS

Several questions were asked that examined long-range planning and planning, in general, by CPA firms. First, the number of firms using these procedures is listed in Table 3.

The behavior of firms varied by size. Those with annual billings less than $1 million were much less likely to be using all three of the above planning activities. Above $5 million in size nearly all CPA firms report adoption of five-year plans, mission statements, and organized plans to create images.

In regard to establishing client fees, the following methods were reported in Table 4. It appears most CPA firms use a cost-based method of determining professional fees. Only about one in three firms appear to be negotiating with clients or considering their competitors' pricing actions.

TABLE 1

CPA Use of Advertising Media	
Newspapers	58%
Specialty Advertising	52%
Direct Mail	50%
Gen. Bus. Magazine	39%
Industry Journals	23%
Technical Journals	21%
Local TV	47%
National TV or Billboards	0%

Advertising Objectives	
Increase Awareness	97%
Enhance Image	92%
Increase Tax Planning Business	87%
Cultivate Public Relations	83%
Increase Advising Business	60%

TABLE 2

Total Years in Business

Category	Percent
Less than 5 years	36
5 to 10 years	21
Between 10 & 20 years	24
Greater than 20 years	19

Firm's Annual Billings

Category	Percent
Less than $50,000	13
$50,001 to $100,000	16
$100,001 to $500,000	53
$500,001 to $1,000,000	9
$1,000,001 to $5,000,000	8
Greater than $5,000,000	1

TABLE 3

Planning Activities by CPA Firms

Five-Year Plan	21%
Mission Statement	20%
Organized Image Plan	25%

TABLE 4

Methods for Setting Fees

Set By Cost	79%
What Client Will Pay	33%
What Competitors' Charge	31%

The authors also wanted to determine what, if any, physical distribution or "place" decisions were being taken by professionals. CPA firms' responses are reported in Table 5. This information infers that over half the firms have decorated their offices for clients, which means that the remaining half either do not have clients visiting their office(s) or felt this was not important. Professional accountants do locate close to principal accounts, which suggests a desire to make transactions convenient for themselves and clients.

Next, CPAs were asked to list the methods used to communicate with clients (see Table 6). The number of CPAs communicating via yellow pages appears to correspond to earlier studies (73 percent vs. 74 percent). However, it does appear that the number of professional accountants using newspapers, radio, TV, and direct mail is higher than previously reported by other professional groups. Also, approximately 27 percent of responding accounting professionals admitted to using some form of paid advertisements.

Accountants also appear to target ads at different client segments. Approximately 23 percent concentrate their ads at a specific customer segment, 43 percent advertise to different segments, and 34 percent reported running global or image advertisements. Another question specifically asked: "What percentage of new clients are

TABLE 5

Place Decisions

Locating Close to Primary Accounts	43%
Opening More Than One Location	15%
Decorating Offices For Clients	52%

TABLE 6

Communication Methods

Method	Percent Using
One-Line Yellow Pages	73%
Block Ads in Yellow Pages	45%
Local Newspaper	31%
Regional Newspaper	17%
National Newspaper	16%
Professional Journals	22%
Company Brochures/Bulletins	46%
Radio	18%
TV	16%

generated by advertising?" It appears that 66 percent of the respondents who advertise do not know or attribute less than 5 percent of their clients to advertising results (see Table 7).

Information about the effectiveness of these advertisements was also sought. Only 28 percent of those firms using advertisements attempt to assess their effectiveness. Of the small number assessing their advertisements, methods reported included: clients were questioned (by 8 firms), advertising costs vs. billings were compared (6 firms), executive judgement was used (2), advertising objectives vs. results (2), and annual review (2). It would seem, therefore, that little objective evaluation of professional advertising is being undertaken.

TABLE 7

Clients Generated by Advertising	
Less than 5%	54%
> 5% but less than 20%	22%
Between 20% and 49.9%	9%
Greater than 50%	3%
Unknown	12%

In an effort to better understand advertising strategies, CPA firms were questioned about the content of their advertisements. Advertising content provides an indication of the purpose of the communication. The majority (83 percent) who advertise stated their advertisements only offered details related to services offered. Approximately 22 percent contained information about the staff's expertise, 10 percent discussed the firm's use of computer software/ auditing, and less than 3 percent provided details about fees.

This information suggests that professionals are attempting to compete on the basis of services offered and staff expertise. Consumers must select professional services based upon perceived expertise or competitive advantage provided by these informational advertisements. This makes consumer choice more difficult since they have less knowledge than professionals about the desired service. Professionals may also believe that advertisements without pricing information are more dignified and acceptable. Placing pricing information directly in ads could, on the other hand, offend professional colleagues and invite unofficial censure and/or criticism.

Next, future use of advertising was examined (see Table 8). Responses were cross-tabulated by years in business/size of firm and anticipated use of advertising. Those firms in business for ten or more years appear less likely to adopt advertising, while younger firms anticipated an increase in firm advertisements. A large number of firms with annual billings of $100,000 to $500,000 reported they would never advertise. However, above $1 million

TABLE 8

Future Advertising Course

Action	Percent
Will never advertise	45
Will begin advertising	22
Will increase advertising	21
Will decrease advertising	4
Will switch advertising medium	3
Will not change advertising	2
All remaining responses	3
	100

per year in billings, the majority of CPA firms (60 percent) plan on increasing advertising expenditures or beginning advertising.

Finally, an effort was made to assess the reasons professionals gave for not advertising. The largest group of non-advertisers (35 percent) felt their firm's billings would grow without using promotional activities. In other words, these professionals believed the competitive environment did not justify the need to advertise or better communicate with potential or current clients. It also appears that many professionals view advertising as being detrimental to their image. Approximately 25 percent of respondents offered this reason. A third group of professionals (13 percent) stated that advertising was not cost effective.

CONCLUSIONS

After examining the data provided by the study, several conclusions are evident. First, overall planning activities by professionals need to be improved. For example, only about 20 percent of professional CPA firms currently have a five-year plan or mission statement. This means that four out of five professionals probably are not conducting environmental analyses or anticipating demographic/

business changes that could severely affect their professional practice.

Second, professionals continue to set fees based primarily on the cost of the service. This infers that professionals still perceive their market from a production view rather than from the customer's view.

Third, the most formal marketing activities pursued by professionals are in the promotional area. That is, professionals have begun using newspapers, brochures/bulletins, radio, and TV to communicate with their clients and publics. However, only a limited number have directed specific marketing communications at one or several customer segments. Most of the firms advertising and promoting their services are doing so without deciding who their prospective clients might be or what services they will need. Professional advertising is informational in nature and only a very small group is competing on price. It also appears that professionals are putting advertising at the forefront of their marketing activities before making the necessary product, pricing, and place decisions.

Fourth, those professionals who advertise are not certain how well their efforts are working. As in other industries, little objective evaluation of advertising appears to be undertaken by professionals.

Fifth, there appears to be a residual feeling by professionals–especially those in business prior to the lifting of the codes of ethics–that almost any advertising will harm the firm's image. Many of these same professionals do not currently perceive a need to advertise in the mass media. As additional professionals enter the marketplace–and from all indications physicians, CPAs, and lawyers either face or will soon face this situation–the need to differentiate one's services from competitors' will become even more important.

Some professionals have made serious marketing efforts since the lifting of the codes of ethics in 1978. These actions have been primarily promotional in nature–advertising in print, radio, and TV. It is now time for professionals to examine where they have been, where they are, and where they want to go. This will require long-range planning. As competition increases, it will be the firms that are aware of customer needs and wants and can respond to market changes most quickly who will survive and prosper. A comprehensive marketing plan and active marketing program will enhance the professionals' chance of success in a dynamic environment.

REFERENCES

Bloom, Paul N. (1984), "Effective Marketing for Professional Services," *Harvard Business Review*, 102-110.

Gelb, Betsy D., Samuel Y. Smith, and Gabriel M. Gelb (1988), "Service Marketing Lessons From the Professionals," *Business Horizons*, September-October, 29-34.

Hite, Robert E. and Joseph A. Bellizzi (1986), "Consumers' Attitudes Toward Accountants, Lawyers, and Physicians with Respect to Advertising Professional Services," *Journal of Advertising Research*, June/July, 45-54.

Hite, Robert E. and Cynthia Fraser (1988), "Meta-Analyses of Attitudes Toward Advertising by Professionals," *Journal of Marketing*, 52, July, 95-105.

Hite, Robert E., and Norman O. Schultz (1987), "A Survey of the Utilization of Advertising by CPA Firms," *Journal of Professional Services Marketing*, 3:1/2, 231-245.

Hite, Robert E., Norman O. Schultz, and Judith A. Weaver (1988), "A Content Analysis of CPA Advertising in National Print Media from 1979 to 1984," *Journal of The Academy of Marketing Science*, 16:3/4, 1-15.

Kotler, Philip and Richard A. Connor, Jr. (1977), "Marketing Professional Services," *Journal of Marketing*, January, 71-76.

Marts, John A., Earl D. Honeycutt, Jr., and Jane Kenan (1989), "How CPA Firms Market Their Services," *Journal of Accountancy*, February, 111-113.

Oliver, Debra D. and Clyde L. Posey (1980), "National vs. Local Accounting Firms: What Are Their Differences of Perception Concerning Advertising?" *Arkansas Business and Economic Review*, 14, Fall, 1-5.

Van Doren, Doris C. and Louise W. Smith (1987), "Marketing in the Restructured Professional Services Field," *The Journal of Services Marketing*, 1:1, Summer, 67-75.

Wheatley, Edward W. (1983), *Marketing Professional Services*, Englewood Cliffs, NJ: Prentice-Hall, Inc.

Chapter 4

Marketing Priorities and Practice Within the Accounting Profession: Does Formalization Make a Difference?

A. Diamantopoulos
S. O'Donohoe
N. Petersen

INTRODUCTION

The relationship between accountants and marketing is relatively recent, and it is arguable as to whether it has yet been firmly established (Morgan, N. 1988; Diamantopoulos, O'Donohoe, and Lane 1989a,b; O'Donohoe, Diamantopoulos, and Petersen 1990). However, it has been well documented in terms of the factors precipitating it, such as the removal of "ethical prohibitions" on advertising from professional codes of conduct, the intensification of competition, and the blurring of boundaries between providers of financial services (Watkins and Wright 1985; Morgan. R. 1990; Diamantopoulos, O'Donohoe, and Lane 1989a). There is also a considerable body of empirical literature concerning the attitudes of accountants and their clients toward advertising (Darling 1977; Dixon and Taylor 1979; Taylor and Dixon 1980; Scott and Rudderow 1983; Traynor 1983/84; Teoh and Gull 1985; Hite and Fraser 1988). More recently, in addition to the many prescriptive articles and books on the subject (reviewed in O'Donohoe, Diamantopou-

This chapter was first published in *Journal of Professional Services Marketing*, Vol. 10(1) 1993.

los, and Petersen 1990), aspects of accountants' marketing practice and organization for marketing have also received empirical attention (Traynor 1983/84; Pincus and Pincus 1986; McLaughlin and O'Kane 1988; Diamantopoulos, O'Donohoe, and Lane 1989a,b, 1990; Marts, Honeycutt, and Kenan 1989; Morgan 1988, 1990; Morgan and Piercy 1990).

The issue of how accounting firms organize for marketing is a particularly interesting one. For Hise (1965), adoption of the marketing concept required, among other factors, an organizational structure whereby all marketing activities were performed by the marketing department. However, the creation and maintenance of a marketing department in itself does not guarantee marketing success. On the contrary, organizations which limit the marketing function to the marketing department may be too restrictive in their interpretation of the marketing concept (Ames 1970; Drucker 1974; Gummesson 1984; King 1985). Indeed, in their recent study of the state-of-the-art of British marketing, Hooley, Lynch, and Shepherd (1990) found no relationship between the formal existence of a marketing department and the marketing approach employed in a cross-section of British companies.

This may suggest that research which considers how accounting firms organize for marketing has little to contribute to an understanding of the substance of professional services marketing. However, N. Morgan (1990) argues that the marketing problems which the professions face are primarily internal, concerned with issues such as market orientation and strategy implementation, rather than those of external communications. In studying "the appointment, role and relative position of the CME [Chief Marketing Executive] and the location, status and function of a marketing department" in accounting and law firms, R. Morgan (1988, 1990) argues that he is focusing on the more tangible elements of strategy implementation. Thus, his approach is similar to research in other sectors by Piercy (1986), Piercy and Alexander (1988) and R. Morgan (1990). Furthermore, it could be argued that within the field of professional services marketing, with the professions' traditional antipathy toward marketing and "self-promotion" (O'Connor 1978; Hanson 1984; Bloom 1984), the establishment of a department or an executive with exclusive responsibility for marketing is a sign of commitment to the marketing concept, and would place such firms at the early stages of marketing evolution (Kotler 1988).

This chapter seeks to enhance understanding of marketing within the professions by an empirical examination of how British accounting firms are organized for marketing. It also seeks to make a contribution to the issue of "trappings versus substance" (Ames 1970) by examining whether firms with a formal marketing facility differ from those without in terms of their perceptions of the marketing environment, the importance which they attribute to elements of the service marketing mix, their actual marketing activities, and their use of external marketing expertise.

METHODOLOGY

Data Collection

Data were collected by means of a five-page mail questionnaire dispatched to what were estimated to be the top 200 accountancy firms, with size being based on the number of partners and branch offices. The sample was drawn from the membership directory of the Institute of Chartered Accountants in England & Wales and the covering letter was addressed to the practice development partner.

A total of 71 usable replies were received, representing an effective response rate of 35.5 percent. This is comparable to the response rates attained in previous similar surveys (e.g., Morgan 1988; Diamantopoulos, O'Donohoe, and Lane 1989a).

Variables

Marketing Formalization

Two dichotomous (yes/no) variables were used to determine whether a formal marketing facility had been established in the firms concerned, notably (a) the existence of a marketing department and (b) the existence of personnel dealing *exclusively* with marketing. The reason for using two variables to describe formal organization for marketing is that some firms may employ marketing personnel but not have a separate department while in other companies a department may exist but may be staffed wholly or partly by staff also undertaking other (i.e., non-marketing activities) in the firm; a similar operationalization of marketing organization/ formalization was used by Morgan (1988) who asked respondents whether they had a marketing department or an individual responsible for marketing in their firms.

Firm Demographics

These include ratio-scaled measures of company size (fee income, number of employees, number of branches) and company age.

Marketing Characteristics

In addition to firm demographics, four sets of variables were used to contrast firms having a formalized marketing facility and firms without such a facility.

Perceptions of the Marketing Environment–these describe the perceived impact of relatively recent developments in the competitive environment of accountancy firms which would be expected to impact on the need for and adoption of marketing concepts and techniques in the sector. Four such developments were included in the questionnaire, notably (a) the removal of restrictions on advertising, (b) the changing client demands away from basic/standard accounting services, (c) the increased competition from non-accountant financial services institutions, and (d) the deregulation of the stock market (Big Bang); the impact of each issue on market competitiveness was assessed by means of a 5-point scale, ranging from 5="greatly affected" to 1="not at all affected".

Importance of Service Marketing Mix Elements–these refer to the relative importance of the various components of accountants' service marketing mix in terms of their contribution to business success. Nine such components were measured on a 5-point scale ranging from 5="very important" to 1="very unimportant" (range of services, new service development, service quality, promotional activities, fee policies, personal contacts, branch locations, number of branches, gathering of market information).

Marketing Activities–these describe concrete actions associated with the implementation of marketing and indicate the extent to which "lip service" on the importance of marketing is actually translated into specific activities. Respondents were asked to indicate the extent to which their firms engaged in fourteen different activities describing the following: research into client needs and wants, research into client perceptions of the firm, analysis of competitors' services and prices, analysis of the economic environment and forecasting fee income, examination of the service range and the customer base, setting and monitoring quantified objectives, training staff in interpersonal skills and personal selling techniques, and using quality control procedures. The frequency of undertaking each activity was measured on a four-point scale, ranging from 4="regularly" to 1="never."

Use of Outside Experts–this describes the degree to which the skills of independent marketing experts are tapped by the firms in the sample. Specifically, respondents were asked to indicate on a four-point rating scale (4="regularly," 1="never") whether they made use of marketing research agencies, advertising agencies, public relations firms, and marketing consultants.

ANALYSIS

Marketing Formalization

As can be seen from Table 1, formalization for marketing is rather low among the respondent firms, with 18 percent having exclusive marketing personnel, 24 percent having a marketing

TABLE 1. Formalization of Marketing

		Marketing Department	
		Yes	No
	Yes	10	3
Exclusive Marketing Personnel	No	7	51

[chi-square=21.1, p=.000]

department, and only 14 percent having both. Thus, overall, only 20 (28 percent) of the firms in the sample can be considered to have some degree of formalization of the marketing function, while the remainder (two and a half times as many) have none.

The low percentage of marketing formalization contrasts sharply with Morgan (1988) where 80 percent of respondents indicated that they had either a department or an individual responsible for marketing. Variation in question wording and sequence would seem to explain at least part of the difference between studies. The inclusion of the word "exclusively" in the marketing personnel question (see methodology section) is a major difference from Morgan (1988) where no such restriction was placed (i.e., one would expect more firms to have *either* full- *or* part-time personnel than the former only). As far as question sequence differences are concerned, the present study placed the question on the existence of a marketing department *after* asking the question on the employment of exclusive marketing personnel. Morgan (1988), on the other hand, used a single either/or question with branching instructing those who answered "no" to skip almost two pages of questions; this branching may have contributed to firms without formalized marketing not replying to his survey. A further plausible explanation of the difference in results is based on the size of the firms responding to the two studies, as marketing formalization is, not unexpectedly, related to the size of the firm (Morgan 1988; see also below). Morgan's (1988) sample of 50 companies was comprised by 40 percent large firms (annual fee income greater than £10 million), 20 percent from medium-sized firms (between £3 and £10 million) and 40 percent small firms (less than £3 million). In contrast, the relevant percentages in the current study were 19 percent, 17 percent, and 64 percent respectively.

The impact of company size on marketing formalization is clearly demonstrated in Table 2, which compares formalized and non-formalized firms in terms of organizational characteristics. A highly significant difference is observed consistently across all three size indicators. Further, inspection of the relevant means reveals that the differences involved are very substantial. Firms with formalized marketing are, on average, twelve times larger in terms of income and eight times larger in terms of employment compared

TABLE 2. Firm Demographics

	Means				
	All Firms	Marketing Formalization		t-value	Sig.[*]
		Yes	No		
Fee Income[**] (£'000)	10,732 (30,708)	29,188 (50,712)	2,252 (3,235)	2.19	.044
Number of Employees	281 (692)	753 (1182)	97 (125)	2.48	.023
Number of Branches	6.0 (5.1)	10.4 (6.0)	4.3 (3.5)	4.32	.000
Company Age (years)	68.0 (36.3)	73.3 (44.4)	66.9 (32.8)	.67	.507

[[*]two-tailed probability; [**]N=54, of which 17 are formalized; figures in brackets are standard deviations]

with the non-formalized group; they also have more than twice the average number of branches. No differences can be discerned with regard to company age.

An important implication of the size differences is that any comparison between formalized and non-formalized firms has to control for the confounding influence of company size, when variables relating to resource/skills availability are involved. Otherwise, any observed variations may merely reflect differences in the practices of large vs. small firms rather than "true" differences due to marketing formalization.

Differences in Marketing Characteristics

Perceptions of the Marketing Environment

According to the firms in the sample, the most important development that has affected the competitive environment of accountancy firms, is the changes in the nature of client demands, while the least important development is the deregulation of the stock market (Table 3). On both these issues formalized firms attach

TABLE 3. Influences Impinging on Market Competitiveness

	Means[#]				
	All Firms	Marketing Formalization		t-value	Sig.[*]
		Yes	No		
Changing Client Demands	3.89 (.60)	4.10 (.45)	3.80 (.63)	2.22	.031
Competition from Non-Accountant Financial Servcs.	2.92 (.84)	3.10 (.97)	2.84 (.78)	1.16	.250
Removal of Advertising Restrictions	2.82 (.96)	2.90 (1.12)	2.78 (.90)	.45	.651
Deregulation of Stock Market	2.00 (.88)	2.35 (1.09)	1.86 (.75)	1.84	.077

[[#]=“greatly affected,” 1=“not affected”; [*]two-tailed probability; figures in brackets are standard deviations]

greater significance than non-formalized ones, however, the *relative* ranking of the four issues within each group is identical.

Importance of Service Marketing Mix Elements

On average, all elements of the service marketing mix are considered important as factors contributing to business success, an exception being the gathering of market information (Table 4). The top ranking for service quality may partly reflect the traditional view that “quality sells itself,” however, the high ratings placed on other factors suggest that the respondents see quality as one of a number of important elements. Consistent with the crucial role of referrals and specialization repeatedly stressed in the literature (see O'Donohoe, Diamantopoulos, and Petersen 1990 for a review), respondents see personal contacts and service range as being of major importance. On the other hand, the low importance attached to the gathering of market information is rather disturbing, especially in the light of the impact that changing clients demands are seen as having on the competitive environment; it is difficult to see how a

TABLE 4. Factors Contributing to Business Success

	All Firms	Marketing Formalization		t-value	Sig.*
		Yes	No		
Service Quality	4.86 (.39)	4.90 (.31)	4.84 (.41)	.55	.583
Personal Contacts	4.73 (.56)	4.70 (.57)	4.74 (.56)	.30	.762
Service Range	4.44 (.65)	4.60 (.60)	4.37 (.66)	1.34	.186
New Service Development	3.93 (.85)	4.05 (.60)	3.88 (.93)	.89	.376
Fee Policies	3.90 (.74)	3.90 (.72)	3.90 (.75)	.01	.992
Branch Locations	3.77 (.80)	3.85 (.67)	3.75 (.85)	.50	.621
Promotional Activities	3.31 (.71)	3.90 (.31)	3.08 (.69)	6.94	.000
Number of Branches	3.31 (.89)	3.35 (.81)	3.29 (.92)	.24	.813
Market Information	2.76 (.84)	3.25 (.85)	2.57 (.76)	3.30	.002

[#5="very important," 1="very unimportant"; *two-tailed probability; figures in brackets are standard deviations]

Means#

firm can effectively respond to such changing demands without proper market intelligence.

Morgan (1988) measured the importance of some similar factors as elements of marketing strategy, which is not the same as business success but one would hope that marketing strategy is designed for success! In this context, there is broad agreement between Morgan (1988) and the present study on service quality (technical service excellence), service range, fee policies, and branch locations; personal contacts were not rated as highly by Morgan's (1988) respondents, but were still rated important on average.

Shifting attention to the differences according to marketing formalization, on most service marketing mix elements there is very close agreement between the two groups of firms. However, there are significant differences with regards to the role of promotional activity and the gathering of market information, with formalized firms placing more importance on both elements. Having said that, even for firms with formalized marketing, market information ranks lowest with an average rating barely above neutral. Bearing in mind that market information is a prerequisite for the successful deployment of the other elements listed in Table 4, the rather "lukewarm" perception even among firms appearing to take marketing seriously is definitely disconcerting.

Marketing Activities

As a first step in the analysis of actual activities associated with the implementation of marketing, a factor analysis was performed on the 14 items describing such activities in order to reduce them to a more manageable number of underlying dimensions; both the Bartlett test of sphericity (p = 001) and the Kaiser-Meyer-Olkin measure of sampling adequacy (KMO = .73) confirmed the suitability of the factor analytic model for the data at hand. Table 5 shows the resulting factor matrix following varimax rotation.

A total of five easily interpretable factors were extracted, together accounting for 70.4 percent of the total variance in the original variables. Factor 1 reflects the *analytical orientation* of the firm as it loads strongly on variables describing different kinds of analyses conducted by the firm; the loading on the use of quality control procedures is consistent with this interpretation as the monitoring of service quality implies analysis of expected vs. actual quality delivered in order to identify deficiencies and take remedial action. Factor 2 can be labelled *staff training* as it describes training activities aimed at sharpening the interpersonal and personal selling skills of staff. Factor 3 refers to *objective setting* as both variables it loads on refer to the establishment and subsequent monitoring of quantified business objectives. Factor 4 refers to the *research use* of the firm, loading highly on variables indicating market research activities. Finally, Factor 5 is captured by a single variable, notably *sales forecasting*. Note that one item, namely the analysis of fee contribution, failed to load sufficiently on any of the extracted dimensions;

TABLE 5. Factor Matrix of Marketing Activities

	Factor 1	Factor 2	Factor 3	Factor 4	Factor 5
Examination of Service Range	.78				
Analysis of Competitors' Prices	.76				
Analysis of Competitors' Services	.50			.66	
Analysis of Economic Environment	.62				
Use of Quality Control Procedures	.59				
Staff Training in Interpersonal Skills		.85			
Staff Training in Pers. Selling		.81			
Set Quantified Objectives			.92		
Monitoring Objective Attainment			.91		
Informal Research into Client Needs/Wants				.78	
Formal Research into Client Needs/Wants				.52	
Formal Research into Client Perceptions of Firm				.58	
Forecasting of Fee Income					.89
Analysis of Fee Contribution by Client/Service					
EIGENVALUE	4.68	1.58	1.38	1.20	1.02
EXPL. VARIANCE	33.5%	11.3%	9.9%	8.6%	7.3%
CRONBACH'S ALPHA	.69	.82	.93	.69	–

it was thus retained in its original form for purposes of further analysis.

As a next step, summated scales were constructed by aggregating the scores of the items identified under each of the first four factors (the fifth factor contained only a single variable which was subsequently in its original form). A reliability analysis produced very good internal consistency estimates of the derived scales as indicated by the relevant alpha coefficients.

Table 6 shows the results of contrasting firms with and without formalized marketing in terms of the various activities described above. Consistent with the observations made earlier on the relationship between company size and marketing formalization, control is exercised over the confounding influence of size through the

TABLE 6. Marketing Activities: Extent of Use

	Means[+]> Marketing Formalization		Main Covariate[*]		Effect	
	Yes	No	F	Sig.	F	Sig.
4 Analytical Orientation	12.80 (12.45)	12.75 (12.99)	2.56	.114	.37	.543
Staff Training	6.30 (6.06)	4.29 (4.53)	5.81	.019	11.23	.001
Objective Setting	6.90 (6.75)	6.37 (6.53)	1.69	.198	.16	.694
Research Use	12.15 (11.69)	9.84 (10.30)	9.70	.003	4.18	.045
Sales Forecasting	3.70 (3.70)	3.96 (3.96)	.00	.973	3.78	.056
Client/Service Fee Contribution Analysis	3.35 (3.25)	3.12 (3.21)	2.45	.122	.01	.881

[*number of employees; figures in brackets are adjusted means, i.e., after controlling for the influence of the covariate]

[+refer to aggregate scores for items loading on each factor. Factors 1 and 4 are composed of 4 items, factors 2 and 3 of 2 items] specification of an ANCOVA (analysis of covariance) design with marketing formalization as the main effect and number of employees as a covariate.

Three significant differences can be detected between the two groups of firms, indicating that firms with a formalized marketing function place more emphasis on staff training, make greater use of market research and forecast their fee income *less* frequently than firms without formalized marketing. The first two differences are consistent with expectations and mirror the findings in Table 4, in which promotional activities (which include personal selling) and gathering of marketing information were the main differentiating factors between the two groups. On the other hand, the lower reported frequency of forecasting activities is rather surprising. One would expect firms with formalized marketing to recognize the importance of forecast monitoring on a regular basis so that timely action can be taken if a material discrepancy between actual and estimated sales is noted.

Use of Outside Experts

The final issue to be examined in this paper relates to the use of external expertise. As Table 7 shows, public relations (PR) firms are used most frequently, which is not surprising given that PR is historically the traditional marketing method for accountancy firms. In this context, PR firms are the only kind of outside experts used by more than half (55 percent) of the respondent companies. This percentage is much greater than the 31 percent reported by

TABLE 7. Use of Outside Marketing Experts

	Regularly		Sometimes/Rarely		Not Used	
	n	%	n	%	n	%
PR Firms	22	31	17	24	32	45
Adv. Agencies	10	14	19	27	42	59
Marketing Consultants	3	4	20	28	48	68
Marketing Research Agencies	3	4	9	13	59	83

McLaughlin and O'Kane (1988), however, the latter study also included some 800 smaller firms in its sampling frame.

Regarding advertising agencies, just 41 percent of the firms have ever used them and only 14 percent use them regularly. This is consistent with the 43 percent usage rate reported by Diamantopoulos, O'Donohoe, and Lane (1989a). Marketing consultants and marketing research agencies do not appear to get much business from accountancy firms; a large majority of the latter never use these experts and only 4 percent use them frequently. This low use is ironic since accountants consider themselves as expert consultants and often recommend other types of professionals to their clients, perhaps these marketing experts do not market their own services effectively to accountants (Kotler and Conner 1977)!

The overlap in usage patterns of the four types of marketing experts is shown in Table 8. It can be seen that most users of other experts also employ the services of PR firms; whether use of the latter also leads to the use of other experts or vice-versa is not known given the cross-sectional nature of the data. Most firms using marketing research agencies also use all three of the other expert groups. This may suggest that accountancy firms initially rely on the other experts for the market research needs and subsequently advance to hire marketing research specialists (again, of course, the usual qualifications relating to inferring causality from cross-sectional data apply). Altogether, the average number of outside experts used by the firms in the sample is 1.45 with 22 firms using none and eight firms using all four types.

As far as the relationship between marketing formalization and

TABLE 8. Cross Use of Outside Experts

And Also Using:	Number of Firms Using:			
	PR Firms	Advert. Agencies	Marketing Consultants	Mkt. Res. Agencies
PR Firms	39	23	18	11
Advertising Agencies		29	15	9
Marketing Consultants			23	11
Marketing Research Agencies				12

use of outside experts is concerned, the results in Table 9 show quite clearly that, after controlling for the impact of resources (indicated by company size), formalized firms are making greater use of PR firms, advertising agencies, and marketing research agencies; with respect to the use of marketing consultants no significant differences are observed. Again, for reasons previously explained, one cannot state with confidence whether formalized firms seek further outside marketing expertise or whether exposure to marketing from outside experts leads the firm to formalize its marketing function. There is *some* suggestion that it is more likely to be the former, as 18 (90 percent) out of the 20 formalized firms use PR firms but only 18 (46 percent) of the 39 PR firm users are formalized; a similar pattern is observed with regards to the use of advertising agencies, the relevant percentages being 70 percent and 48 percent respectively.

An issue highlighted by the results in Table 9 is that the use of any kind of outside expert is a cost-incurring activity and hence dependent upon the availability of resources. This is indicated by the significant F-values for the covariate (reflecting company size) in all four analyses. Further, inspection of the observed and adjusted mean values indicates that the distance between the mean usage

TABLE 9. Extent of Use of Outside Marketing Expertise

	Means[#]		Covariate[*]		Main Effect	
	Marketing Formalization					
	Yes	No	F	Sig.	F	Sig.
PR Firms	3.20 (3.07)	1.98 (2.11)	2.85	.096	7.56	.008
Advertising Agencies	2.60 (2.44)	1.57 (1.73)	6.44	.013	5.63	.020
Marketing Consultants	1.95 (1.83)	1.41 (1.53)	4.82	.032	1.46	.230
Mkt. Research Agencies	2.05	1.84	36.25	.000	12.66	.001

[[#]="used regularly," 1="not used"; [*]number of employees; figures in brackets are adjusted means, i.e., after controlling for the influence of the covariate]

rates of formalized and non-formalized firms is always smaller once the adjustment for company size is made. This confirms the importance of controlling for size as the differences between the two groups of firms would be otherwise exaggerated and possibly misleading; for example, if size is not taken into account in the comparison relating to the use of marketing consultants, a t-test applied to the observed mean values produces a highly significant result (t-value = 2.32, p = .023, two-tailed probability).

DISCUSSIONS AND CONCLUSIONS

According to the accounting firms participating in this study, the removal of advertising restrictions was not a factor impinging greatly on market competitiveness. This is not surprising, as there has been relatively little advertising by accountants (*Accountancy* 1984; Watkins and Wright 1985), and several studies have shown accountants regard advertising as a relatively unimportant promotional tool (Traynor 1983/84; Diamantopoulos, O'Donohoe, and Lane 1989a,b). This supports the suggestion of Morgan and Piercy (1990) that the removal of advertising restrictions from accountants' codes of practice were important more on a symbolic rather than practical basis.

The external factor impinging most on market competitiveness was thought to be changing client demands. This may indicate that an important aspect of the marketing concept (i.e., customer orientation) has been adopted within the accounting profession. However, researching those needs emerged as such a low priority that accountants' ability to monitor, let alone respond to those changing needs is doubtful. Gathering market information was the marketing activity considered to contribute least to business success, and research into client needs or perceptions was not conducted on a regular basis. Therefore, it seems that the accounting firms are paying lip service to the concept of customer orientation rather than implementing it.

Less than a third of the firms in this sample had established a marketing department or appointed personnel with exclusive marketing responsibilities. As those firms which had formalized the marketing function had on average significantly higher fee income and employee levels, as well as more branches than those which had not formalized, it could be argued that formalization is a luxury which only the largest firms could afford. There are certain parallels with the finding of Diamantopoulos, O'Donohoe, and Lane (1989a) that the availability of financial resources had a significant influence on accounting firms' advertising practices. The larger firms were more likely to advertise in the first place, to use advertising agencies, and to be more systematic in their approach to advertising. However, further analysis (Diamantopoulos, O'Donohoe, and Lane 1989b) found that the mere availability of financial resources was no substitute for the expertise gained from the use of advertising agencies. Furthermore, not all those who could afford to use an advertising agency chose to do so, and these "agency decliners" were less systematic in the planning of advertising programs. In this context, this raises the issue of whether differences in marketing priorities and practices within the accounting profession could indeed be attributed to the formalization of the marketing function, or whether such differences could be accounted for simply by firm size. In order to examine this question, comparison of formalized versus non-formalized firms was undertaken, controlling for the effect of size. This revealed a number of significant differences. Firstly, firms which had formalized marketing appeared to be more sensitive to forces within the marketing environment. They rated key external factors as impinging more on market competitiveness than did those which had not formalized. The ranking of the factors, however, was the same for the two groups.

In terms of perceptions regarding the contribution of marketing activities to business success, formalized firms attached significantly greater importance to promotion and the gathering of market information. As promotion (and, to a lesser extent, market research) is traditionally an area for which marketing departments have significant responsibility (Ames 1970; Hooley, Lynch, and Shepherd 1990), one would expect firms with such departments to consider these activities particularly important. Even among the formalized firms, however, it was disappointing to note that gathering market information was considered the least important marketing activity.

Moving from perceptions to the actual marketing activities undertaken most regularly, formalized firms placed more emphasis than non-formalized firms on market research and staff training. Again, one would expect to see market research conducted on a regular basis by firms with individuals or departments with exclusive responsibility for marketing. The emphasis which formalized firms place on staff training is consistent with the importance of personnel in the provision of services (Gronroos 1978; Berry 1980; Lovelock 1981; Bateson 1989), and could be considered to form part of an internal marketing program, which the services marketing literature recommends (George and Wheiler 1986; Dumesic and Ford 1983). Less encouraging is the finding that although forecasting fee income was undertaken on a regular basis by the sample as a whole, it was a *less* common activity among formalized firms. This is ironic, as it is a service performed by accountants for their clients in order to assist the planning process. One would expect a key contribution of marketing departments or personnel in accounting firms to be the development of business plans, which would require some forecasting input.

The final area which this chapter addressed was the use which accounting firms made of external expertise. Overall, public relations consultants were the most commonly employed (reflecting the profession's traditional preference for public relations as a form of communication with clients) and market research agencies the least (reflecting the low importance attached to research among the firms surveyed). Formalized firms used external experts (including marketing consultants!) to a greater extent than non-formalized firms. This could be attributed to the greater financial resources available in formalized firms. However, controlling for the effect of size, formalized firms still used external expertise to a significantly greater extent than their non-formalized counterparts.

Overall then, the findings suggest that formalization of the marketing function does impact on marketing priorities and practice within the accounting profession. Despite the reservations expressed within the marketing management literature about "bolt-on" marketing departments (King 1985), it appears that in this case, the formalization of marketing is accompanied by an enhanced awareness of the marketing environment, greater use of staff training and market research, and greater use of external expertise. However, even among formalized firms, the need to research client needs and perceptions (particularly at such a turbulent time within the financial services industry), does not appear to be sufficiently appreciated. Without a commitment to research, a true customer orientation, and thereby marketing effectiveness, are likely to prove elusive.

This chapter has dealt with the impact of formalization on market perceptions and broad areas of marketing activities within the accounting profession. In future research, it would be useful to move beyond the general to an in-depth investigation of issues relating to the practical implementation of marketing activities, by considering for example, the extent to which formalization influences decisions and policies regarding the promotional mix and budget, new service development, and pricing.

REFERENCES

Accountancy (1984), Not exactly opening the floodgates. 95.11. 5.

Ames B (1970), Trappings vs. substance in industrial marketing. *Harvard Business Review.* 48.4. 93-102.

Bateson J (1989), *Managing services marketing.* Dryden Press, Orlando.

Berry L (1980). Service marketing is different. *Business,* 25.3.

Bloom P (1984), Effective marketing for professional services. *Harvard Business Review.* 65.5. 102-110.

Darling J (1977), Attitudes towards advertising by accountants. *Journal of Accountancy.* 143.2. 48-53.

Diamantopoulos A, O'Donohoe S and Lane J (1989a), Advertising by accountants–an empirical study. *Managerial Auditing Journal.* 4.1. 3-10.

Diamantopoulos A, O'Donohoe S and Lane J (1989b), A comparison of advertising practices within the accounting profession. *The Service Industries Journal.* 9.2. 280-296.

Diamantopoulos A, O'Donohoe S and Lane J (1990), Modelling advertising decisions by accountants: A path analysis. *British Accounting Review.* 22. 3-26.

Dixon B and Taylor D (1979), Advertising: attitudes and reactions of New Zealand accountants. *The Accountants' Journal.* 58.10. 337-340.

Drucker P (1974), *Management tasks, responsibilities and practices.* Heinemann.

Dumesic R and Ford N (1983), Internal practice development: an overlooked strategy for marketing professional services. *The Practical Accountant.* 15.12. 39-44.

George W and Wheiler K (1986), Practice development–a services marketing perspective. *The CPA Journal.* 56.10. 30-43.

Gronroos C (1978), A service oriented approach to the marketing of services. *European Journal of Marketing.* 12.8. 588-601.

Gummesson E (1984), The marketing of professional services–25 propositions. In: C Lovelock (ed.), *Services Marketing,* Prentice-Hall. 125-132.

Hanson J (1984), The impact on the accounting profession of relaxing advertising rules. *Admap.* 6.314-317.

Hise R (1965), Have manufacturing firms adopted the marketing concept? *Journal of Marketing* 29.7. 9-12.

Hite R and Fraser C (1988), Meta-analysis of attitudes toward advertising by professionals. *Journal of Marketing.* 52.3. 95-105.

Hooley G, Lynch J and Shepherd J (1990), The marketing concept: putting theory into practice. *European Journal of Marketing,* 24.9. 6-24.

King S (1985), Has marketing failed or was it never really tried? *Journal of Marketing Management.* 1.1. 1-19.

Kotler P (1988), *Marketing management: analysis, planning, implementation and control.* Prentice-Hall, Englewood Cliffs.

Lovelock C (1981), *Services marketing.* Prentice-Hall, Englewood Cliffs.

Marts J, Honeycutt E and Kenan J (1989), How CPA firms market their services. *Journal of Accountancy.* 167.2. 111-113.

McLaughlin N and O'Kane B (1988), Practice promotion and the PR consultant. *Accountancy.* 102.4. 85-86.

Morgan N (1988), Marketing in professional accounting firms. In: T Robinson and C Clarke-Hill (eds.), *Marketing: past, present and future.* Proceedings of the Annual Conference of the Marketing Education Group, Huddersfield Polytechnic, 541-559.

Morgan N (1990), Communication and the reality of marketing in professional service firms. *International Journal of Advertising.* 9. 283-293.

Morgan N and Piercy N (1990), Barriers to marketing implementation in professional service firms. In: A Pendlebury and T Watkins (eds.), *Recent developments in marketing.* Proceedings of the Annual Conference of the Marketing Education Group, Oxford Polytechnic. 956-972.

Morgan R (1990), Marketing professional services: an empirical investigation into consulting engineering services. In: A Pendlebury and T Watkins (eds.), *Recent developments in marketing.* Proceedings of the Annual Conference of the Marketing Education Group, Oxford Polytechnic. 973-995.

O'Connor J (1978), The discrete capability factor in marketing professional services. *Industrial Marketing Management.* 7.5. 308-310.

O'Donohoe S, Diamantopoulos A and Petersen N (1990) Marketing by accountants: principles and practice–A review of the literature. In: H Muhlbacher and C Jochum (eds.), *Advanced Research in Marketing,* Proceedings of the 19th Annual Conference of the European Marketing Academy, Innsbruck. 1597-1616.

Piercy N (1986), The role and function of the chief marketing executive and the marketing department. *Journal of Marketing Management.* 1.3. 265-289.

Piercy N and Alexander N (1988), The status quo of marketing organisation in UK retailing: a neglected phenomenon of the 1980's. *The Service Industries Journal.* 8.2. 155-176.

Pincus K and Pincus J (1986), Public relations: what CPA firms are doing. *Journal of Accountancy.* 162.5. 128-138.

Scott R and Rudderow D (1983), Advertising by accountants: how clients and practitioners feel about it. *The Practical Accountant.* 16.4. 71-76.

Taylor D and Dixon B (1980), Advertising: attitudes and reactions of New Zealand Accountants, part II. *The Accountants' Journal.* 59.2. 25-28.

Teoh H and Gull F (1985), Perceptions of Australian finance managers on the impact of advertising in the accounting profession: some empirical evidence. *Accounting and Finance.* 25. 41-55.

Traynor K (1983/84), Accountant advertising: perceptions, attitudes and behaviours. *Journal of Advertising Research.* 23. 35-41.

Watkins T and Wright M (1985), Firm and industry effects of advertising accountancy services. *The Service Industries Journal.* 5.3. 306-321.

Chapter 5

Has the Household User Profile for Accounting Services Changed with the Changing U.S. Environment During the Eighties?

Antonio L. Que
Carl S. Farinacci
Barbara C. Garland

INTRODUCTION

From the late 1970s to the present, many changes have been taking place in the environment impacting accounting service firms as well as in their increasing orientation to the marketing concept. The lifting of the ban on advertising by certified public accountants has generated widespread interest in the marketing and advertising literature concerning consumer client, business client, and accountant attitudes, copy strategy and content, and other advertising practices of accounting firms (Darling 1977; Upah and Uhr 1981; Traynor 1984; Hite and Bellizzi 1986; Hite, Schultz, and Weaver 1988; Hodge, Brown, and Lumpkin 1990; Fouland, Peacock, and Pelfrey 1991; and Thompson, Smith, and Jordan 1991). More recently, marketers have turned their attention less toward advertising and selling and more toward target marketing, market segmentation, and marketing planning for accounting firms (Ferguson and

This chapter was first published in *Journal of Professional Services Marketing*, Vol. 9(1) 1993.

Higgins 1989; Tootelian and Gaedeke 1990; Honeycutt and Marts 1990; Hodge, Brown, and Lumpkin 1990).

Accounting literature, too, has increased its coverage of practical guidelines to accountants in the use of advertising, selling, direct marketing, and strategic planning, so that most of the practitioner-oriented journals contain regular columns which explain how to deal with marketing like "Marketing CPA Services" in *The CPA Journal*. Then, too, many of the theoretically oriented journals in accounting and taxation also contain articles which blend marketing and accounting and which are exploring predictors of demand and profiles of the customer-base, instead of just advertising and selling (Wheatley 1983; Slemrod and Sorum 1984; Liebtag 1986; Long and Caudill 1987; Collins, Milliron, and Toy 1990).

Indeed, there is a small, but growing, body of literature which addresses the predictors of accounting service use, including pricing strategy (Ferguson and Higgins 1989), taxpayers' objectives (Collins, Milliron, and Toy 1990), demographics like income level, source of income, age, race, and education (Slemrod and Sorum 1984; Liebtag 1986), product and task-related variables like marginal tax rate, number of dependents claimed, and difficulty of completing the tax return (Long and Caudill 1987). As yet, there has been no historical study which focuses on changes in the customer-base over time.

Given the well-publicized demographic changes in the US environment and the myriad of changes in tax law over the past decade, it is quite possible that the year in which some of the above studies were conducted could influence the results. For example, the percentage of adult persons completing high school increased from 66.5 in 1980 to 76.2 in 1988 while the percentage completing college increased from 16.2 to 20.3. Per capita GNP (in constant dollars) increased from $11,995 to $19,810 in the same period; the median age increased from 30.0 to 32.3; the number of single parent households headed by a woman increased from 14.6 percent to 16.3 percent, while married couples fell from 82.5 percent to 79.5 percent (US Department of Commerce 1990). It is possible that the profile of any services' users will have changed as these demographics change.

Similarly, there have been significant changes in the tax law. For example, the Tax Reform Act of 1986 included the following:

- The tax rates are changed drastically.
- The deduction for personal interest paid is phased out.
- The deduction for sales tax paid is revoked.
- The deduction for miscellaneous items is subjected to a two percent floor.
- Income averaging is revoked.
- The number and severity of penalties is increased.
- The political contributions credit is revoked.
- The deduction for IRA contributions is subjected to a complex reduction formula.
- A young child's investment income is subjected to tax at the parents' rate.
- The long-term capital gain deduction is revoked.

These items have taken taxpayers years to understand. The consumer household is faced with re-learning each year's new tax rules and regulations and unlearning the old year's; the income tax forms are convoluted, given their intrinsically simple purpose. It is possible that the accounting service user profile may change in response to an increasingly confusing and difficult task.

It is the purpose of this study to examine the historical changes in the profile of accounting service users. By comparing the predictive ability of a set of standard demographics on purchase data from 1980 to the same set from 1989, it will be possible to determine whether these changes have yet become of sufficient magnitude to alter forecasting and targeting practices. As previous research indicates education, income, race, and age have already been tested (Slemrod and Sorum 1984; Liebtag 1986). All of these variables are present in a government database.

One of the few accessible sources of historical data on consumer purchasing is the Interview Survey of Consumer Expenditures, produced by the Bureau of Labor Statistics (BLS). Although public use tapes are available for one major survey in the 1960s and one in the 1970s, until the 1980s the format and methodology of the survey do not facilitate comparison. In the first quarter of 1980, the BLS began to conduct quarterly retrospective interviews of household durables, income, and expenditures every quarter, instead of annual retrospective interviews once a decade. Data from both 1980 and 1989 are now available to be public (US Department of Labor 1980; US Department of Labor 1989). At the time of writing for this study of accounting services, given the time lag inherent in any secondary data from the government, the data are as current as possible.

Other variables relating to product or to consumer motives or attitudes which were studied in previous research are unfortunately not included in the database. However, the type of residence (rural or urban), the number of earners in the family, marital status, home ownership, and taxes paid are included and can be added to the predictor set.

METHODS

The Interview Survey of Consumer Expenditures is a nationwide probability sample of US households, in which one-fifth of the respondents are replaced each quarter. A household is first given an anchoring interview, and then it is interviewed for four quarters in succession before being dropped from the sample. This study of accounting services analyzes only those households from 1980 that continued from first quarter to fourth quarter of 1980 in order to analyze the total spending for the year for the same group of respondents–794 in all and 193 households using accounting services. The same procedure was used in 1989, for a total of 939 and 277 households using accounting services. Documentation on the tapes from the BLS indicates that in both years, the response rate was over 70 percent (US Department of Labor 1980; US Department of Labor 1989).

The criterion variable is the dollar amount spent on accounting services for one year; when the model tested includes data for one year only, dollars are current dollars. However, when the model tested includes pooled data from both years, this amount has been adjusted by the consumer price index to counteract the effect of inflation on the value of the dollar. Again, in the pooled model only, all other dollar amounts in the predictor set have been similarly adjusted–annual family after tax income and annual taxes paid. For all models, other predictors include number of earners in the household and age of household head plus a set of dummy variables for residence (urban = 1, rural = 0), gender of household head (male = 1, female = 0), race of household head (black = 1, other = 0), education of household head (some college = 1, other = 0), marital status (married = 1, other = 0), and home ownership (yes = 1, no = 0).

The data analytic technique is regression with three models specified. The model for the 1980 sample and the model for the 1989 set have the same predictor set exactly, in order to show the strength of these relationships in the two years separately. Since changes have taken place in tax policy, social structures, and marketing practices within accounting firms, the model may not be equally powerful in predicting consumer spending on accounting services. A third model is also tested, which pools the data from the two years and includes a dummy variable for time (1 = 1989, 0 = 1980). The purpose of this third model is to provide a significance test on the slope of the two equations, essentially to determine whether or not time makes a difference in the stability of the predictor set.

Since the units of measure include dollars, years, number of people, and dummy variables, the standardized Beta weights are reported in addition to the raw coefficients. In this way, the relative strength of each predictor can be assessed within a model as well as across models. T tests on the difference of the individual parameters from zero are also included for each model. For all significance tests, an alpha of .05 is used.

RESULTS

Table 1 presents a profile of the two samples. In 1980, the typical buyer is a forty-six-year-old, married, white, urban, male home-owner without a college education; his family has an average of 1.8 earners, who jointly bring home $21,303 (current dollars) and pay $2,921 in taxes. The 1980 buyer has more earners in the family, brings home more money, pays more taxes, is younger, and has a greater tendency to be white and to own a home than the non-buyer. Buyers and non-buyers in 1980 follow the national trends in terms of marital status, gender, residence, race, and education.

In 1989, the typical buyer is a fifty-year-old, married, white, urban, male home-owner without a college education; his family

TABLE 1. Profile of the Samples

HOUSEHOLD HEAD CHARACTERISTICS	1989		1980	
	NON-BUYERS	BUYERS	NON-BUYERS	BUYERS
NUMBER OF HOUSEHOLDS	662	277	601	193
MARITAL STATUS				
% MARRIED	57.70	71.84[a]	63.39	72.02
WIDOWED	14.65	10.47	13.48	11.40
DIVORCED	11.48	10.47	9.65	7.77
SEPARATED	2.57	2.17	3.00	2.07
SINGLE	13.60	5.05	10.48	6.74
EDUCATION				
% SOME COLLEGE	38.82	46.93[a]	33.78	35.23
NO COLLEGE	61.13	53.07	66.22	64.77
HOME OWNERSHIP				
% OWN HOME	66.16	85.56[a]	66.89	82.38[a]
DO NOT OWN	33.84	14.44	33.11	17.62
RACE				
% WHITE	86.86	91.70a	81.03	97.41[a]
BLACK	11.03	5.05	15.14	2.59
OTHER	2.11	3.25	3.82	0.0
GENDER				
% MALE	62.54	76.17[a]	67.55	70.47
FEMALE	37.46	23.83	32.45	29.53
RESIDENCE				
% URBAN	88.97	84.84b	82.36	84.46
RURAL	11.03	15.16	17.64	15.54
AGE	50	50	50	46[a]
INCOME	26,277	35,252[a]	14,847	21,303[a]
TAXES PAID	2,113	3,876a	1,979	2,921[a]
NUMBER OF EARNERS	1.4	1.6[a]	1.4	1.8[a]

KEY: a = prob of chi-square <= .05
       b = prob of chi-square <= .10

has an average of 1.6 earners, who jointly bring home $35,252 (current dollars) and pay $3,876 in taxes. The 1989 buyer, like the 1980 buyer, has more earners in the family, brings home more money, pays more taxes, and has a greater tendency to be white and to own a home than the non-buyer. However, the 1989 buyer is not significantly different in age from the non-buyer. Unlike the 1980 buyer, the 1989 buyer *is* significantly different from the non-buyer in the likelihood of being male, married, more often college educated, and more often an urban-dweller. Buyers and non-buyers in 1989 still follow the national trends in terms of marital status, gender, residence, race, and education, however, there are a few differences in the figures, which deserve comment. More minority buyers appear in 1989; more highly educated buyers appear in 1989; more divorced buyers appear in 1989, and; more male buyers appear in 1989.

Table 2 presents the results of the tests on individual parameters in both the 1980 and 1989 separate models' tests. In the 1980 model, only taxes and education are significant predictors of household expenditure on accounting services. The size of the Beta weights indicates that taxes are the most important, followed by college education. The higher the taxes, the higher is the spending on accounting services; clearly, the motivation to pay a lower but still fair amount of taxes is important. If the head of household has at least some college education, the amount of spending is also higher. Income is not a significant predictor at the .05 level, although it is close to significant. What is really interesting is the sign of the Beta weight on income–negative–which could imply that it is the lower income households that are likely to spend more rather than the higher income households.

In the 1989 model, in addition to taxes and education, which are still significant, other important predictors of household expenditure on accounting services include the intercept term, income, and age. The size of the Beta weights indicates that taxes are still the most important, followed by college education, age, the intercept term, and income. Again, the higher the taxes, the higher is the spending on accounting services. Similarly, if the head of household has at least some college education, the amount of spending is also higher. The older the head of household, the greater the amount of

TABLE 2. Separate Models' Individual Parameter Results

VARIABLES	1989				1980			
	RAW ESTIMATE	STANDARDIZED B	T	PR> T	RAW ESTIMATE	STANDARDIZED B	T	PR> T
INTERCEPT	-223.49500	0.00000	-2.309	0.0217	4.88733	0.00000	0.108	0.9140
INCOME	0.00134	0.14174	2.212	0.0278	-0.00169	-0.21062	-1.952	0.0524
TAXES	0.00999	0.32059	5.214	0.0001	0.01089	0.36604	3.874	0.0001
# EARNERS	-2.47461	-0.00913	-0.150	0.8807	1.37191	0.01409	0.165	0.8688
URBAN	33.03654	0.04020	0.741	0.4595	9.15256	0.02306	0.386	0.7001
MALE	2.71688	0.00393	0.064	0.9494	-4.28990	-0.01656	-0.198	0.8433
BLACK	-0.83045	-0.00062	-0.011	0.9910	11.99734	0.01613	0.227	0.8206
COLLEGE	122.21180	0.20592	3.641	0.0003	58.26131	0.23550	3.202	0.0016
MARRIED	53.51577	0.08166	1.282	0.2010	31.78052	0.12072	1.323	0.1876
OWN HOME	26.18584	0.03123	0.563	0.5737	0.38267	0.00123	0.016	0.9869
AGE	3.10481	0.16630	2.747	0.0064	0.40471	0.05405	0.681	0.4969

spending. In addition, income is now a significant predictor at the .05 level, although its sign is now positive instead of negative. Therefore, the higher the income, the greater is the spending on accounting services, as might be expected. Since the sign of the Beta weight for the intercept term is negative, the earlier variables in combination overestimate the spending level.

Table 3 provides the comparative results on the two models as wholes. Although both models are significant, the power of the model with the 1989 data is almost tripled, as is indicated by the adjusted r-squared values of 24.32 percent versus 9.63 percent. In current dollars, the average amount spent on accounting services more than doubled, from $70.66 to $161.53. Much of this is the result of inflation as shown by the adjusted constant dollars–$85.75 in 1980 versus $130.27 in 1989.

Tables 4 and 5 clearly indicate that the predictor set is relatively stable over time, since in the pooled model the probability of the t statistic is greater than .05 and the overall model is significant and can explain over twenty percent of the variance in spending. Furthermore, taxes and college education remain the important predictors (with the largest Beta weights and a significance level below .05). In addition, age and the intercept term are important in the pooled model even though they were not important in the 1980 model (of course, the pooled model has many more observations and only one variable added). Income is not significant in the combined model perhaps because the 1980 data implied an inverse relationship and the 1989 data a direct relationship, but marital

TABLE 3. Separate Models' Regression Overall Results

OVERALL MODEL	1989	1980
F VALUE	9.868	3.046
PROB > F	0.0001	0.0014
DEP MEAN	$161.53	$70.66
R-SQUARE	27.06%	14.34%
ADJ R-SQ	24.32%	9.63%

TABLE 4. Pooled Model Individual Parameter Results

VARIABLES	1989 + 1980 WITH $ VALUES ADJUSTED FOR INFLATION			
	RAW ESTIMATE	STANDARDIZED B	T	PR > T
INTERCEPT	−1.05241	0.00000	−2.135	0.0333
INCOME	0.00071	0.07735	1.469	0.1425
TAXES	0.01008	0.32506	6.604	0.0001
# EARNERS	−0.07040	−0.03928	−0.831	0.4064
URBAN	0.18121	0.03176	0.753	0.4518
MALE	−0.09626	−0.02059	−0.421	0.6736
BLACK	−0.02614	−0.00251	−0.060	0.9525
COLLEGE	0.81247	0.19522	4.428	0.0001
MARRIED	0.45834	0.10024	1.962	0.0503
OWN HOME	0.10495	0.01860	0.425	0.6711
AGE	0.01529	0.11817	2.550	0.0111
TIME	0.30835	0.07382	1.748	0.0811

TABLE 5. Pooled Model Overall Regression Results

OVERALL MODEL 1989 + 1980 WITH $ VALUES ADJUSTED FOR INFLATION	
F VALUE	12.313
PROB > F	0.0001
DEP MEAN * 100	$111.99
R-SQUARE	22.82%
ADJ R-SQ	20.97%

status approaches significance, perhaps because of the increased sample size.

CONCLUSIONS

What has emerged most clearly from this historical analysis is the critical importance of the amount of taxes and of the achievement of at least some college education as predictors of the amount of spending. Although the decade of the 1980s has witnessed many changes in tax policy, in the marketing of accounting services, and even of some basic demographic characteristics of the population, these changes have not yet been translated into different predictors of household spending on accounting services. However, the 1989 model probably is a better indicator of future trends; indeed, as the relative affluence of the former baby-boomers increases with middle-age, spending on accounting services should also increase. As some of the other social changes which now affect relatively few households begin to diffuse through more of the population, the predictor set could well be expanded to include divorced households, Asian-American households, and multiple-income households.

LIMITATIONS OF THE STUDY
AND SUGGESTIONS FOR FUTURE RESEARCH

Clearly, the limitation of the historical data set to demographic and financial variables makes it impossible to test differences in spending related to different motivations in using the service, different levels of satisfaction in previous agency-client relationships, different types of accounting services, differences in fee structure, and differences in advertising and promotional practices. Many of these variables have been included in recent surveys, but there are no longitudinal data available which include them. Business researchers need to begin now to build such longitudinal databases, so that historical trends may be tracked in future research. With such databases, the effect of changes in tax policy on consumer patronage could also be studied.

REFERENCES

Collins, Julie H., Valerie C. Milliron, and Daniel R. Toy (1990), "Factors Associated with Household Demand for Tax Preparers," *The Journal of the American Taxation Association*, (Fall), 9-25.

Darling, John R. (1977), "Attitudes toward Advertising by Accountants," *Journal of Accountancy*, 143 (February), 48-53.

Ferguson, Jeffery M. and Lexis F. Higgins (1989), "Effects of the Price of Tax Preparation Services and the CPA Credential on the Perception of Service Quality," *Journal of Professional Services Marketing*, 5:1, 87-99.

Fouland, Sherman, Eileen Peacock, and Sandra Pelfrey (1991), "Advertising by Accountants: Attitudes and Practices," *Journal of Professional Services Marketing*, 6:2, 97-112.

Hite, Robert E. and Joseph A. Bellizzi (1986), "Consumers' Attitudes Toward Accountants, Lawyers, and Physicians with Respect to Advertising Professional Services," *Journal of Advertising Research*, June/July, 45-54.

Hite, Robert E., Norman O. Schultz, and Judith A. Weaver (1988), "A Content Analysis of CPA Advertising in National Print Media from 1979 to 1984, *Journal of the Academy of Marketing Science*, 16:3/4, 1-15.

Hodge, Thomas G., Michael H. Brown, and James R. Lumpkin (1990), "The Use of Marketing Plans and Advertising Among Accounting Firms: Is This Profession a Viable Candidate for Marketing?" *Journal of Professional Services Marketing*, 6:1, 43-52.

Honeycutt, Earl D. and John A. Marts (1990), "Marketing by Professionals as Applied to CPA Firms: Room for Improvement?" *Journal of Professional Services Marketing*, 6:1, 29-42.

Liebtag, Bill (1986), "Marketing to the Affluent," *Journal of Accountancy*, 162 (August), 65-71.

Long, J. and S. Caudill (1987), "The Usage and Benefits of Paid Tax Return Preparation," *National Tax Journal*, 40 (March), 35-46.

Slemrod, J. and N. Sorum (1984), "The Compliance Cost of the U.S. Individual Income Tax System," *National Tax Journal*, 5 (Fall), 87-98.

Thompson, James H., L. Murphy Smith, and Robert E. Jordan (1991), "The Changing Face of Accounting Advertising," *Journal of Professional Services Marketing*, 6:2, 113-128.

Tootelian, Dennis H. and Ralph M. Gaedeke (1990), "Marketing of Professional Services as Applied to Tax Professionals: Represenation of the Client, Public, or Profession?" *Journal of Professional Services Marketing*, 6:1, 17-28.

Traynor, Kenneth (1984), "Accountant Advertising: Perceptions, Attitudes, and Behaviors," *Journal of Advertising Research*, 23:6 (December/January), 35-40.

Upah, Gregory D., and E. B. Uhr (1981), "Advertising by Public Accountants: A Review and Evaluation of Copy Strategy," *Marketing of Services*, James H. Donnelly and William R. George, eds. Chicago: American Marketing Association.

US Department of Commerce (1990), Bureau of the Census, *Statistical Abstract of the United States, 1990*, 110th edition, Washington, DC.

US Department of Labor (1980), Bureau of Labor Statistics, "Interview Survey."

US Department of Labor (1989), Bureau of Labor Statistics, "Interview Survey."

Wheatley, Edward W. (1983), "Auditing Your Marketing Performance," *Journal of Accountancy*, 56 (September), 68-75.

Chapter 6

The Small Accounting Firm:
Managing the Dynamics
of the Marketing Function

Carmen C. Reagan
Thomas A. Gavin

BACKGROUND

The accounting profession, like other segments of the financial services industry, is undergoing tremendous change. Changes are taking place to address new, or least previously unrecognized, needs of clients. Altering the composition of services has important implications for managing the marketing function of the CPA firm.

The purpose of this paper is to report on an exploratory study designed to:

- determine the present service mix of small CPA firms and the activities used to market those services, and
- determine future services planned by these same firms.

Implications for firms' management and marketing functions which result from change in services are also provided.

THE STUDY

Partners from 16 small accounting firms in the Southeast met as a focus group and were asked to complete a questionnaire and engage

This chapter was first published in *Journal of Professional Services Marketing*, Vol. 3(3/4) 1988.

in a two-hour dialogue concerning the implications of marketing professional accounting services.

The questionnaire asked each accountant to:

- indicate the frequency with which he/she engaged in 27 marketing activities using a scale of (1) "continuously" through (5) "never."
- indicate the extent to which the firm had and/or planned to develop expertise in 16 areas using a scale of (1) "substantial level of expertise" through (5) "less than slight level of expertise."

Tables 1 and 2 illustrate that this group of accountants plans to offer more of all but three of the listed services. Table 1 provides the median scores of present and proposed service activity; Table 2 provides an indication of the magnitude of the difference between present and proposed service activity.

Presently, as shown in Table 1, a substantial portion of participants' billable time is spent providing accounting services and preparing compilations and tax returns. A moderate amount of time is spent in IRS representation, engaging in audits, and computer and management consulting services. Little time is spent in analysis of tax shelters, reviews, estate planning, personal financial planning, business valuation, operation audit, mergers and acquisitions, liquidations, reorganizations, and litigation support services.

Respondents foresee an expansion in the breadth of services offered. Table 2 shows increased activity (+) is planned for 13 services, no change is planned for tax preparation, and a small decrease in activity (–) is planned for compilations and analysis of tax shelters. The cumulative net increase in services to be provided is substantial. From the perspective of managing an accounting firm, the projected growth in services will affect the planning, organizing, directing, and controlling activities of firms. More traditional services, referred to by some as Type I services, will be de-emphasized. However, the range of consulting (Type II) services will be expanded. These include business valuation, computer consulting, and personal financial planning. These areas, unlike auditing practice, are not services in which the accounting profession has had a legislative monopoly. Focus group partners plan not only

TABLE 1. Present and Planned Services of Small CPA Firms

ACTIVITY	PRESENT*	PLAN*
1. Compilations	1.50	1.83
2. Tax Preparation	1.50	1.50
3. Small Business Accounting	2.00	1.50
4. IRS Agency Representation	3.17	2.50
5. Audits	3.17	2.70
6. Computer Consulting	3.67	2.33
7. Management Consulting	3.70	2.50
8. Analysis of Tax Shelters	4.00	4.61
9. Reviews	4.10	3.83
10. Estate Planning	4.30	3.50
11. Personal Financial Planning	4.33	3.17
12. Business Valuation	4.50	3.50
13. Operation Audit	4.70	4.61
14. Mergers and Acquisitions	4.70	4.61
15. Liquidations/Reorganizations	4.77	4.30
16. Litigation Support	4.77	4.61

*Median scores on a scale ranging from (1) "substantial" through (5) "less than slight."

to provide financial data to the client but to add value by offering advice and counsel on how to interpret and use the financial data provided.

As accountants change their offerings to better serve clients in financially related matters, they must (a) make an effort to educate the clients as to the repositioning of the accountant's role as an advisor and (b) shift the responsibility for nonreport Type I activities to paraprofessionals and clients.

TABLE 2. Degree and Direction of Change of Services Offered

DEGREE	DIRECTION	TYPE OF SERVICE
Slight	0	Tax Preparation
(0–<.5)	+.089	Mergers and Acquisitions
	+.089	Operational Auditing
	+.162	Litigation Support
	+.267	Reviews
	–.333	Compilations
	+.467	Audits
	_.473	Litigations/Reorganizations
Moderate	+.500	Small Business Accounting
(≥.5–<1.)	–.611	Analysis of Tax Shelters
	+.667	IRS Agency Representation
	+.800	Estate Planning
Substantial	+1.000	Business Valuation
(≥1.0 – <1.5)	+1.200	Management Consulting
	+1.334	Computer Consulting
	+1.166	Personal Financial Planning

REPOSITIONING

What Is Repositioning?

The orange juice industry successfully repositioned its product from solely a breakfast drink to an anytime snack. The banking industry has expanded its services to include brokerage and non-traditional single transaction financial services. Similarly, accountants must encourage clients to contact them anytime a financial question arises. Accountants may assume clients will educate themselves as to their need for consulting services and who provides such services most effectively. However, clients are generally quite busy and find it difficult to be knowledgeable or expert about every facet of business. Accountants must educate clients about the value of consultory services they provide.

Repositioning requires the use of multiple strategies. These include target marketing, product development, promotion, pricing, and placing products in the market. These tasks are much more difficult than positioning new products/services because clients have entrenched beliefs which must be undone and redirected.

Table 3 indicates the current marketing strategy of the accountants in the sample. They were asked to indicate the frequency with which they engaged in each of the marketing activities mentioned; responses are recorded on a scale of (1) "very frequently" to (5) "never." The sequence of categories listed in the table follows the current marketing philosophy assumed for a typical target market. First, the target market should be identified and described; this is followed by the development of a marketing mix which includes the formulation of product, promotion, place, and price strategies.

The table appears to reflect a fairly accurate composite of what is commonly believed to be the marketing strategy of the smaller CPA firm. Those activities most often thought of as more or less frequently pursued are reflected within each of the categories of marketing strategy activities. The median scores of the group of accountants indicate they most frequently use referrals, participation in community activities, and personal selling to market their services; least frequently used are printed advertising in the Yellow Pages, newspapers, magazines, and direct mail.

Personal selling, as a market strategy, is the most expensive form of communication. These costs are increasing at a faster rate than advertising costs.[1] It is a costly way to initially develop client beliefs about services and firms, especially with large groups of prospective clients. It is also costly to employ it as the only repositioning tactic. Accountants need to consider making greater use of target market identification and analysis and employing advertising as an approach to repositioning the firm in the minds of clients.

A Three-Step Process

Repositioning requires making use of a three-step approach. These steps consist of position analysis, image change techniques,

TABLE 3. Current Marketing Strategy

		Median Score
I.	Target Marketing Identification and Analysis	
	A. Evaluate Client Needs	2.125
	B. Define Specific Target Markets	2.833
	C. Estimate Size of Client Base	2.929
	D. Determine Shares of Market	3.257
	E. Determine Firms' Image Among Clients	3.300
	F. Study Clients By Service	3.500
II.	Product Mix	
	A. Determine Which New Services Are Needed	2.700
	B. Periodically Reexam Services	2.833
	C. Study Profit Trends	3.250
III.	Promotion Mix	
	A. Cultivate Referrals	1.500
	B. Participate in Community Activities	1.500
	C. Personal Selling	1.750
	D. Provide Newsletters	2.100
	E. Engage in Public Speaking	2.786
	F. Speak at Seminars	3.125
	G. Develop Communication Strategy	3.500
	H. Develop Publicity	4.000
	I. Provide Brochure	4.500
	J. Advertise in Yellow Pages	4.500
	K. Advertise through Direct Mail	4.700
	L. Advertise in Newspaper	4.773
	M. Advertise in Magazines	4.857
	N. Participate in Trade Shows	4.885
IV.	Place and Price Mix	
	A. Evaluate Price Policies	2.167
	B. Analyze Price Structure of Competition	3.300
	C. Analyze Location	3.300

*Median Score on a scale ranging from (1) "very frequently" to (5) "never."

and re-analysis. The last step is a control technique to determine if the second step was successfully completed.

First, accountants need to know the present position they occupy in the minds of clients. Clients can be given a description of different accounting services and asked to rate the similarity of the services to those offered by bankers, lawyers, stockbrokers, life insurance agents, and bookkeeping and computer processing centers. The information provided through such an analysis can be used to determine if the clients' perception of accounting services is consistent with that of the accountant.

If the analysis reveals that clients recognize accountants as financial advisors, referrals and personal selling efforts should be continued as a primary method of communication. However, if the analysis suggests that clients do not perceive the accountant as an advisor it will be necessary to pursue a marketing strategy to change clients' perceptions. Image change strategies should include a comprehensive mix of advertising, personal communications, and a pricing mechanism to position advisory services as an additional offering.

Advertising

Advertising can initiate a new way of thinking. The role of advertising would be: to make clients aware of advisory services; to get them to question why they should go to another professional (when they could just ask their present accountant); and to encourage them to ask for referrals and more in-depth personal communication.

Individual firms should consider placing an ad in the Yellow Pages in sections for accounting and financial services (other than merely listing name and phone number in the standard format), developing brochures to send to clients, and various forms of direct mail. National and state accounting groups can assist members by developing magazine, newspaper, and television advertisements which reveal the generic advisory services of accountants.

Advertising is an efficient method of communicating when the goal is to formulate new ways of thinking about a service; it is also one of the most effective at capturing clients' attention. Information gathering and processing research indicates that individuals first scan the environment for visual cues which lead them to initiate requests for personal, verbal communications or be more receptive when the marketer calls or visits. Visual media also help prepare the client for personal communications by introducing technical terminology necessary for the client to understand the sender's (accountant's) message.

Personal Communications

Personal sources and messages need to be prepared to answer questions and handle requests raised through advertising. Those making referrals should be informed of the accountant's desire to increase consulting activities. Special groups can be informed through public speaking engagements and seminars; personal contacts can be made with present and potential clients who serve as opinion leaders for other clients. Also, participation in community activities which reinforce the role of the accountant should continue.

Pricing

Pricing policies need to be evaluated. Accountants should estimate the value clients place on advice while, at the same time, being cognizant of prohibitions established by Codes of Ethics at state and national levels.

Communicating the appropriate value to the client is difficult. The importance of price as it affects the demand for the services will vary based on the client's involvement with financial data.

Clients identified as information seekers are not likely to consider price until it goes beyond reasonable expectations. However, those who have yet to recognize the importance of financial advice will be very price sensitive.

As clients are introduced to the services, they should be told that additional charges are required for advisory services. Advisory services should be listed as separate items on the billing statement. This establishes in the client's mind that advice was given and that it has a value separate from other, more traditional services.

A second position analysis should be made after a reasonable period to determine if the marketing efforts were successful in reorienting the consumer to think differently about accounting services.

THE DYNAMICS OF SHIFTING
FROM TYPE I SERVICES

As accountants increase advisory services, others need to perform the more routine, Type I activities. Responsibility for less complex and nonreport services can be shifted to paraprofessionals within the firm or to clients themselves.

In service organizations, such as accounting firms, it is critical that the staff develop appropriate client expectations. In turn, the staff must meet these expectations through quality service.

The accounting firm's staff must be taught and continually motivated to accept the new directions in service offering and the marketing of those services. For some staff, these new responsibilities may represent job enhancement; for others, the changed and increased work load may lead to frustration, dissatisfaction, and possibly job turnover. Principals of the firm should anticipate change in employees' attitudes and behaviors as the firm's services evolve. If the staff does not accept change, the firm will not be successful in repositioning itself in the market. A three-step internal marketing effort must be established to analyze staff members' attitudes about change, to implement planned management strategies, and to reanalyze the success of those strategies.

Given new, less expensive computer technology, clients can be encouraged to assume more of a role for preparing financial data. Clients can be assisted by having accounting firm staff available to analyze selected past and proposed transactions and other data of the client. Accountants should be willing to provide training to clients to facilitate the learning, execution, and repositioning processes. Clients must believe that their assumption of selected accounting activity will allow the accountant to better serve them.

CONCLUSION

Accountants anticipate expanding their offering of advisory (Type II) services to present and potential clients. To be successful, they must reposition their services in the minds of clients. Repositioning requires a broad range of marketing activities including the three-phase position analysis, image change techniques, and re-analysis.

Accountants need to shift responsibility for some Type I activities to paraprofessional staff members and/or to the clients themselves. They should prepare strategies which recognize clients' resistance to change. Adequate instruction to the accounting staff and client personnel is necessary if a successful shift in responsibilities is to be achieved.

NOTE

1. "Survey: Business Sales Calls Costing $229.70" (1986), *Marketing News*, American Marketing Association, Chicago, Vol. 20, No. 16, Aug. 1.

PART TWO:

PERSPECTIVES ON MARKETING

Chapter 7

Priorities and Perceptions from the Client Point of View: Opportunities for Effective Marketing of an Accounting Practice

Nora Ganim Barnes
Helen Ann LaFrancois

INTRODUCTION

The focus of this study is to examine how effectively accountants are meeting the needs of their clients. While such an issue has been informally discussed, virtually no research has been done which systematically examines major characteristics of a practice and satisfaction levels of clients. This study presents findings which should be of value to those practitioners striving to build and improve their practices through the use of marketing strategy. The incorporation of a marketing orientation should be fundamental in maximizing client satisfaction.

LITERATURE REVIEW

Recently several articles have appeared in financial services/accounting publications stressing the importance of incorporating marketing techniques in their planning and evaluation process.[1,2]

This chapter was first published in *Journal of Professional Services Marketing*, Vol. 3(1/2) 1987.

Many of those address specific marketing issues. *The Practical Accountant* reviews advertising decisions including media selection, frequency, and ad content.[3] *The Journal of Accountancy* suggests firms do a "marketing" audit as part of their regular evaluation process.[4] The implication here is clearly that the marketing of one's services is an important function of any firm.

Very few articles present marketing research or empirical data on the marketing of financial and accounting services. One survey discusses responses of selected clients in order to determine their understanding of the profession's role and responsibilities.[5] The only article which actually surveys clients' satisfaction levels appeared in 1984.[6] The study reviews responses to an extensive questionnaire examining virtually every aspect of an accounting practice. The study, however, confines itself to one CPA firm, and did not use any statistical sampling techniques.

The study presented here attempts to systematically examine client satisfaction with the financial and accounting services they are provided. In addition, the marketing implications of the findings are discussed and suggestions are made to help incorporate a marketing orientation into the accounting service field.

DESIGN AND METHODOLOGY

A nonexperimental survey design was used for the study. Data was collected through a mail questionnaire. The instrument was designed to have clients rate different characteristics of an accounting practice in terms of their importance. A second five-point scale had respondents evaluate their firms actual performance on the same set of characteristics. The variables chosen for the questionnaire were determined after an extensive review of the literature as well as discussions with selected accountants. Other information gathered included the type of services utilized, frequency of use, and complete demographic information for private clients and a business profile for all others. The questionnaires were sent out with cover letters explaining to the participant their selection and assuring them anonymity. Questionnaires could only be identified by participating accounting firms.

SAMPLING PROCEDURE

The 1985 National Directory of Certified Public Accountants was used as a basis for selecting potential participants for this study. The directory includes information on location only, but through telephone interviews data was collected on size of the firm, number of professionals employed, type of clientele, and type of services offered. Fourteen firms were selected from this information as potential subjects based on all the characteristics mentioned. One objective of the sampling procedure was to get a range of firms which represented a diversity of clients. Such a sample would differentiate this study from all other published literature on the subject. Eight of the 14 firms agreed to participate for a response rate of 56 percent. While the final eight firms have good representation on most dimensions, we were not able to enlist a West Coast accounting firm. The other major regions of the continental U.S. are represented to various degrees.

Each participating firm provided a systematic random sampling of their clients. A total of 483 questionnaires were returned with response rates varying from 20 percent to 60 percent per firm.

The CPA firms participating in the study are from eight states, including Alabama, Colorado, Maryland, New Hampshire, North Carolina, Ohio, Pennsylvania, and Rhode Island. The largest firm has 23 professionals, working out of three branches for 4,000 clients. The smallest has one professional working out of one branch for 100 clients. Clients in all cases include a range from businesses requiring full accounting services including third-party audits as well as tax preparation and individuals who require only tax return preparation once a year. (See Table 1.) Clients using the firm for family/personal affairs are predominantly male, 36-45 years old, married and with two children. He is a professional/technical person with a spouse who works full time. Their combined incomes are $40,000-$50,000 per year. (See Table 2.)

Clients using the firm for corporate/business affairs are mainly corporations with approximate annual gross sales of less than $250,000 and less than five full-time employees. (See Table 3.)

FINDINGS

Perceived Importance vs. Actual Performance Ratings

Aggregate responses for all clients from all firms were examined using their responses to the two scales mentioned. The characteristics rated in the top third on both scales were the same. Clients perceive accuracy and reliability, thoroughness of statements, ability to meet deadlines, interpretation of statements, and performance of auditors to be the most important of the 16 characteristics evaluated. In addition, those same characteristics were rated as the highest in terms of their actual performance by accounting firms. It is interesting to note, however, that while the same characteristics top both lists in rank order, the differences between the mean scores are significant in every case. T-tests were performed on the mean scores for each of the 16 characteristics as they were rated on the perceived importance scale and the actual performance scale. (See Table 4.) It appears that firms are focusing on some of the important issues, but their actual performance is significantly less than clients seek.

The discrepancies are more obvious in the ranking of other variables. Some characteristics are viewed as relatively less important although they are performed at a high level of satisfaction. More seriously, some characteristics are viewed as more important and are evaluated significantly lower in actual performance. In both these cases, not only were there significant differences in the mean scores, but the rank order of the variables was very different (see Table 5).

TABLE 1. Profile of Participating Firms

STATE	PROFESSIONALS	BRANCHES	CLIENTS
Alabama	2	1	330
Colorado	14	3	1200
Maryland	1	1	125
New Hampshire	23	2	4000
North Carolina	2	1	200
Ohio	8	2	300
Pennsylvania	1	1	100

TABLE 2. Clients Using Firms for Family/Personal Business

Sex:	Number	%
Male	236	73.8
Female	69	21.6
Age:		
16-25	2	.6
26-35	43	13.0
36-45	93	28.1
46-55	89	26.9
56-65	57	17.2
Over 65	34	10.3
Marital Status:		
Married	268	82.2
Single	34	10.4
Other	12	3.7
Number of Children:		
0	47	15.9
1	39	13.2
2	95	32.2
3	58	19.7
4	31	10.5
5	14	4.7
6	9	3.1
Employment:		
Full time	255	77.3
Part time	13	3.9
Retired	41	12.4
Not currently employed	7	2.1
Total Family Income:		
$10,000-$19,999	29	9.0
$20,000-$29,999	40	12.4
$30,000-$39,999	46	14.2
$40,000-$49,999	50	15.5
Over $50,000	144	44.6
Type of Employment:		
Professional/Technical	155	43.8
Managerial/Administrative	123	34.7
Support services	12	3.4
Other	47	13.3

TABLE 3. Clients Using Firms for Corporate/Business Purposes

	Number	%
Type of Business:		
Sole Proprietorship	78	22.6
Partnership	26	7.5
Corporation	204	59.1
Other	17	4.9
Approximate Gross Annual Sales:		
Less than $250,000	115	38.9
$250,000-$499,999	46	15.5
$500,000-$999,999	30	10.1
$1,000,000-$3,999,999	56	18.9
$4,000,000-$6,999,999	23	7.8
$7,000,000-$9,999,999	6	2.0
$10,000,000-$12,999,999	5	1.7
$13,000,000-$15,999,999	7	2.4
Over $16,000,000	8	2.7
Number of Employees:		
Less than 5	144	43.8
6-15	77	23.4
16-25	23	7.0
26-50	30	9.1
51-100	29	8.8
101-200	18	5.5

Those characteristics being "over performed" include convenient location of the office, appearance of the office, availability of computer services, pleasant personality of staff, and reputation of the firm. In all cases the differences were significant and each variable was considered less important than other variables, yet better performed in actuality than other variables.

Of more serious concern are those variables being "under performed." In these cases the variables were deemed more important while their actual performance was rated as relatively low. These variables include assistance in tax and financial planning, understanding the client's business, notification of new laws, communication skills of professionals, accessibility of professionals, timely and relevant reports, and notification of new changes in tax

TABLE 4. Results of T-Test Analysis on Practice Characteristics

Characteristics	n	means	S.D.	t-values
Accuracy & Reliability				
Perceived Importance	475	3.98	.158	12.87**
Actual Evaluation		3.67	.519	
Ability to Meet Deadlines				
Perceived Importance	470	3.78	.457	10.41**
Actual Evaluation		3.37	.761	
Thoroughness of Statements				
Perceived Importance	469	3.95	.248	12.58**
Actual Evaluation		3.61	.566	
Pleasant Personality				
Perceived Importance	472	3.23	.687	−9.29**
Actual Evaluation		3.56	.577	
Reputation of Firm				
Perceived Importance	463	3.46	.666	−2.88*
Actual Evaluation		3.56	.551	
Appearance of Office				
Perceived Importance	425	2.74	.777	−16.75**
Actual Evaluation		3.46	.590	
Performance of Auditors				
Perceived Importance	260	3.70	.498	6.11**
Actual Evaluation		3.46	.604	
Communication Skills				
Perceived Importance	472	3.61	.542	5.07**
Actual Evaluation		3.44	.645	
Accessibility of Professionals				
Perceived Importance	467	3.61	.543	4.79**
Actual Evaluation		3.44	.688	
Interpretation of Statements				
Perceived Importance	455	3.76	.478	9.56**
Actual Evaluation		3.42	.719	
Availability of Computer				
Perceived Importance	369	2.95	.831	−9.65**
Actual Evaluation		3.39	.655	
Understanding Client's Business				
Perceived Importance	456	3.72	.517	10.74**
Actual Evaluation		3.32	.748	

TABLE 4 (continued)

Characteristics	n	means	S.D.	t-values
Location of Office				
Perceived Importance	429	2.59	.797	−16.25**
Actual Evaluation		3.30	.645	
Notification of Changes				
Perceived Importance	463	3.56	.642	6.18**
Actual Evaluation		3.30	.802	
Timely & Relevant Reports				
Perceived Importance	437	3.60	.596	7.67**
Actual Evaluation		3.29	.766	
Assistance in Tax Planning				
Perceived Importance	434	3.63	.559	12.35**
Actual Evaluation		3.05	.902	

* $p<.01$
** $p<.001$

laws. In each of these cases the differences were significant between perceived level of importance and actual level of performance. Clients are reporting a frustration in several important aspects of the accounting services they experience.

The graph in Figure 1 depicts the relationship between the mean scores on both scales for each of the 16 variables examined. As noted, obvious discrepancies exist. Those discrepancies in a negative direction indicate a potential source of client dissatisfaction.

Those discrepancies in the positive direction may indicate a need for the firm to reevaluate its emphasis in order to maximize its effectiveness. Some marketing strategy should be employed in order to minimize or avoid cognitive dissonance for the client.

It is important to note that satisfied clients translate into larger practices when one considers the fact that almost one half of all referrals to an accounting firm are from family or friends. This is consistent with the published literature on the buying of services. The high risk nature of services seems to mandate the more secure search through informal and trusted channels.[7]

An unhappy client can result in the loss of that client as well as potential others that would have been referred.

TABLE 5. Final Rankings Compared

Actual Performance		Perceived Importance
1	Accuracy and reliability	1
2	Ability of firm to meet deadlines	3
3	Thoroughness of statements and tax returns	2
4	Pleasant personality	13
5	Reputation of the firm	12
6	Appearance of the office	15
7	Performance of the auditors	6
8	Communication skills	7
9	Accessibility of Professionals	8
10	Interpretation of statements and/or tax returns	4
11	Availability of computer services	14
12	Understanding client's business	5
13	Location of office	16
14	Notification of new or proposed changes in laws or practices	11
15	Timely and relevant reports	10
16	Assistance in tax or financial planning	9

One other finding consistent with the literature on services has to do with fees. In this study 87 percent of the respondents report fees to be fair for the services being provided. In the service area there is a willingness to pay more to assure quality.

IMPLICATIONS AND CONCLUSIONS

The implications of these findings are surprising. For all 16 variables under investigation, significant differences were reported

FIGURE 1. Comparison of Mean Scores Between Perceived Importance and Actual Evaluation of Performance

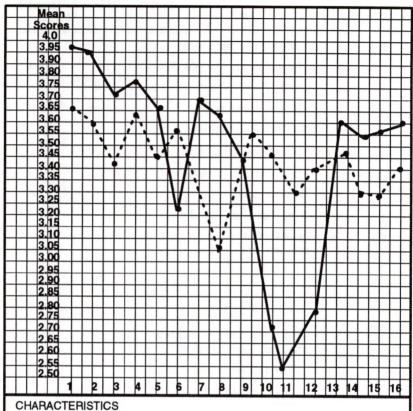

CHARACTERISTICS

1. Accuracy
2. Thoroughness
3. Interpretation
4. Deadlines
5. Auditors
6. Personality
7. Understanding
8. Planning
9. Reputation
10. Appearance
11. Location
12. Computer
13. Accessibility
14. Notification
15. Timely
16. Communication

—— Importance

- - - - Actual Evaluation of Performance

between the perceived importance of the variable, and the actual performance of that variable from the client's point of view. While some of these differences were in a positive direction (client's were getting performance on variables they considered less important) many important differences involved characteristics considered more important yet being performed at a relatively lower level.

1. Accounting firms should continue to emphasize their skills in the areas of accuracy and reliability, thoroughness, ability to meet deadlines, interpretation of statements, and the performance of their auditors. These provide a good basis for development of a marketing plan. Any promotion or literature undertaken by the firm should include details on these items. Personnel decisions should concentrate on maintaining excellence on these dimensions.

2. Clients should be encouraged to make referrals. As noted, an important source of new business is word of mouth communication between family and friends. Accountants might benefit from marketing techniques now being used by other professionals with regard to referrals. It is not uncommon to send thank-you notes, flowers, or some other acknowledgement to a client who has recommended your firm to another.

3. A CPA firm should consider enlarging and upgrading their staff, being more accessible to clients, and developing a better understanding of the client's business, rather than renovating or redecorating the office. Again, literature or promotions should stress this orientation rather than decor or location characteristics.

4. Firms should not be overly concerned with fee structure. It appears not to be a major concern in the professional service area. Emphasis should be placed on those variables rated most highly with minimal focus on fees.

5. Client's consider some aspects of a practice to be performed at a higher level than necessary for their satisfaction. Having computer services or pleasant personalities may be helpful for the firm's image. It may also become a source of frustration for the client who is not receiving a satisfactory level of performance on other dimensions. Here the firm needs to assess its priorities and survey its clients in order to better match expectations with performance. A disparity between the two can result in what marketers refer to as a "dissonant" client who is unhappy and will disseminate unfavor-

able information about their experience. Marketing research should become an integral part of any long-range plan.

In conclusion, clients are interested in quality work and efficient services to help them maintain or develop a healthy financial status. Those firms which are innovative and can incorporate a marketing perspective into their strategic planning will be the most successful in the years to come.

NOTES

1. Denny, Robert. "Marketing Accounting Services: An Introduction," *The National Public Account*, September, 1982, 14-17.

2. "Practitioners Forum," *The Journal of Accounting*, October, 1983, 112-115.

3. Smith, Clarence C. "Advertising and Marketing: Should You and How?" *The Practical Accountant*, March, 1985, 49-53.

4. Wheatley, Edward W. "Auditing Your Marketing Performance," *The Journal of Accountancy*, September, 1983, 68-70.

5. Guerrasio, Michael E. "Accounting and Auditing," *CPA Journal*, October, 1984, 96-98.

6. Axline, Larry L. "Are Your Clients Satisfied?" *The Journal of Accountancy*, July, 1984, 84-90.

7. Berry, Leonard L. "Services Marketing is Different," in *Services Marketing*, ed. C. H. Lovelock, Prentice-Hall, Englewood Cliffs, NJ, 29-36.

Appendix

I. How important are the following characteristics of an accounting firm to you?

	Very Important	Somewhat Important	Somewhat Unimportant	Very Unimportant	Does not apply
1. Accuracy and Reliability	____	____	____	____	____
2. Thoroughness of statements and/or tax returns	____	____	____	____	____
3. Interpretation of statements and/or tax returns	____	____	____	____	____
4. Ability of firm to meet deadlines	____	____	____	____	____
5. Performance of auditors during an audit	____	____	____	____	____
6. Pleasant personality of the acctg. professional	____	____	____	____	____
7. Understanding the client's business	____	____	____	____	____
8. Assistance in tax or financial planning	____	____	____	____	____
9. Reputation of the firm	____	____	____	____	____
10. Appearance of the office	____	____	____	____	____
11. Location of the office	____	____	____	____	____
12. Availability of computer services	____	____	____	____	____
13. Accessibility of the professionals	____	____	____	____	____

Appendix (continued)

	Very Important	Somewhat Important	Somewhat Unimportant	Very Unimportant	Does not apply
14. Notification of new or proposed changes in laws or practices	_____	_____	_____	_____	_____
15. Timely and relevant reports	_____	_____	_____	_____	_____
16. Communication skills of the professional	_____	_____	_____	_____	_____

II. How would you evaluate some of those same charactersitics using your accounting firm?

	Excellent (1)	Good (2)	Fair (3)	Poor (4)	Does not apply (5)
1. Accuracy and reliability	_____	_____	_____	_____	_____
2. Thoroughness of statements	_____	_____	_____	_____	_____
3. Interpretation of statements and/or tax returns	_____	_____	_____	_____	_____
4. Ability of firm to meet deadlines	_____	_____	_____	_____	_____
5. Performance of auditors during an audit	_____	_____	_____	_____	_____
6. Pleasant personality of the acctg. professional	_____	_____	_____	_____	_____
7. Understanding the client's business	_____	_____	_____	_____	_____
8. Assistance in tax or financial planning	_____	_____	_____	_____	_____

	Excellent (1)	Good (2)	Fair (3)	Poor (4)	Does not apply (5)
9. Reputation of the firm	_____	_____	_____	_____	_____
10. Appearance of the office	_____	_____	_____	_____	_____
11. Location of the office	_____	_____	_____	_____	_____
12. Availability of computer services	_____	_____	_____	_____	_____
13. Accessibility of the professional	_____	_____	_____	_____	_____
14. Notification of new or proposed changes in laws or practices	_____	_____	_____	_____	_____
15. Timely and relevant reports	_____	_____	_____	_____	_____
16. Communication skills of the professional	_____	_____	_____	_____	_____

III.	Very Fair	Fair	Unfair	Very Unfair	Does not apply
1. Are the fees usually	_____	_____	_____	_____	_____

2. Have you recommended us to others? _____

3. In your opinion, what additional services should be added? _____

4. In your opinion, what is the most favorable characteristic about your accounting firm

_____

_____

Appendix (continued)

5.   How did you first hear about your firm?

     _____ lawyer   _____ other accountant   _____ family

     _____ banker   _____ friend   _____ phone book

     _____ other

6.   Which of the following services do you utilize? (Check as many as apply)

     _____ auditing

     _____ tax advice/returns

     _____ management services (analysis, surveys, advice, etc.)

     _____ financial planning

7.   How often do you make use of the indicated services per year?

     _____ auditing

     _____ tax advice/returns

     _____ management services

     _____ financial planning

Chapter 8

Different Perspectives on the Marketing of Accounting Services

Paul W. Allen
Danny R. Arnold

INTRODUCTION

Traditional accounting activities range from basic bookkeeping services to large-scale audits. The possibilities for marketing these services have increased in recent years due primarily to changes in American Institute of Certified Public Accountants (AICPA) ethical standards regarding advertising and solicitation. In response to legal pressure from the Federal Trade Commission (FTC), the AICPA made rule changes in 1978, 1979, and 1983 that served to free CPAs to advertise or solicit for business in a conservative and professional manner. The accounting profession, however, has been slow to adopt new marketing strategies in accordance with the relaxed standards.

A 1990 consent agreement between the AICPA and the FTC may have the most profound effect on accounting practice since the AICPA's formation over 100 years ago. Under the agreement, a CPA is allowed by the AICPA to do things never permitted before. The marketing cry of the 1960s, "Innovate or Perish," could well characterize the accounting profession in the 1990s.

This chapter was first published in *Journal of Professional Services Marketing*, Vol. 7(2) 1991.

This chapter explores how the AICPA-FTC agreement could impact the marketing of accounting services. The text presents a hypothetical debate between a marketer and a CPA. An intermediary poses questions, based on the consent agreement, for the debate. Note that the purpose of this chapter does not include exploring applicable state laws which might impose more rigid standards on CPAs than does the AICPA-FTC agreement, nor does it address accountant liability insurance contracts that may exclude coverage for certain activities permitted by the agreement.

THE AICPA-FTC AGREEMENT

In March 1989 the AICPA entered into a consent agreement with the FTC to refrain from maintaining or enforcing certain prohibitions regarding contingent fees, commissions, referral fees, advertising, solicitation, and trade names. In summary form, the agreement allows a CPA to:

1. accept disclosed commissions from non-audit clients for the sale of (a) computer hardware/software products, (b) securities, (c) real estate, and (d) insurance.
2. accept contingent fees from non-audit clients based on cost savings of management advisory services (MAS).
3. pay or accept disclosed referral fees.
4. solicit any potential client by any means, including direct solicitation (without being false or deceptive).
5. advertise using (a) self-laudatory or comparative claims, (b) testimonials or endorsements, and (c) advertisements not considered by the AICPA to be professionally dignified or in good taste (without being false or deceptive).
6. use *any* trade name (without being false or deceptive).

THE DEBATE

The following hypothetical debate probes the potential marketing opportunities which could emerge from changes included in the agreement. The marketer (MKT) in the debate seeks to maximize the potential opportunities, while the CPA is conservatively cautious and brings out the negative aspects of pursuing new marketing angles. The debate is initiated by an intermediary (INT). All dialogue is indented.

Contingent Fees

A contingent fee as defined by the agreement refers to a fee established for the performance of any service according to an arrangement in which no fee will be charged unless a specified finding or result is attained, or in which the amount of the fee is otherwise dependent upon the finding or result of such service. The agreement permits a CPA to accept contingent fees from non-audit clients. This would allow an accounting firm to enter into a contingent fee arrangement with a client for whom the firm provides management advisory services (MAS).

INT: What opportunities or threats do you see on the horizon for accountants who engage in such practice?

CPA: A contingent fee arrangement is too uncertain because CPAs may or may not get paid. Everything depends on the results or findings of the MAS engagement. For example, if the arrangement provides that the accounting firm receive 10 percent of operating costs saved for the client over the next five years, no income from the engagement would result if the client's operating costs go up. Also, any income would be delayed until the operating results are in.

Even though accountants for the most part are aversive to risk, some accounting firms will undoubtedly take the risk of foregoing income in order to have the chance of making the big gain in the case of very favorable MAS results. These firms will likely perish if a large percentage of their income is generated from contingent fee arrangements because bills must be paid in a timely manner and cash flow from contingent fee engagements would not be dependable.

MKT: That perspective is right, as far as it goes. However, if the contingency factor or results are specified appropriately, should not the CPA be paid based on delivery–either something or nothing? Further, if a broader view is taken, some accounting firms may be able to gain a competitive advantage by building contingent fees into their pricing strategy.

The psychological role of prices for services is greater than it is for tangible products because consumers often depend on price as the sole indicator of service quality. With this in mind, an accounting firm with an established track record of saving money for a particular client due to MAS services rendered to the client may be able to successfully establish a pricing strategy of charging a fixed fee for MAS work plus a fee contingent on *estimated* cost savings from MAS work performed. In this situation, the accounting firm would be assured of a fixed income and have the prospect of realizing a great deal more. Furthermore, the contingent fee would not be delayed since it would be based on estimated cost savings instead of actual. There would be many potential scenarios in which a contingent fee could be coupled with a fixed fee. A firm with a strong reputation for reaping benefits to its MAS clients may be able to easily find new clients willing to pay a contingent fee based on estimated cost savings.

Commissions

The agreement defines a commission as compensation, other than a referral fee, paid to a CPA for recommending or referring any product or service to be supplied by a person other than the CPA. No commission is involved when a practitioner actually takes title to goods and in turn markets them to a client at a profit or where the CPA actually renders the service to the client for a fee.

The service marketer must strive to provide a bundle of benefits that satisfies the needs of customers. The AICPA-FTC agreement permits CPAs to enlarge their bundle of services by accepting commissions as long as their independence is not compromised. Such commissions could come from the sale of computer hardware/software, securities, real estate, or insurance.

INT: What service/product strategy with regard to these types of commissions should CPA firms adopt?

MKT: For companies interested in continued growth and profits, successful new service/product strategy should be viewed as a planned totality that looks ahead for some years. For the marketer of accounting services, the development of new and innovative services and marketing techniques is of paramount importance in maintaining a competitive posture in a dynamic, growth-oriented environment.

CPA firms must respond to these commission-related opportunities by making the necessary arrangements to extend their service lines accordingly. Short-range and long-range goals should be established. A firm must decide whether to employ in-house training programs for selected personnel or to bring trained outsiders in so that the firm has the necessary expertise in computers, investments, real estate, and/or insurance to effectively compete in these areas. Surely the CPA community does not have the prejudicial view that marketers of these services are unprofessional, or that CPAs who dabble in these services would suffer a tarnished professional image. Actually, the professional aura of CPAs could even give them a competitive advantage in marketing certain services–consumer perceptions can be very powerful. CPA firms must also actively seek out other opportunities for commissions than the ones mentioned earlier.

There is undoubtedly money to be made by accounting firms that posture themselves to compete for commissions. Unlike the introduction of new tangible consumer products, for which the acceptance rate is generally low, the introduction of these commission-related services should have a high acceptance rate. These services are not new–only the delivery vehicle is new. With proper planning CPA firms can successfully enter these service markets and gain a piece of the action by tapping their existing

MAS or tax client base, as well as targeting new clients. The accounting firm may also enlarge its tax or MAS client base with new clients attracted through the providing of new services.

CPA: It would be useless to argue that growth could not be achieved through engaging in permitted commission-related activities. However, a CPA should recognize that acting as a sales agent in order to receive commissions makes the CPA liable to the client for express or implied warranties. Only when the accounting firm is well acquainted with the product or service of the supplier should the CPA consider accepting commissions.

The proliferation of computers since the 1960s has transformed the nature of information flow in most companies to the extent that CPAs must have considerable knowledge of computer hardware and software in order to perform traditional accounting services. Thus, many CPA firms may already be in position to receive commissions for referring clients to the computer equipment that best meets their particular needs.

In other words, accounting firms should be hesitant to adopt an aggressive service strategy which involves adding commission-related areas primarily because of the potential liability involved. However, many firms may have adequate knowledge about computers to successfully increase profits from commissions for the sale of computer hardware and software. To sell insurance, real estate, or investments the CPA must meet the appropriate licensing requirements. Accountants should stay within the boundaries of accounting and leave the business of selling insurance, real estate, and securities to those already specializing in those areas.

Referral Fees

The agreement defines a referral fee as compensation for recommending or referring any CPA service to any person. Referral fees may be paid or received by the CPA. The distinction between a commission and a referral fee is that a referral fee is based on the CPA supplying a recommended service, while commissions are applied when the supplier is someone other than the CPA. Medical doctors, for example, are noted for receiving kickbacks from pharmaceutical firms for recommending certain products or services to their patients. Typically, referral fees are ultimately paid for by the patient or customer.

INT: Would this be the recommended pricing strategy for a CPA who pays referral fees to obtain clients who have been referred by a lawyer, that is, charging the referral fees back to the accounting clients?

CPA: Yes, assuming a CPA is unethical enough to charge a client for services not actually rendered. Even though the agreement requires that such a referral fee arrangement be disclosed to the client, each CPA must consider whether this is an *acceptable* pricing strategy. A better strategy for some CPAs may be to pay the referral fee without charging it back to the client, even though this would mean accepting a lower profit margin.

Although not related to the specific question, CPAs might consider specializing in certain areas of tax, for example, and then referring clients to each other without involving referral fees. Certainly firms involved in such an arrangement could not keep tabs of who benefitted more than who.

MKT: CPAs should charge back referral fees to their clients, most definitely! CPAs are not above doctors. Passing costs on to someone else is a part of any business transaction. Referral fees are definitely not unethical as long as the customer receives value. When a lawyer charges a CPA a referral fee which is passed on to the client, the customer is actually paying for the lawyer's knowledge regarding CPAs' ability and skill, and for the implied piece of mind that comes with the lawyer's and their own subsequent confidence in the CPA.

Solicitation

Webster defines solicitation as a "moving or drawing force." The agreement permits a CPA to solicit any potential client by any means, including direct solicitation.

INT: What opportunities for effectively promoting accounting services do you foresee relative to the agreement's allowance of in-person, uninvited solicitation of potential clients?

MKT: Personal selling is a potentially powerful tool in the marketing of services because it allows consumers and salespeople to interact directly. CPAs can sell their services much more effectively via personal solicitation than they can by advertising in a newspaper. Actually, many accountants are already excellent salespeople–they manage to get the job done without asking directly. Direct solicitation should allow them to become even better.

Although the question does not address soliciting existing clients or potential clients who contact the accounting firm, I would strongly suggest that accountants employ direct solicitation in these situations. Consumers that enter into a service transaction generally interact with a service firm's employees. Customer contact personnel can be trained to take advantage of this opportunity to reduce customer uncertainty, give reassurance, reduce dissonance, and promote the reputation of the accounting firm.

CPA: I agree with the entire response of my fellow-debater in a sense. I must add that even if uninvited in-person solicitation was practical, it should not be regarded as a promotional opportunity by the CPA. These potential clients would generally be clients of other CPAs. Although competition in general is a positive thing, accounting is a unique profession in that accountants must retain a high level of objectivity. Practitioners who knowingly try to steal away clients from other CPAs when contact is uninvited would find it difficult to maintain the level of objectivity that they should. They would likely find themselves making statements to clients that would be difficult to back up with action.

MKT: Balderdash!

Advertising

The consent order permits CPAs to advertise by using self-laudatory or comparative claims, testimonials or endorsements, and advertisements not considered by the AICPA to be professionally dignified or in good taste.

Professional service providers such as doctors, lawyers, and CPAs were restricted from advertising until recent years. Consumers are beginning to adjust to seeing professionals, particularly lawyers, advertise their services. Lawyers sometimes advertise on TV, for example, by offering legal services related to divorce or bankruptcy–sometimes lawyers try to attract customers by stating that if they do not win the case the client will not pay.

Most advertising by accountants to this point has been done via newspapers or accounting journals, but Big Six accounting firms are starting to advertise on television. A large number of CPAs, however, have never advertised because they view advertising as highly unprofessional. Thus, advertising is largely unfamiliar territory to much of the accounting profession. As a result of the AICPA-FTC agreement, CPAs can use more competitive forms of advertising.

INT: Will CPAs who continue refraining from advertising be able to effectively compete in light of the agreement?

CPA: I believe that they will. Just as many CPAs feel that advertising accounting services is highly unprofessional, many accounting service consumers view advertising the same way. Many people are shocked at the lack of professionalism of lawyers who advertise legal services for divorce on television as though they are encouraging married couples to split up. Along the same vein, many potential consumers of accounting services would be turned off to see CPAs holding themselves out as accounting specialists, comparing their track records with those of other CPAs, bragging on themselves while putting other CPAs down, using biased testimonials, accepting endorsements, or using advertising that is not in good taste like running a TV spot during an X-rated movie. The agreement's loosening of restraints on advertising may ironically result in less advertising by the accounting profession. CPAs who want to be careful to protect their professional image may respond by becoming even more hardened against advertising.

MKT: I must disagree with my fellow-debater. The main reason professional service providers balk at advertising is that it is new to them. Innovations must always go through a diffusion phase before they are widely accepted and advertising innovations are no different. Although any given CPA may rightfully be hesitant to be the first one to advertise in a form permitted by the AICPA-FTC agreement, CPAs will ultimately move into the advertising arenas. After the initial shockwaves fade away, advertising will become acceptable to consumers and necessary for CPAs to maintain a competitive posture.

Even though CPAs could advertise in some forms prior to this agreement, they were still handcuffed to some degree. The agreement really makes advertising wide open for CPAs now. Consumers tend to value word-of-mouth communications more than company sponsored communications. This is especially true for services and, therefore, accounting firms should attempt to stimulate and to simulate word-of-mouth communications. This can be accomplished by encouraging consumers to tell their friends about satisfactory performance. Word-of-mouth can be simulated through communication messages using a testimonial format like television advertisements that feature consumers who vouch for the benefits of a service offered by a particular firm. Receiving open endorsements by organizations like the Chamber of Commerce could not hurt an accounting firm's image.

Perhaps the greatest contribution of advertising involves fostering competition and its benefits to consumers. How does a small firm which offers high quality products and services become large quickly? Advertising. Without advertising, competition is less and established firms have the small firm or CPA exactly where they want them—down, with a long road up. Another more subtle potential contribution of advertising involves actually increasing word-of-mouth communications among CPA clients. In particular, people are more likely to talk about a low quality CPA or attorney if they advertise. Without advertising, people tend to keep their "bad decisions" to themselves.

Overall, the changes resulting from the agreement suggest that the accounting profession must start establishing an advertising strategy that encompasses the promotional avenues opened by the agreement. CPAs who ignore these opportunities may see their clients drawn away by the sophisticated advertising techniques of other CPAs.

Trade Names

The agreement defines a trade name as a name used to designate a business enterprise. The agreement provides that CPAs can use any trade name that is not false or deceptive. This would permit a CPA firm to use a business name denoting specialization or to use fictitious names in the trade name.

INT: How do trade names fit in relative to the marketing of accounting services?

MKT: Trade names would be used primarily as promotional devices. Trade names are often prominently displayed on signs outside the doors of an accounting firm. The traditional trade names found on these signs could be lengthened to include a listing of the services offered, for example, Jones and Edwards, CPAs–Audit, Tax, MAS, Computer Hardware/Software, Real Estate. CPAs who have particular expertise in dealing with estate taxes, for example, could identify themselves in the trade name as Estate Tax Specialists.

CPA: A trade name should truthfully describe the form of business, that is, proprietorship, partnership, or professional corporation and should be used as a promotional tool within these boundaries.

SUMMARY

The impact of the AICPA-FTC agreement on the marketing of accounting services may be uncertain for some time but is sure to be pervasive. CPAs should study the agreement's potential implications and decide how to react in the short-range and long-range with regard to planning their marketing strategies.

Chapter 9

Professional Tax Service Marketing from a Consumer Buyer Behavior Perspective

James R. Dalkin

CURRENT ENVIRONMENT

Marketing tax services has traditionally been limited to personal selling and referral marketing. One notable exception is the national tax firm of H&R Block, which has advertised primarily through the television media. However, many tax professionals perceive marketing as an unnecessary evil. Indeed, "a substantial portion of tax professional's billable time is spent providing accounting services and preparing compilations and tax returns."[1] When marketing does take place, a study (Reagan and Gavin, 1988) found "accountants indicate they most frequently use referrals, participation in community activities, and personal selling to market their services; least frequently used are printed advertising in the Yellow Pages, newspapers, magazines and direct mail."[2]

Another factor that adversely affects the professional marketing concept is that "many of today's professionals have negative images of 'marketing.'"[3] Research originated by Kotler and Connor and highlighted by Honeycutt and Marts suggests that professionals must cope with the following three significant forces:

This chapter was first published in *Journal of Professional Services Marketing*, Vol. 10(2) 1993.

1. Assaults on Professional Codes of Ethics.
2. Changing Expectations of Clients.
3. Increased Competition.

The forces are further complicated by the following:

1. Disdain of Commercialism–Few professionals view themselves as business people. Many claim to be motivated by providing service to clients and, therefore, do not enjoy discussing fees.
2. Association Codes of Ethics–Professional bans against advertising, direct solicitation, and referral commissions were banned. These bans have been declared illegal since 1978, but their influence remains.
3. Equating Marketing with Selling–Most professionals make the mistake of viewing marketing as selling. Marketing is a much larger force than selling.[4]

Furthermore research (Marts, 1991) demonstrates that "professionals have always done some marketing yet its application has usually been fragmented. Professional governing bodies and their codes of ethics have been restrictive in terms of allowing marketing in any comprehensive or systematic manner. There exists a fear marketing will debase or demean the professionals, adversely affect consumer confidence or even threaten the quality of services. However, evidence has proven that this has not occurred. Further, some of the confusion that marketing entails is perhaps contributing to the reluctance of professionals in embracing the concept."[5]

Based upon a literature review, the environment appears to be in a paradox: the professionals are reluctant to market, yet the industry has become market-driven and a firm's survival depends on marketing. Nevertheless, marketing without focus may prove to be futile and a financial drain on the tax professional. As professionals learn to accept the need to market, they will need to learn how to successfully market their services. Recent research indicates those who do engage in marketing have little confidence in its results. In a study by Honeycutt and Marts, "66 percent of the respondents who advertise do not know or attribute less than 5 percent of their clients to advertising results."[6] Clearly, tax professionals must gain confidence that their marketing efforts are worthwhile in order for the marketing concept to receive greater acceptance. Learning which marketing techniques will be successful is critical for professionals attempting to market their services.

METHOD

Before a marketing strategy can be formulated, whether it includes advertising or not, a study of consumer behavior should be undertaken to understand attitudes and views toward professional service marketing. Given the importance of qualitative methodologies to aid market research, the research included a focus group interview with six randomly selected subjects. Areas of inquiry included demographic and socioeconomic backgrounds, attitudes toward methods of professional service advertising, criteria for selecting a tax return preparer, and other important factors focusing on the buying behavior process for tax services.

Participants were required to complete a questionnaire prior to group questioning. The group included the following: naval officer, real estate agent, college administrator, attorney, engineer, and retired teacher. Four members of the group had completed college and an additional two completed graduate level work. The income level ranged from $30,000 to $145,000 with the median $37,500 and the mean $59,750. Two of the participants had less complicated returns as judged by preparation of either a 1040A or not itemizing deductions. The others all itemized deductions on their return. Five of the participants had previously used a tax return preparer, while one prepared his own return.

Five members in the focus group believed their return was either too difficult to prepare themselves or would require too much of their own time to prepare. Of the attributes the participants would have preferred in their tax return professional, most indicated that return preparation promptness was the single most important attribute. The price range participants were willing to pay for tax return preparation services was $50 to $800 dollars with a median of $100 and a mean of $236.

Focus group members indicated that a certified public accountant (CPA) was the single most important professional qualification in selecting a tax return preparer. Other options discussed included a tax "literate" person, an enrolled agent, and an attorney at law. The nature of practice whether it be a national firm (such as H&R Block), local practitioner, or accounting firm did not play an important role in their decision selection process.

The factors affecting selection of tax return preparers were further analyzed. All members of the group indicated that a referral provided the best form of advertising. There appeared to be a universal disdain for mass advertising techniques including phone solicitation and direct mail. While the participants objected to the term "direct mail" a "personalized letter" did not meet with the same negative reaction. The group rated qualification, convenience, and cost in order of relative importance, respectively. However, participants clearly did have a limit to what amount they were willing to pay.

Another important aspect was establishing a personal relationship with their tax return preparer. The group indicated they wanted a relationship where they felt free to call upon their accountant and ask questions. This was especially important for the retired participant who considered her tax return preparer a "friend."

CONSUMER PERCEPTION

The focus group's consumer behavior was generally validated by the current research. Previous research has found that, fundamentally, "many clients do not care about the professional service firm, they buy the individual."[7] Based upon feedback from the focus group, most participants placed a high value on a personal relationship with their professional. Group members relied heavily upon subjective types of information when considering a tax professional. Important subjective attributes include quality of work, truthfulness, and competency.

To validate subjective attributes, group members relied heavily on information provided by "personal" sources of information. In a study (Murdock highlighted by Mangold), "it was found that word of mouth was the most effective source for communicating information that related to such subjective attributes as competence, reputation, and possession of up-to-date knowledge."[8]

Selection of a tax return preparer was a high involvement decision for members of the focus group. Although members were willing to spend only $100 on average for tax return preparation, the decision process was more involved than most products within a similar price range. The Mangold study found "personal sources of information are more important to a selection when the perceived risk associated with a decision is high."[9] This risk includes physical, financial, or emotional risk and is typically associated with the professional service sector. When the perceived risk associated with a purchase is high, then, personal sources can be expected to have a dominant, or decisive impact on the purchase decision.

THE SEARCH PROCESS

As part of the selection process, potential seekers of professional tax services undergo a prepurchase search process. The nature of this process is affected by the consumers' educational, occupational, and demographic background. Freiden and Goldsmith found that new residents rely heavily on informal social contacts to learn about products and services. Freiden and Goldsmith also found that personal information sources tended to dominate the search process for professional services. In addition, consumers purchase professional services with less frequency than products and once a relationship has been established changes do not occur often.

In general, focus group participants had retained the same tax professional for a number of years. Thus, in the search process, focus group members selected their tax return preparer on a permanent basis. Group participants would only change their preparer under certain circumstances including physical relocation or dissatisfaction with the quality or cost of the preparation service. Thus, once a selection was made, focus group members were not likely to "try" new brands, which is a more common behavior with low cost product purchases. This factor partially explains the high involvement characteristics for tax return preparation services.

SEARCH LIMITATIONS

The lack of established marketing channels and limited information or quality ranking of tax professionals contributes to a more difficult search process. The search for satisfactory solutions in the product area includes a wide range of consumer information sources. The search for professional services is more confined. Due to the particular characteristics of the services, typical "search qualities" are non-existent or irrelevant to the consumption experiences. The consumer often lacks information on price, amount of time needed to secure the service, or even what the environment in which the service is delivered is like.

"Researchers have confirmed that the credibility of personal information sources encourages their use in situations of high perceived risk. This physical, financial or emotional risk is typically associated with the professional service sector. Professional service alternatives tend to be fewer and more difficult to locate. Other than listings in the yellow pages, consumers tend to be unaware of professional directories or other listings and advertising is still limited."[10] Focus group participants perceived a lack of information to perform their search for professional tax services. To compensate for this lack of information, participants would first inquire with an individual with whom they perceived to be knowledgeable of "good" tax preparers. None of the focus group members considered using professional listings to select their tax professional.

DECISION PROCESS

The decision process for selection of professional services must be examined on a more fundamental level. "There exists some fundamental differences in the nature of products and services."[11] Product and service marketing paradigms have been developed that "begin with consumers' recognition of a discrepancy between the existing states of affairs and a desired state of affairs. Seeking potential solutions requires a distinctly different process from that point on."[12] Many of the differences in the buyer behavior process are engendered by the different nature of the exchange transactions. Professional service marketing can be viewed in "the exchange concept as a central paradigm for the consumer behavior process. In this new domain, theorists and researchers were forced to consider how consumer decisions like giving blood were similar to decisions to buy a television set or a hamburger. They recognized that, at the most fundamental level, all of these decisions involve the exchange of bundles of costs for bundles of benefits."[13]

The first concept in the buying process for an intangible service involves identification and awareness of the service. Following identification of the service, the buyer must then be sufficiently influenced in order to be persuaded to purchase the product. Thus, information and influence must be present for the adoption process to be successful.

Social psychology examines concepts such as motivation which would influence buyer behavior in service marketing. A variety of factors influence an individual's decisions and purchase marketing behavior. The nature of the communication, the credibility, and the level of trust in the organization delivering the service are all primary factors that may influence an individual's decision. This corresponds to the responses from the focus group concerning the need for trust and credibility in selecting a tax return preparer.

The manner in which marketing communication is delivered also plays an important role in determining its effectiveness. Important factors include whether a communication is more persuasive if designed to appeal to the audience's reasoning ability or to arouse the audience's emotions. Other variables involve whether people are more swayed by a communication if tied to a vivid personal experience or if bolstered by a great deal of clear and unimpeachable statistical evidence. "The overwhelming weight of experimental data suggests that, all other things being equal, the more frightened a person is by a communication, the more likely he or she is to take a positive preventive action."[14]

INFLUENCING CONSUMERS

Given that marketing for services such as tax return preparation do not offer physical products, buyer behavior must be influenced through other means. Often advertising campaigns that play heavily on the range of human emotions can foster strong reactions from the targeted audience. For example, a campaign for tax services would want to evoke emotions of trust and the need for financial security.

For the tax professional, the implication is that marketing should be developed to highlight anxieties toward preparing one's own return. However, while a marketing campaign stating that an individual improperly preparing his own return may be put in jail would arouse the fear emotion, it would be considered in poor taste. However, a marketing effort stating that individuals would sleep well at night knowing their return was properly prepared by a qualified professional would better deliver the same message.

The acceptance of a service marketing concept can largely be influenced by the perceived trustworthiness of the communication. For example, if the communicator is believed to be less than respectable, the level of belief will be significantly reduced. In this environment, potential consumers rely heavily on professional qualifications as a methodology for initially evaluating a professional. The focus group indicated that a public accountant certification was an important designation for their tax return preparer. Interestingly enough, the CPA designation does not accurately reflect on an individual's ability to prepare a tax return. However, the designation has a high value in society as consumers perceive an individual with such a designation to be qualified.

In addition, concepts delivered by individuals or groups who are considered experts in the field generate a much higher level of acceptance. Thus, a marketing campaign that highlights an individual with high community or professional standing can provide further persuasion. For example, an advertisement that aligns a tax return professional with a highly esteemed organization would further persuade a potential consumer.

IMPLICATIONS AND CONCLUSION

The focus group provides valuable insight into the consumer behavior selection process for tax services. First, tax professionals must make their name available to be considered in the preselection process. Research found that methods employed by potential consumers were not sophisticated and consumers were not often aware of sources that listed professionals.

Additionally, subjective types of information play a significant role in the purchase decision. Tax professionals must be aware of customers' primary selection criteria before designing a marketing program. Marketing of tax services must address subjective issues such as quality, personal relationships, and qualifications of the potential preparer. "Quality becomes a matter of a subjectively perceived quality which is also influenced by the professional's ability to sell oneself and the results. The professional should be able to bring about a degree of increased certainty for the client in an area where uncertainty is felt." [15]

A marketing program must meet the subjective concerns of the potential customer. The focus group's opinions indicate that the "old" methods of marketing professional services through personal selling which includes referrals tend to have the most credibility in the buying behavior process. Thus, the process that is currently the most widely accepted by professionals may be the most effective. However, "personal selling as a marketing strategy is the most expensive form of communication." [16]

While personal selling may be the most direct and effective method, tax professionals should consider employing additional techniques to supplement personal selling. Clearly, commercial sources such as direct mail or phone solicitation do not have enough credibility and would either be discarded or considered a negative by recipients.

Successful options may include developing referral contacts with individuals who regularly meet with those in need of professional services. For example, to market to new residents who would likely be in need of professional services, a tax return professional should establish relationships with real estate agents, who may be considered a credible personal referral source. Such a relationship would reduce the amount of time expended on meeting all "new" residents, which provides more credibility than a form letter stating "Welcome new resident . . . My firm offers superior tax services."

Many tax professionals have avoided direct mail and other forms of direct advertising. The focus group clearly indicated that impersonal direct mail or phone solicitations would not be successful. However, the focus group did not object to the idea of a "personalized" letter. There appears to be a perception gap between the negative view toward direct mail and that of a personal letter. The implication is that a professional could engage in less costly forms of advertising than personal selling. Any "personalized" letter would need to address the critical factors in the buying behavior process toward tax services. A critical success factor for "personalized" letters would be the message. Specifically, the letter would need to emphasize quality, the preparers qualifications, and relationships with clients. Other attributes, such as costs play a less significant role in the first contact. In fact, addressing cost may adversely affect perceptions of quality. For example, a tax professional who issues a "personalized letter" emphasizing cost may be viewed as less qualified.

The marketing of professional tax services has not been developed to its potential. Tax professionals have heard they "need" to market, but have received little direction "how" to successfully market. A lack of direction combined with a historical negative association with professional services marketing has stagnated marketing efforts for many tax professionals. Professionals need to be educated on the buyer behavior process as it relates to professional services. Once these professionals become more comfortable with the critical success factors of marketing, including delivery of the proper message for their services, marketing of professional tax services will become more accepted as a successful tool to develop a tax practice.

NOTES

1. Reagan, Carmen C., and Gavin, Thomas A., "The Small Accounting Firm: Managing the Dynamics of the Marketing Function," *Journal of Professional Services Marketing*, Vol. 3 1988, p. 306.

2. Reagan and Gavin, p. 309.

3. Honeycutt, Earl D., Jr., Marts, John A., "Marketing by Professionals as Applied to CPA Firms: Room for Improvement?" *Journal of Professional Services Marketing*, Vol. 6(1) 1991, p. 29.

4. Honeycutt and Marts, p 31.

5. Crane, F.G., "Part One: Generic Professional Services Marketing Articles," *Journal of Professional Services Marketing*, Vol. 5(1) 1989, p. 4.

6. Honeycutt and Marts, p. 39.

7. Webster, Cynthia, "Strategies for Becoming Marketing-Oriented in the Professional Services Arena," *Journal of Professional Services Marketing*, Vol. 2 1987, p. 19.

8. Mangold, Glynn W., "Use of Commercial Sources of Information in the Purchase of Professional Services: What the Literature Tells Us," *Journal of Professional Services Marketing*, Vol. 3 1987, p. 13.

9. Mangold, p. 9.

10. Barnes, Nora Ganim, "The Consumer Decision Process for Professional Services Marketing: A New Perspective," *Journal of Professional Services Marketing*, Vol. 2 1986, p. 42.

11. Barnes, p. 41.
12. Barnes, p. 41.
13. Kassarjian, H.H., and Robertson, T.S., *Handbook of Consumer Behavior*, (New Jersey: Prentice-Hall, 1991) p. 486.
14. Aronson, E., *The Social Animal*, (New York: W.H. Freeman and Company, 1988) p. 83.
15. Webster, p. 17.
16. Reagan and Gavin, p. 311.

BIBLIOGRAPHY

Ahmed, Zafar U, "A Strategic Plan for Marketing Accounting Services," *CPA Journal*. Vol: 60. October 1990. pp. 50-57.

Aronson, E. *The Social Animal*. New York: W.H. Freeman and Company, 1988.

Barnes, Nora Ganim. "The Consumer Decision Process for Professional Services Marketing: A New Perspective," *Journal of Professional Services Marketing*. Vol: 2. 1986. pp. 39-45.

Crane, F. G. "A Practical Guide to Professional Services Marketing," *Journal of Professional Services Marketing*. Vol: 5. 1989. pp. 3-15.

Freedman, Art., "Part 1: How to Create a Tax Marketing Culture," *Practical Accountant*. Vol: 23. May 1990. pp. 12-22.

Freiden, Jon B., and Goldsmith, Ronald E. "Correlates of Consumer Information Search for Professional Services," *Journal of Professional Services Marketing*. Vol: 4. 1988. pp. 15-27.

Honeycutt, Earl D., and Marts, John A. "Marketing by Professionals as Applied to CPA Firms: Room for Improvement?" *Journal of Professional Services Marketing*. Vol: 6. 1990. pp. 29-41.

Johnson, E.M. et al. *Profitable Service Marketing*. Illinois: Dow Jones-Irwin, 1986.

Kassarjian, H. H., and Robertson, T. S. *Handbook of Consumer Behavior*. New Jersey: Prentice-Hall, 1991.

Mangold, Glynn W., "Use of Commercial Sources of Information in the Purchase of Professional Services: What the Literature Tells Us," *Journal of Professional Services Marketing*. Vol: 3. 1987. pp. 5-15.

Pope, Ralph A. "Marketing Financial Planning Services: Highlights of a Survey of CPAs," *Journal of Professional Services Marketing*. Vol: 3. 1988. pp. 297-303.

Reagan, Carmen C., and Gavin, Thomas A. "The Small Accounting Firm: Managing the Dynamics of the Marketing Function," *Journal of Professional Services Marketing*. Vol: 3. 1988. pp. 314.

Tootelian, Dennis H., and Gaedeke, Ralph M. "Marketing of Professional Services as Applied to Tax Professionals: Representation of the Client, Public, or Profession?" *Journal of Professional Services Marketing*. Vol: 6. 1990. pp. 17-27.

Webster, Cynthia. "Strategies for Becoming Marketing-Oriented in the Professional Services Arena," *Journal of Professional Services Marketing*. Vol: 2. 1987. pp. 11-25.

Chapter 10

Effects of the Price
of Tax Preparation Services
and the CPA Credential
on the Perception of Service Quality

Jeffery M. Ferguson
Lexis F. Higgins

INTRODUCTION

Concern with marketing principles has become more and more common among those who market accounting services (George and Wheiler 1986). Many firms marketing such services first become aware of marketing basics through the design and development of promotional programs. However, as their familiarity with marketing progresses, accounting firms recognize the need for application of marketing research projects designed to gain a better understanding of their target markets. This understanding leads to market segmentation strategies, assists in planning the marketing mix, and helps determine overall marketing strategy for the firm.

An understanding of customers' perception of price and quality relationships is one important ingredient for designing effective marketing programs. This information helps the accounting firm understand and sometimes predict how its particular target market(s) will react to certain pricing strategies such as price cuts, special deals, coupons, and promotional appeals. Specifically, a well-designed research project can help the firm answer such ques-

---

This chapter was first published in *Journal of Professional Services Marketing*, Vol. 5(1) 1989.

tions as: Do customers believe paying a higher price necessarily means receiving higher service quality? Does the title used by a firm create a certain perception of quality and price expectations among prospective customers?

This chapter provides a discussion of such a study. We describe the process of doing a study of customers' perception of price and quality relationships in a specific market for accounting services. We discuss this study from the perspective of consultants who have done such studies for accounting firms in a metropolitan area. The chapter outlines the research questions identified, describes the research process applied to address the research questions, and discusses results of the study.

Two of the specific research questions tested in this study are:

1. Does the price charged by an accounting firm have an impact on how present and potential customers perceive the quality of the tax preparation services offered?
2. Does the credential of the individual that prepares the taxes have an impact on expected quality of the services provided?

These and other research questions are described and addressed in more length in this study. We now turn to a description of how the study was planned and designed.

RESEARCH DESIGN

Previous research (Monroe 1973) has shown that price and brand information may have a significant impact on the perception of product quality. In the area of public accounting, the CPA credential may act as a brand which signifies a certain level of service quality. Research by Wood and Ball (1978) suggests that potential clients do use the CPA credential as an indicator of general technical expertise. However, isolating the degree of impact on the CPA "brand" can be a difficult task. Since many factors affect a customer's assessment of service quality, any study of price and credential effects must be carefully designed to isolate these factors. Otherwise, the specific impact of price and credential cannot be known. Additionally, care must be taken to ensure that the study does not intrude into the situation in a way that creates as well as measures attitudes, or elicits atypical roles or responses from the subjects. Such problems frequently occur in surveys when subjects know the purpose of the study. They may take a cooperative posture and answer in ways which do not reflect their true judgments.

In order to minimize the aforementioned problems, a 3 × 3 between-subjects factorial design was used. This design features three levels of price and three different credentials of the accounting service provider. The subjects were given booklets containing an advertisement for a fictitious tax preparer. The advertisement contained information about the tax preparer and his service. His professional credential was prominently placed at the top of the ad while the price was in the body of the ad (see Figure 1). Subjects were told that the purpose of the study was to determine consumers' perceptions of different service firms. They were instructed to read the ad and then answer questions about the tax preparer.

Subjects

The participants in the study consisted of a convenience sample of 247 adults living in the Colorado Springs, Colorado area. As

FIGURE 1. Sample Advertisement

JOHN PETERS

Certified Public Accountant (CPA)

"My goal is personalized tax service for you."

John Peters will prepare your taxes in the comfort of your home or office for $125 per hour.

Special emphasis is placed on tax preparation and planning with related services for the individual and small business. Experience with all forms of taxation problems provides the background for doing your taxes quickly and accurately.

Call 485-4491 for an appointment.

All forms and postage included.

---

shown in Table 1, these individuals represent a broad cross-section of taxpayers.

Procedure

Booklets were put in random order before being distributed to ensure random assignment of treatments to each respondent. Each booklet contained an instruction sheet, an advertisement containing the experimental treatments, and a questionnaire concerning the tax service.

Independent Variables

The price of the tax preparation service was manipulated by identifying one of three rates ($15, $50, or $125 per hour) in the body of the ad. These rates represent the range of rates typically charged for tax services in Colorado Springs.

TABLE 1. Subject Demographics. n = 247

Sex		Marital Status	
Male	46.7%	Married	62.8%
Female	53.3%	Single	37.2%
Age		**Household Income**	
Under 20	2.0%	Under $10,000	6.6%
20-29	35.0%	$10-20,000	19.0%
30-39	32.9%	$20-30,000	21.9%
40-49	17.5%	$30-40,000	16.9%
50-59	6.8%	$40,000 Up	35.5%
65 or Over	5.7%		
		Formal Education	
Occupation		**Completed**	
Prof. Tech.	26.4%	Some high school	1.6%
Mgr., Prop.	12.6%	High school grad	24.7%
Sls., Cler.	35.4%	Some college	32.8%
Skilled	10.2%	College grad	21.1%
Semiskilled	4.1%	Grad school	19.8%
Unskilled	1.2%		
Retired	2.4%		
Unemployed	.4%		
Homemaker	2.8%		
Student	4.5%		

The professional credential of the tax preparer was listed as either Bookkeeper, Tax Advisor, or CPA. These titles represent the most frequently used professional credentials appearing in the yellow pages. The idea behind using them was to expose potential customers to the same kind of choices they are likely to encounter when searching for a tax service. An example of the ad is shown in Figure 1.

Dependent Variables

The multiple dependent variables used in this study were designed to measure whether or not the price and professional credential of the tax preparer would affect the perceived quality of the service. Individual questions were designed to measure beliefs, attitude, and intentions regarding the service. A seven-point Likert scale (1 = strongly disagree, and 7 = strongly agree) was used to measure each variable. The specific questions asked were as follows:

1. John Peters is qualified to provide income tax services.
2. John Peters is experienced in the area of tax preparation.
3. The service provided by John Peters is useful to me.
4. John Peters is a highly qualified tax preparer.
5. I would like to have Mr. Peters prepare my next tax return.
6. The service provided by John Peters is worth the price.

The questions were designed to measure all three levels of the hierarchy of effects. Questions 1 and 2 measure the subjects' beliefs about the tax service. Questions 3, 4, and 6 measure attitude toward the service, and Question 5 measures the intention to use the service in the future.

ANALYSIS AND RESULTS

The presence of multiple dependent measures suggests the use of MANOVA when the dependent variables are correlated due to measuring the same underlying factor or being collected from the same subjects (Hair, Anderson, Tatham, and Grablowsky 1979). This is due to the likelihood of Type I error through the use of repeated applications of ANOVA.

To determine if MANOVA was appropriate, the data were first factor analyzed using principal component analysis with a varimax rotation. A single factor, which might be called "service quality," was identified with an Eigenvalue greater than one (3.708). All six dependent variables had factor loadings greater than .676 and a reliability of α.87.

Price Effects

The mean ratings for the different price treatments on the six dependent variables are shown in Table 2. Multivariate analysis of variance revealed a significant main effect ($F = 3.78$, $p < .001$) for price. Univariate analysis of variance showed significant differences only for the variable "service is worth the price." To determine where the differences lie among the three levels of price, a least significant difference (LSD) multiple ranges test was con-

TABLE 2. Ratings of the Tax Service as a Function of Price

Variable	PRICE ($ Per Hour)			
	$15	$50	$125	F
Peters is qualified	3.83	3.88	3.78	.05
Peters is experienced	3.96	3.97	3.85	.12
Service is useful	3.97	3.62	3.57	1.49
Peters provides high quality tax service	3.24	3.30	3.15	.22
Want Peters to do my return	2.67	2.59	2.33	1.18
Service is worth the price	3.77[A]	2.90[B]	2.26[C]	18.10*

* $p < .001$

Means with different letter superscripts are significantly different from each other.

ducted. The results showed significant differences (p < .05) among all three prices. The lower the price, the greater the perceived worth of the service. These findings show no evidence that consumers use price as a predictor of service quality.

Credential Effects

The mean ratings for the different credential treatments on the six dependent measures are shown in Table 3. Multivariate analysis of variance revealed significant main effects (F = 4.07, p < .001) for professional credential. Univariate analysis of variance found significant differences (p < .001) for measures of the qualifications of Peters (Question 1), experience of Peters (Question 2), and the perceived quality of the service provided (Question 4). For all three of these variables the LSD test showed the evaluation of CPA to be significantly (p < .05) more positive than the evaluations for either bookkeeper or tax advisor. There were no significant differences between the evaluations of the bookkeeper and the tax advisor.

TABLE 3. Ratings of the Tax Service as a Function of Credential

| Variable | CREDENTIAL | | | |
	Bookkeeper	Tax Advisor	CPA	F
Peters is qualified	3.33^A	3.39^A	4.79^A	22.71*
Peters is experienced	3.57^A	3.73^A	4.51^B	8.51*
Service is useful	3.59	3.52	4.06	2.59
Peters provides high quality tax service	2.91^A	3.00^A	3.80^B	9.27*
Want Peters to do my return	2.46	2.36	2.79	1.83
Service is worth the price	2.75	2.88	3.30	2.42

*p < .001

Means with different letter superscripts are significantly different from each other.

Price and Credential Interactions

There were no significant price-credential interactions. That means, for example, that price did not have a greater impact on the perception of a CPA than on the perceptions of a bookkeeper or tax advisor.

DISCUSSION AND MANAGERIAL IMPLICATIONS

This section discusses the managerial implications of the study's findings. The discussion is especially targeted to both CPA and non-CPA firms that market accounting services involving tax preparation and consultation services to consumers.

Price/Quality Relationship for Accounting Services

The results of the study indicate that the consumers surveyed considered other information more important than price when establishing perceived quality of the accounting service. If one considers the overall image of an accounting service similar to the evaluation of the brand of a tangible product, this finding is consistent with other studies of consumer evaluation of price/quality relationships. It is also consistent with the research which suggests that customers use CPA as an indicator of technical competence (Wood and Ball 1978). Based on this finding, the following important implications appear:

Special pricing deals to consumers may not negatively impact the perceived quality of the services offered by an accounting firm. Promotional pricing such as lowered prices for early tax preparation, direct mail coupons for reduced prices, and special prices for ancillary services may all stimulate demand for services without reducing a previously established high-quality image of an organization. However, a firm may have difficulty maintaining a high-quality image if low price is the *sole* theme of its promotional campaign. Before instituting any promotion based on price, a firm needs to consider how the promotion fits in with the overall image the firm wishes to communicate to clients and potential clients.

Management attention to the design of services is essential. Because the study indicates that other, more important cues are being used by consumers in evaluation of overall service quality, those cues must be addressed in an orderly way and monitored to ensure a favorable impact on consumer attitudes toward the services provided. Parasuraman, Zeithaml, and Berry (1985) through executive interviews and focus-group interviews, determined several determinants of service quality. Table 4 lists these determinants along with questions for evaluating your firm's service offering. Accounting firms, both CPA and non-CPA, should establish a program to identify specific measures of these determinants for their present and potential clients and try to determine the relative importance of each determinant to clients. The firm should also develop a process for monitoring how well the quality of these dimensions is controlled in the delivery of the firm's service. For example, regarding "Access" as a determinant of service quality, how often is a present or potential client unable to call the accounting firm due to a busy telephone line, and how often are they put on hold when they call? When a client encounters a busy telephone line several times or is put on hold, the perceived quality of the firm's service will suffer. This may seem like a trivial matter to the CPA firm because it does not deal with its technical expertise. However, customers use an array of attributes as determinants of quality CPA services. A review of the service quality dimensions listed in Table 4 will help a CPA firm evaluate how well it has integrated these dimensions into the customer service program.

Importance of the CPA Credential

The study found that the CPA designation was significant in how quality was evaluated. While this may not be surprising to many, we are not aware of any previous studies that empirically tested this relationship. Also, it is important to examine the implications of this finding for both the CPA firm and the non-CPA firm. In a marketing sense, we might say that the CPA credential is well understood by consumers as a branding device for accounting services and is used in assessing the image and quality of the accounting services offered.

Implications for Firms
with the CPA Credential

The firm should build on the favorable credential/service quality perception of consumers by exploiting the presence of the credential to its fullest. There are other potential uses of the credential in addition to displaying it in promotional materials and on company logos. Advertising themes may be used that make the designation more prominent by using copy that points out that preparation of all taxes is done or supervised by a Certified Public Accountant. Informational programs on what "CPA" means (e.g., continuing education, accuracy, reliability, professional competence, etc.) also help in building awareness for the firm and its credentials. Also, other components of service quality mentioned in Table 4 should be managed with the designation in mind. Because the relationship between quality dimensions seems to be synergistic, the total image of the firm should be managed to take full advantage of the CPA credential. Many managers in accounting firms may aver that these steps are already being followed. However, the key to gaining the full potential represented by this approach is a well-planned and implemented process that considers both the strengths of the CPA designation and the delivery of the highest quality possible in the other service dimensions pointed out in Table 4.

Implications for Firms
without the CPA Credential

The study findings indicate that firms without the CPA designation will not suffer from aggressively promoting lower prices and package pricing deals. However, other dimensions of the service may be more effective in building business. For price to serve as a competitive advantage for these firms, the total service offered must be designed to instill confidence in the overall organization. These firms can compensate for the lack of the CPA credential by carefully assessing their most substantial competitive advantages such as more personalized service, quicker service delivery, and precise market segmentation.

Remember that the CPA credential is not a prerequisite for executing the service quality dimensions listed in Table 4. Like Avis,

TABLE 4. Determinants of Service Quality as Applied to Accounting Services*

Reliability
- Is the quality of your accounting service consistent?
- Can your clients have confidence that their taxes will be done correctly the first time?

Responsiveness
- Do your employees act promptly in returning calls and setting appointments?

Competence
- Is the knowledge and skill of all personnel that interact with the customer appropriate for that interaction?
- Is tax research in your firm managed effectively?

Access
- Can clients easily talk to an appropriate person in your firm? (For example, do clients often get a busy signal or are they put on hold when telephoning your office?)
- Do your hours of operation and location match the needs of present and potential clients?

Courtesy
- Are your customers always treated politely and considerately both on the telephone and in person by all contact personnel?

Communication
- Do your tax preparation personnel consider the knowledge of each customer when writing them or talking to them? (For example, the same statement might seem confusing to one client and condescending to another.)
- Do your tax preparation personnel effectively explain the approximate cost of your service and the expected time for completion of tax returns?

Credibility
- Does your organization make it clear to your clients that the organization exists to effectively meet their needs and your reputation is partially a function of how well this is done? Does all your market communication instill present and potential clients with confidence in the integrity of your firm?

Security
- Does your firm attempt to free each client of risk or doubt in the preparation of his/her taxes? (For example, is there ever any question in the client's mind regarding confidentiality?)

Understanding/Knowing the Customer
- Do you have a system by which the individual needs of each client are determined?
- Do you provide personal, individualized attention to each client or are they made to feel "like a number"?
- Do you take the opportunity to recognize your long-term clients or do you ignore them in favor of seeking new clients?

Tangibles
- Does your office and the appearance of your personnel project the image that your firm is seeking?
- Are your written communications projecting a feeling of quality?

*Adapted from Parasuraman, Zeithaml, and Berry (1985).

these firms may have to try harder. Customers respond more to how you treat them than they do to who you are. Without the instant credibility of having a CPA, more effort will have to be expended to ensure that customers "experience" quality in the various ways they interact with the firm.

CONCLUSION

In this chapter we discussed three general topic areas. First, we reported the findings of a study that addressed two major questions regarding accounting services. We examined the price/quality perceptions of accounting services among consumers and explored the impact of the CPA credential on perceived quality of the service. Second, we described some managerial implications of the findings as they related to both research questions. Third, we adapted the findings of a previous study to the present study and presented the determinants of service quality in a table with questions that accounting firms should address regarding their service quality.

The findings of the study and its managerial implications and the table presented, all indicate that it is imperative that accounting firms closely examine the quality of their service offering before implementing communications programs designed to build the firm's client base. A close look at an accounting firm's performance on each dimension of service quality and a process for improving weak areas and constantly monitoring those areas is an important prerequisite to any communications or promotion program.

Future research should examine the price/quality and CPA credential questions in other sampling contexts. Also, the managerial implications of the findings in this study should be extended to provide some clear guidelines for implication of the program we recommend here.

REFERENCES

George, William R. and Kent W. Wheiler. 1986. Practice development: A service marketing perspective. *CPA Journal* 56 (October): 30-43.

Hair, Joseph F. Jr., Rolph E. Anderson, Ronald L. Tatham, and Bernice J. Grablowsky. 1979. *Multivariable Data Analysis*. Tulsa: The Petroleum Publishing Company.

Monroe, Kent B. 1973. Buyer's subjective perceptions of price. *Journal of Marketing Research* 10 (February): 70-80.

Parasuraman, A., Valarie A. Zeithaml, and Leonard L. Berry. 1985. A conceptual model of service quality and its implications for future research. *Journal of Marketing* 49 (Fall): 41-50.

Wood, Thomas D. and Donald A. Ball. 1978. New rule 502 and effective advertising by CPA's. *Journal of Accountancy* (June): 65.

Chapter 11

Comparing Accountants' Perceptions Toward Marketing and Advertising in Hong Kong and Malaysia: A Preliminary Study

Thomas C.H. Wong
Oliver H.M. Yau
Abdul Latif Shaikh Mohamed al-Murisi
Abdul Aziz Abdul Latif

INTRODUCTION

The existing literature on attitudes toward advertising and marketing has progressed along two distinct streams of research. Studies in the first stream explore attitudes toward marketing and advertising from the viewpoint of consumers (Barksdale and Deaden 1972, Hite and Bellizzi 1986, Hite and Kiser 1985) Overall, two types of results were obtained. First, it was found that consumers had negative attitudes toward advertising and marketing in general. Criticisms mainly focused on advertising, deceptive advertising, insufficient information, and proliferation of advertising. Second, consumer attitudes about professional advertising were generally favorable. Consumers believed that advertising would not lower professional image (Hite and Bellizzi 1986).

The second stream of research comprises a number of studies that explore professionals' viewpoints of advertising and marketing (Allen and Arnold 1991, Folland, Peacock, and Pelfrey 1991,

This chapter is also being published in *Journal of Professional Services Marketing*, Vol. 11(2) Fall, 1994.

Jackson and Tod 1991, Honeycutt and Marts 1990, Hite and Fraser 1988, Hite and Schultz 1987, Hite, Schultz, and Weaver 1988, Stevens, McConkey, and Loudon 1990, Thompson, Smith, and Jordan 1991, Yau 1987, Yau and Sin 1985, Yau and Wong 1987). It was found that professionals tended to be more conservative than consumers. Most studies indicated that professionals still held negative attitudes toward advertising their services.

Studies in the above two streams were mostly conducted in the USA. Yau and Wong (1987) have indicated that economic and cultural forces would have impacts on professionals' attitudes toward advertising. However, little has been done comparing professionals' attitudes toward advertising. Hence, this chapter attempts to examine how CPA firms in different countries perceive the concepts of advertising and marketing. More specifically, the main points are (a) to better understand how accountants perceive the effects of advertising and marketing of their services on professional ethics; and (b) to compare Hong Kong accountants' perceptions toward marketing and advertising with those in Malaysia.

BACKGROUND

Professional accounting associations were established during the late nineteenth century. Like other professional bodies, a feature of their structure is self-discipline. A code of ethics is imposed upon members in order to protect the interests of the public and the reputation of the profession. Since the earliest years, one of the tenets of that code has been restriction on self-promotion through advertising or publicity. This restriction had gained virtually universal support from the public and the profession until the 1970s. Nowadays, professional accounting bodies in most English-speaking countries have relaxed restrictions on advertising and other marketing activities to varying degrees.

Reasons for Development

The development of marketing, especially advertising, by professional accountants in most developed or developing countries followed more or less the same pattern as the US profession whose members initiated the change. The driving force behind the change came mainly from government. The US accounting professions were challenged by the Federal Trade Commission and later by the Justice Department on the issues of price fixing, anti-trust law, and conspiracy in restraint of trade. The British accounting professions were challenged by the Monopolies Commission, and by the Office of Fair Trading on restrictive trade practices.

In the 1970s the British accounting professions presented a united front against the arguments of the Monopolies Commission that restrictive trade practices resulted from prohibition of promotional activities. In 1983, the Council of the Institute of Chartered Accounting in England and Wales changed their attitude toward advertising and agreed that the present rules were unsatisfactory in many respects and that publicity and advertising should be permitted. This line of thinking was shared and supported by large accounting firms. One of the possible reasons which brought about this drastic change was that large accounting firms, which are major international enterprises, were heavily hit by stagflation in the 1970s. Suffering from a combination of lower earnings and rising overheads, these major firms had to look for opportunities to increase market share. The territory of the smaller practice did not escape attention. The large firms saw that liberalization of advertising and some marketing activities was the surest way of gaining much of the smaller firms' business. Another reason for the change of attitude was the competition from non-accounting sectors, such as banks and financial institutions, which had provided services traditionally rendered by chartered accountants. Non-accounting firms were able to use all media to advertise their services whereas professional accounting firms were not allowed to compete equally. Thus, professional accountants found that there was a need to inform the general public of all services which their profession was able to offer and thereby to ensure that the profession did not lose ground to those without professional qualification or professional responsibility.

The Accounting Profession in Hong Kong

The Hong Kong Society of Accountants (HKSA) was established in 1973 by the Professional Accountants Ordinance. There are three classes of membership: student, associate, and fellow. In addition practicing certificates were issued to those who have obtained appropriate experience and passed the required examinations. In December, 1988, HKSA had about 12,000 student members, 4,500 associates and fellows, and 400 accounting firms. Among these accounting firms, 95 percent have fewer than 50 staff members. All the "big eight" firms have offices in Hong Kong. The largest of them has about 800 staff members. The average size of the "big eight" firms is around 400 staff members.

Since the 1970s, Hong Kong has built herself into one of the major financial and industrial centers of the world. The success of Hong Kong is largely attributed to the "non-intervention" policy of the government. As such, business is able to operate under minimum government regulation. Nevertheless, accountants in Hong Kong are not allowed to advertise within this environment of free trade and free competition. Statement 1.205B, Professional Ethics: Advertising, of the Hong Kong Society of Accountants states, "A member should not advertise his professional services or skills." A member of the HKSA may be restricted to place an advertisement under these situations. The development of accounting standards in Hong Kong was or has been very much in line with their development in the United Kingdom. The direction of the HKSA is no doubt influenced largely by its counterpart in the UK. It would be surprising therefore to see that both institutes have different views on the issue of advertising and marketing.

The Accounting Profession in Malaysia

Malaysia was formerly a colony of the United Kingdom. The development of the accounting profession in Malaysia was also very much influenced by the professional accounting associations in the United Kingdom. A well-organized accountancy profession started in Malaysia when a group of qualified accountants returned from the United Kingdom in the pre-Second World War period and established the Association of Chartered and Incorporated Accountants (ACIA). However, their activities were stopped in 1940-1945 during World War II.

In 1958, 20 local accountants who were members of the ACIA incorporated the Malaysian Association of Certified Public Accountants (MACPA) and the Malaysian branch of the Association of Certified and Corporate Accountants (ACCA). The MACPA is responsible for controlling accounting standards in Malaysia. The Accounting and Auditing Standards Committee of the MACPA has been assigned the responsibility of studying every standard issued by the International Accounting Standards Committee (IASC). The approved standards will then become mandatory to all MACPA members. However, as a private body which was hampered by its relatively small membership, MACPA was unable to address many issues faced by the accountancy profession.

In 1967, recognizing the need for legal regulation, the government, through the Accountants Act 1967, established the Malaysian Institute of Accountants (MIA). However, for the first 20 years of its incorporation, the MIA was dormant except in the activity of registering its members.

Since 1973, the idea of integration to strengthen the profession had been deliberated by the Councils of the MACPA and the MIA. Unfortunately, in July 1985, the Amendment Bill to the Accountants Act 1967 to effect the merger of the two bodies was rejected by the Cabinet. Despite this setback, the MACPA and the MIA continued to work toward unification of the profession.

April 1987 saw a new dimension in the accounting profession in Malaysia when the joint working committee's proposed co-operation arrangement was accepted by the Council of the two bodies. Under this arrangement, all technical standards for the accountancy profession in the country would be jointly developed by them and issued as joint statements to members of both bodies. Through the consolidation of resources and efforts, the two bodies will minimize duplication of effort and work together for the good of the accountancy profession in Malaysia.

THE STUDY

The Samples

The Hong Kong sample was drawn from the Hong Kong Yellow Pages telephone directory which provided a list of 360 CPA firms.

One hundred twenty firms were drawn by systematic sampling. Eighty successful interviews resulted, for a response rate of 75 percent. This response rate is acceptable when it is compared with those in similar studies in Hong Kong. (Sin, Cheng, and Yau 1986.) The CPA firms in the sample were largely small firms with only one partner (68.75 percent). Only 6.25 percent of them had four or more partners. Results also indicate that 93.75 percent of them were small firms with 50 or fewer staff members and only 6.25 percent had more than 50 staff members. These findings are very close to those of the population.

The Malaysian sample was drawn by using a systemic 1 in 3 sampling technique using the Directory of Accountants, Tax Consultants, and Tax Advisers (as of 30 September, 1988) as the sampling frame. Structured questions were sent to the senior partners of 416 CPA firms. Out of the 416 questionnaires posted, 68 envelopes marked "moved" or "no such person" were returned. Eighty-six successful responses were received which give an acceptable response rate of 20.67 percent (Kerlinger 1973).

Measurement Instrument

Apart from the demographic profile of respondents, 27 statements were tailored to analyze the CPAs' perception of marketing and advertising. These 27 statements were classified into five categories: (1) promotion, (2) products/services, (3) price, (4) customers, and (5) ethics of accounting services, and were evaluated by respondents on a 5-point Likert-scale, ranging from strongly disagree (1) to strongly agree (5). To make the analysis simple, responses on all statements were recoded in three categories: "agree," "uncertain," and "disagree."

FINDINGS

After eliminating the uncertain responses, each statement of the 27 items was subject to a two-tailed z-test. For the two samples, the hypothesis was tested at the alpha level of 0.05. The results show that all statements are significant at 0.05, except for statements 3 and 8 for the Hong Kong sample. In order to compare the perceptions of the two samples employed in the analysis, a T-test was used to compare their mean scores. At the level of 0.05, 14 out of the 27 statements were found to have significant difference between the two samples.

Attitudes toward promotion. Accountants in both countries showed a significant difference in opinion on statement 1, "all accounting firms should be allowed to advertise." (See Table 1.)

TABLE 1. Attitudes Toward Promotion

| Statement | Mean Score | | |
	Hong Kong (N=80)	Malaysia (N=85)	T-Value
1. All accounting firms should be allowed to advertise.	2.088	2.810	−3.40**
2. We will not advertise even if it is allowed.	3.150	3.024	.53
3. Sales turnover can be increased through aggressive advertising campaigns.	2.962	3.048	−.39
4. Our company needs a marketing department.	1.788	2.424	−3.18*
5. Advertisements will ruin our company's goodwill.	3.175	2.602	2.60*
6. Sponsoring academic exhibitions or contests can improve goodwill.	3.825	3.512	1.66
7. Our service quality is the best promotional tool.	4.663	4.702	.39
8. Direct mailing is the best way to make our company known to the public.	2.900	2.602	1.44
9. Personal selling will have a limited effect on promotion of our services.	2.575	2.655	−.37

* significant at the level of 0.05
** significant at the level of 0.01

In Hong Kong, 71.25 percent of the respondents disagreed with this statement whereas in Malaysia only 44.7 percent disagreed. In addition, the Hong Kong respondents disagreed more strongly that "accounting firms should have marketing departments" than their counterparts in Malaysia. In the same vein, Hong Kong accountants agreed more than the Malaysian accountants that "advertisements will ruin our company's (accounting firm) goodwill." Being professional, these two groups of respondents all agreed very strongly that "Our service quality is the best promotional tool."

Attitudes Toward Product/Service. A total of 94.2 percent of the Malaysia respondents agreed that "accounting firms tailor their services according to the needs of the clients" whereas 82.5 percent in Hong Kong agreed with this statement. (See Table 2.) In the same direction, Malaysia accountants showed much stronger disagreement with the statement, "differences between the quality of competing firms are insignificant and unimportant," than their Hong Kong counterparts.

Attitudes Toward Pricing. The two groups of respondents showed a significant difference in opinion in 4 out of the 6 state-

TABLE 2. Attitudes Toward Product/Service

| Statement | Mean Score | | T-Value |
	Hong Kong (N=80)	Malaysia (N=85)	
10. We need to increase the provision of a variety of services.	3.738	4.024	−1.49
11. We tailor our services according to the needs of our clients.	4.138	4.518	−2.59*
12. Quality of services is not important.	1.563	1.235	1.93
13. Differences between the quality of competing firms are insignificant and unimportant.	2.413	1.624	4.13**

* significant at the level of 0.05
** significant at the level of 0.01

ments in this section. (See Table 3.) The Malaysian accountants showed much stronger agreement than the Hong Kong accountants with the statement, "higher quality services deserve higher price." In addition, they tended to believe more that "customers in general pay more attention to price than quality (62.8 percent)," and also "accounting firms always revise their pricing policy (52 percent)." However, a contradiction was shown in that the Malaysian accountants agreed more than the Hong Kong accountants that "lower prices cannot attract more customers."

Attitudes Toward Customers. This section shows a very significant difference in opinion between the two groups of respondents. (See Table 4.) Three out of the 4 statements showed significant difference at the level of 0.01. It was found that both groups had mixed feelings about their primary objective, whether to make money or to provide services to satisfy customers. However, the Malaysian accountants seemed to be more customer-oriented than

TABLE 3. Attitudes Toward Pricing

Statement	Mean Score		T-Value
	Hong Kong (N=80)	Malaysia (N=85)	
14. Lower price cannot attract more customers.	2.713	3.323	−2.40*
15. Higher quality services deserve higher prices.	4.200	4.698	−3.65**
16. Customers in general pay more attention to price than quality.	3.300	3.577	−2.03*
17. We always revise our pricing policy.	3.025	3.518	−2.33*
18. When we price our services we consider our competitors' pricing policy.	3.113	3.259	−.67
19. We price our services after considering our market position.	2.925	3.329	−1.89

   * significant at the level of 0.05
   ** significant at the level of 0.01

TABLE 4. Attitudes Toward Customers

Statement	Hong Kong (N=80)	Mean Score Malaysia (N=85)	T-Value
20. The primary objective of our company is to make money.	3.875	2.843	4.87**
21. Customers are always right.	2.275	2.386	−.57
22. When clients complain about our services, we try our best to effect a satisfactory remedy.	3.825	4.643	−5.79**
23. We provide marketing training courses to our accountants.	1.850	2.725	−4.35**

* significant at the level of 0.05
** significant at the level of 0.01

their Hong Kong counterparts. A total of 95.3 percent of the Malaysian respondents indicated that "they will try their best to effect a satisfactory remedy when their clients complain about their service," whereas only 70 percent of respondents in Hong Kong agreed with the statement. However, they all disagreed with the statement that "customers are always right" and significant differences were not shown in this regard. However, most Hong Kong respondents (76.25 percent) indicated that they disagreed with statement 23 which was concerned with the provision of marketing training courses to the accountants of their firms, whereas only 62 percent of their Malaysian counterparts showed disagreement. Although it appears that in general, Hong Kong accountants are less customer-oriented, 72.5 percent of the Hong Kong accountants agreed that the primary objective of their accounting firm is to make money whereas only about half of the Malaysian accountants agreed with this statement. Hong Kong accountants, therefore, tended to be more profit-oriented than their counterparts in Malaysia.

Attitudes Toward Ethics. The findings show that accountants in both countries in general are ethical. (See Table 5.) A total of 92.8 percent of the Malaysian respondents disagreed with the statement that "in order to satisfy our customers, we may do something that

TABLE 5. Attitudes Toward Ethics

| Statement | Mean Score | | |
	Hong Kong (N=80)	Malaysia (N=85)	T-Value
24. If we are too aggressive in promoting our services, there will be undesired effects upon our professional image.	3.575	4.048	−2.33*
25. MIA/HKSA should relax the rules against advertising and promotion.	2.638	2.940	−1.39
26. Word of mouth is not enough to inform customers about our services.	2.775	3.012	−1.04
27. In order to satisfy our customers, we may do something that they request, even though it is unethical.	1.675	1.268	2.91*

* significant at the level of 0.05
** significant at the level of 0.01

they request, even though it is unethical," whereas 80 percent of the Hong Kong accountants showed disagreement. However, only 63.25 percent agreed with the statement "that if we are too aggressive in promoting our services, there will be undesired effects upon our professional image," whereas more than 70 percent showed agreement with the same statement. On the other hand, only 28.75 percent agreed that the HKSA should relax the rules against advertising and promotion whereas 41.7 percent of the Malaysian accountants agreed that the MIA should relax the rules against advertising and promotion.

DISCUSSION AND IMPLICATIONS

The findings of the comparison between the opinions of accountants in Hong Kong and Malaysia on marketing and advertising suggest several broad conclusions:

1. In general, accounting firms in Malaysia are more aggressive in marketing their services.
2. Accounting firms in Malaysia are more market-oriented because they recognize the fact that there are significant and important differences between competing firms.
3. Accounting firms in Malaysia are price conscious, therefore, they revise their pricing policy in order to remain competitive.
4. Accounting firms in Malaysia in general are more customer-oriented. They will try their best to effect a satisfactory remedy when clients complain about their services. In order to remain competitive, they would provide marketing training to their accounting staff.
5. In general, accountants in both countries are ethical, and they are not particularly in favor of the idea of relaxing the rules against advertising and promotion.

In general, the success of Hong Kong in becoming one of the financial and industrial centers of the world is largely attributed to the "non-intervention" policy of the government. Business is able to operate under minimum government regulations. Under this kind of business environment, business firms enjoy a very high degree of freedom in conducting their business. Likewise, professionals there should be very market- and customer-oriented. However, the findings show that the Malaysian accountants are in fact more market- and customer-oriented in all aspects.

There are several possible reasons that explain why Hong Kong accounting firms were not as market- and customer-oriented as their counterparts in Malaysia.

First, Hong Kong has been lacking the necessary catalyst to facilitate changes of attitudes toward marketing and advertising. During the 1970s and 1980s, Hong Kong has enjoyed a very steady economic growth which has made CPA firms complacent with their present situations. CPA firms have been enjoying steadily flourishing business since the People's Republic of China opened its doors in 1978.

Second, because of the fast expanding market in Hong Kong and China, it is apparent that "Big Eight" (now "Big Six") firms do not need to cannibalize market share from small CPA firms in order to maintain their huge operating expenses.

Third, it seems that the business of large CPA firms in Hong Kong has not been affected by competitors such as banks, financial companies, and other management consulting firms, which offer many of the services traditionally provided by CPA firms. This may be due to the rapidly expanding market potential as a result of the economic growth in Hong Kong and China. Hence, there has been no pressure for change of the advertising and promotion rules.

Traditionally, Hong Kong has been regarded as more liberal than Malaysia because of government's laissez-faire policy. The findings indicate that Hong Kong accountants were not as market-oriented which may be attributed to the factors of a buoyant economic environment, absence of government pressure, and absence of competition from non-accounting companies. Further research should operationalize these constructs and relate them to accountants' attitudes toward advertising across a number of countries. Also, the cultural values of accountants can be incorporated as a predictor variable to explain differences in accountants' perceptions among countries.

BIBLIOGRAPHY

Abdul Latif, S.M.A. and Abdul Aziz, A.L. (1990), "Perceptions of CPAs Towards Marketing and Advertising: A Malaysian Experience," Proceedings of the Second Asian-Pacific Conference on International Accounting Issues, Vancouver, B.C. Canada, October 11-13, 88-91.

Allen, P.W. and Arnold, D.R. (1991), "Different Perspectives on the Marketing of Accounting Services," *Journal of Professional Services Marketing*, Vol. 7 (2), 15-134.

American Institute of Certified Public Accountants (1988), "Rule of Conduct 502–Advertising and Other Forms of Solicitation."

Barksdale, H.C. and Deaden, W.R. (1972), "Consumer Attitudes Towards Marketing and Consumerism," *Journal of Marketing*, 36, 28-35.

Folland, S., Peacock, E. and Pelfrey, S. (1991), "Advertising by Accountants: Attitudes and Practice," *Journal of Professional Services Marketing*, Vol. 6 (2), 97-111.

Hite, R.E. and Bellizzi, J.A. (1986), "Customers Attitudes Toward Accountants, Lawyers and Physicians with Respect to Advertising Professional Services," *Journal of Advertising Research*, June/July, 45-54.

Hite, R.E. and Fraser, C. (1988), "Meta-Analysis of Attitudes Toward Advertising by Professionals," *Journal of Marketing*, 52, (July), 95-105.

Hite, R.E. and Kiser, E. (1985), "Consumers' Attitudes Towards Lawyers with Regard to Advertising Professional Services," *Journal of the Academy of Marketing Sciences*, Spring, 321-339.

Hite, R.E., and Schultz, N.O., (1987), "A Survey of the Utilization of Advertising by CPA Firms," *Journal of Professional Services Marketing*, Vol. 3 (1/2), 231-245.

Hite, R.E., Schultz, N.O., and Weaver, J.A. (1988), "A Content Analysis of CPA Advertising in National Print Media From 1979 to 1984," *Journal of the Academy of Marketing Science*, 16 (3/4), 1-15.

Honeycutt, E.D. and Marts, J.A. (1990), "Marketing by Professionals as Applied to CPA Firms: Room for Improvement," *Journal of Professional Services Marketing*, Vol. 6 (1), 29-42.

Hong Kong Society of Accountants, Statement 1.205B (1986), "Professional Ethics: Advertising."

Institute of Chartered Accountants in England and Wales (1986), "Revised Guidelines on Publicity and Advertising." *Accountancy*, September.

Jackson, M. and Tod, A. (1991), "Attitudes Towards Marketing: The Case of Queensland Solicitors," *Asia Pacific Business: Issues and Challenges*, Proceedings of the Academy of International Business Southeast Asia Conference, Singapore: National University of Singapore, 254-260.

Kerlinger, F.N. (1973), *Foundation of Behavioral Research*, N.Y.: Holt, Rinehart and Winston.

Oliver, D.D. and Posey, C.L. (1980), "National vs Local Accounting Firms: What Are Their Differences of Perception Concerning Advertising," *Arkansas Business and Economic Review*, 14 (Fall), 1-5.

Schweikart, J.A. (1987), "Attitude Measurement and Instrumentation in International Accounting Research," *International Journal of Accounting*, 22 (2), Spring, 131-141.

Sin, L.Y. M., Cheng, D.W.L. and Yau, O.H.M. (1986), "Occupational Stress of Managers in an Oriental Culture: A Causal Analysis," Proceedings of the Academy of International Business Southeast Asia Regional Conference, Taipei, 664-778.

Stevens, R., McConkey, C.W., and Loudon, D.L. (1990), "A Comparison of Physicians' and Attorneys' Attitudes Toward Advertising," *Journal of Professional Services Marketing*, Vol. 5 (2), 115-125.

Thompson, J.H., Smith, L.M. and Jordon, R.E. (1991), "The Changing Face of Accounting Services," *Journal of Professional Services Marketing*, Vol. 6 (2), 113-127.

Yau, O.H.M. (1987), "Consumer Rights: The Perception of Business Managers in Hong Kong," in Hawes, J.M. and Glisan, G.B. (eds.), *Developments in Marketing Science*, Vol. X, 146-150.

Yau, O.H.M. and Sin, L. (1985), "Attitudes Towards Advertising Among Executives in the People's Republic of China," in *Proceeding of the Annual Conference of the European Marketing Academy*, Bielefeld, West Germany, 248-256.

Yau, O.H.M. and Wong, T. (1987), "How Do CPA Firms Perceive Marketing and Advertising? A Hong Kong Experience," *European Journal of Marketing*, 24:2, 43-54.

Chapter 12

Clients' Selection and Retention Criteria: Some Marketing Implications for the Small CPA Firm

Ellen Day
Luther L. Denton
Jerome A. Hickner

INTRODUCTION

The very survival of some small CPA firms may be threatened by the increased competition among firms providing accounting and financial services. The growth in franchised accounting and tax services, in particular, has posed new challenges for the small CPA firm. To survive and prosper in this increasingly competitive environment, small CPA firms must adopt a marketing perspective in order to compete more effectively. While a thorough discussion of strategic marketing planning is beyond the scope of this chapter, we will focus on certain aspects of the client-CPA relationship that are critical to success. Specifically, the purpose of this chapter is to describe how particular marketing principles can better enable the small CPA firm to retain current clients and attract new ones, based on the findings from a recent study.

The Marketing Concept

Fundamental to marketing is the "marketing concept," which, very simply, means being customer-oriented. It means that products

This chapter was first published in *Journal of Professional Services Marketing*, Vol. 3(3/4) 1988.

and services should be designed to satisfy actual customer needs and wants. But to do so first requires an understanding of those needs and wants. For accounting services the marketing concept implies more than merely conducting audits, preparing tax returns, etc.

Certainly the client needs and wants such services, but the client also needs and wants more, e.g., assurance that the services are performed competently and on time. A particular problem in marketing accounting (and other professional) services is that the client typically lacks the expertise to perform the services for him/herself; therefore, the client may not be able to evaluate the competency of the CPA on the basis of objective criteria (i.e., those criteria used by certification boards). Therefore, the client typically relies on more subjective and/or intangible cues to assess competency. But the client will want even more. He/she will want to feel that the CPA is trustworthy and that the CPA values the client's business. In short, client needs and wants go beyond the mere performance of accounting services and extend to the psychological needs as well. Hence, the effective marketing of accounting services requires looking at the CPA firm from the client's perspective. Only then can the CPA develop a competitive edge essential for long-term success.

FACTORS THAT INFLUENCE
THE SELECTION OF A CPA FIRM

Implicit in the marketing concept is understanding what factors influence customer choice. One study (George and Solomon, 1980) identified factors influential in the choice of a CPA firm, which are presented in Table 1. The findings from this study suggest that among critical considerations are proximity of the CPA firm to the client, favorable recommendations from business associates, specialization in a particular industry, and availability of related services. The importance of the marketing concept is underscored by the fact that 60 percent of the respondents indicated that aggressiveness of the CPA firm (i.e., a strong client orientation), influenced their choice.

While the results of this study may be of general interest to CPA

TABLE 1. Major Factors Influencing Selection of a CPA Firm

FACTORS	INFLUENTIAL*
CPA firm has offices in areas where business units are located	78%
Recommendation of other clients of CPA firm	72
Recommendation of CPA firm by third-party referrals	69
Specialization in the industry by CPA firm	69
Related services such as management consulting offered by the CPA firm	66
Aggressiveness of the CPA firm	60
Current client list of the CPA firm	58
CPA firm is one of the eight largest	57
Fee estimate given by the CPA firm	56
Personal friendship with members of the CPA firm	54

*Percentage of respondents indicating that the factor was influential in their selection of a CPA firm

Adapted from: William R. George and Paul J. Solomon, "Marketing Strategies for Improving Practice Development," *The Journal of Accountancy*, Vol. 149, No. 2 (February 1980), pp. 79-84.

firms, it is not clear that these findings hold for large and small CPA firms alike. Because respondents comprised middle and upper management primarily of large businesses (listed in Dun and Bradstreet's *Million Dollar Directory*), the relevance of this study to the small CPA firm is questionable. Therefore, we conducted research in which information was obtained only from those most likely to constitute the target market for the small CPA firm: small businesses and individuals/professionals.

Factors Influencing the Selection of a Small CPA Firm

Data in our study were collected in semi-structured personal interviews with 25 owners and/or managers of small businesses (including manufacturing, service, and retail firms) and 25 individuals (the majority of whom were professionals) who presently use a CPA firm. While respondents comprised a convenience sample, we carefully selected the respondents to ensure a cross-section of clients.

When asked, "What was the primary reason for choosing the CPA firm you currently use?" both sets of respondents gave similar answers. The reasons were simple: The CPA firm had been recommended to the client and/or the client knew the CPA (or someone else in the firm) personally. As can be seen in Table 2, the two reasons appear to be of approximately equal importance among businesspeople, whereas individuals were more likely to respond that knowing the CPA or someone else in the firm influenced their choice.

When asked about other factors that influenced their selection, the personality of the CPA was mentioned most frequently by both sets of respondents. Specifically, respondents mentioned the CPA's interpersonal skills, aggressiveness, interest in the client, ability to explain procedures in terms the client could understand, willingness to give advice, and perceived honesty.

While there were many similarities between the findings from our study and that of George and Solomon, some differences were revealed. For example, among the factors that were important to large clients but not to small businesses and individuals were: specialization in the industry, the availability of related services, the

TABLE 2. Reasons for Selecting a Small CPA Firm

	INDIVIDUALS (% Mentions)	BUSINESSES (% Mentions)
PRIMARY REASON(S)*		
Recommendation	36	56
Knew Someone in the Firm	56	52
SECONDARY REASONS(S), If Any		
Personality of CPA	28	40
Qualifications of CPA	24	28
Recommendation	—	12

*Because some respondents gave more than one reason, column subtotals may exceed 100 percent.

current client list of the CPA firm, whether the CPA firm was one of the eight largest, and fee estimates. George and Solomon also found that location of CPA offices was very influential in the selection of a CPA firm, although our respondents did not not mention this criterion. However, it should not be concluded that location (i.e., physical accessibility) is unimportant to smaller clients. Rather, this difference between the two findings is undoubtedly due to the fact that the majority of our respondents were located in a mid-sized city in which all businesses are quite accessible. Hence, proximity of the CPA firm was not likely to have been a real concern to those comprising our sample.

FACTORS THAT INFLUENCE THE RETENTION OF A CPA FIRM

Client satisfaction is unquestionably the key determinant in retaining current clients, and one indicator of client satisfaction is whether the client recommends the firm to another individual or business. Hence, respondents were asked if they had ever recommended the CPA firm they were currently using. Virtually all of the businesspeople responded yes, as did the large majority of individuals/professionals in our sample. When asked why, by far the most frequent response related to perceptions of overall service quality. Specifically, respondents stated that their CPA was doing a good job, possessed extensive knowledge of accounting practices and tax law, was accessible, and/or completed projects on time. Many of the businesspeople added that the CPA's personality also determined whether they recommended him/her. Among the personality characteristics that would lead to a recommendation were the CPA's honesty, friendliness, willingness to answer (even simple) questions, and ability to explain concepts in easy-to-understand terms.

Reasons for Changing CPA Firms

While attracting new clients is important to CPA firms, retaining current clients is relatively more important for two reasons. First, it can be costly in terms of time and effort to attract new clients.

Second, clients who leave the firm often do so because they are dissatisfied. Since positive word-of-mouth "advertising" is so critical to a CPA's practice, it is essential that deliberate steps be taken to insure client satisfaction.

In exploring reasons for client dis/satisfaction, respondents were asked what would cause them to switch to another CPA firm. For both individuals and businesses, the most frequent reason given was poor service. When asked to elaborate, respondents typically cited incompetence, apparent lack of interest in the account, and lengthy turnaround time as reasons for switching. Many of the businesspeople also indicated that personality problems could force a switch. Those problems included CPAs who were too passive, who made the client feel dumb, who acted as if the client was a pest, who were dishonest, and/or violated the client's trust.

A somewhat surprising finding was that while competency was rarely mentioned as a selection criterion it was a consideration in retaining or recommending a firm. There are at least three plausible explanations for this apparent inconsistency. First it is likely that competency is assumed by virtue of certification, i.e., it is taken as a given–at least initially. Second, competency is difficult, if not impossible, to judge prior to the rendering of services. Third, a potential client would assume that a positive recommendation would inherently imply competency.

MARKETING IMPLICATIONS
FOR THE SMALL CPA FIRM

The findings from our study, along with results of previous research, clearly lead to two strong conclusions: (1) that new business overwhelmingly is generated through referrals and (2) that maintaining high service quality is essential to retaining current clients. Of course these two points are inextricably linked in that referrals are generated largely through satisfied clients. Therefore, we will discuss the issue of service quality first, then referrals.

Projecting and Maintaining a Quality Image

When respondents in our study were asked why they were satisfied with their current CPA firm, the majority responded simply that their CPA was doing a good job, although few could articulate what "doing a good job" meant. This (very typical) situation can be perplexing to professionals, since such vague judgements do not easily translate into specific activities that will help build a quality image. Researchers who have studied issues related to consumer/client perceptions and evaluation of service quality (e.g., Parasuraman, Zeithaml, and Berry, 1985), have found that many factors contribute to a quality image, such as those presented in Table 3. While competency of course is essential, many other chacteristics of the firm and its personnel also shape perceptions of quality.

In reviewing the determinants of service quality, it is clear that the major responsibility for maintaining and projecting a quality image falls on the professional and support personnel. It is also

TABLE 3. Determinants of Service Quality

RELIABILITY = consistency of performance; dependability

RESPONSIVENESS = willingness/readiness of personnel to provide timely service

COMPETENCE = possession of the necessary skills and knowledge to perform the service

ACCESSIBILITY = approachability; ease of contact

COURTESY = politeness; respect; consideration of client; friendliness

COMMUNICATION = keeping clients informed in language they can understand; listening to clients

CREDIBILITY = trustworthiness; honesty; having client's best interests at heart

SECURITY = confidentiality

UNDERSTANDING/KNOWING THE CLIENT = making the effort to understand the client's needs

TANGIBLE CUES = physical appearance of personnel and office

Adapted from A. Parasuraman, Valarie A. Zeithaml, and Leonard L. Berry, "A Conceptual Model of Service Quality and Its Implications for Future Research," *Journal of Marketing*, Vol. 49, No. 4 (Fall 1985), p. 47.

clear that all members of the CPA firm must be people-oriented as well as performance-oriented.

While quality of performance may be evaluated along specific objective criteria, it is more likely that the client will form some overall perception of quality. Often these perceptions are quite subjective. That is, clients may evaluate the quality of the CPA firm along many intangible dimensions–even along dimensions that do not directly relate to the quality of the services rendered, for example, courteousness or friendliness of contact personnel. Certainly the intangibles can help a firm develop a competitive advantage over other firms offering basically the same services. In particular, in order to differentiate itself from other, especially larger, firms, the small CPA firm can emphasize a more personal interest in and attention to clients.

Internal Marketing and Impression Management

Internal marketing (see, e.g., Winston, 1985/6) becomes essential in projecting a quality image. Not only should all personnel be well trained in performing assigned tasks, but also they should be made aware of their critical role in projecting a quality image. Whether the client feels that his/her account is valued by the firm and whether the client feels confident that the job will be done accurately and on time depends in large part on the interpersonal skills of the contact personnel. Indeed, most determinants of service quality are related to the notion of "impression management." Long delays in returning phone calls or curt responses by a staff member, for example, may be interpreted by the (potential) client as indifference toward both the client and the performance of services. As mentioned before, many of the respondents in our study indicated that they considered personality factors when selecting and recommending their current CPA firm. While such factors have little to do with quality of performance, per se, obviously the attitudes and demeanor of the personnel influence the client's opinions of the firm.

Impression management also involves a careful assessment and planning of the more tangible cues that contribute to clients' perceptions of quality. The physical appearance of the office and staff, for example, can convey unintended messages to clients, especially new or potential clients. If the office appears in disarray, the client may well become concerned that records may be lost or difficult to find or that crucial reports are not likely to be completed on time. Even the location and outside appearance of the office influence a client's perception of quality. In short, tangible cues must match the standards that are set for the service itself.

Ensuring Client Satisfaction

Continuity of service also contributes significantly to client satisfaction. That is, clients prefer dealing with the same people in a CPA firm, especially because of the amount of proprietary information a client must disclose to the CPA. With turnover of personnel, the client can become frustrated in having to explain his/her particular problems and needs to a new person. Moreover, the client is likely once again to become concerned about competency, trustworthiness, and other factors critical to the relationship. The importance of continuity is underscored by the fact that a CPA who leaves a firm typically takes many accounts with him/her.

While client satisfaction is largely dependent upon his/her perceptions of quality, it is also dependent upon the client's expectations with respect to services performed. That is, satisfaction–or dissatisfaction–results from (often implicit) comparisons of what was delivered with what was expected. The importance of communications in the formation of client expectations cannot be overemphasized. By explaining what a particular service entails, how much it will cost, and when it can be done, the CPA can help ensure that the client has realistic expectations. Very simply, the likelihood of client satisfaction can be greatly increased by providing adequate information to the client–in a language the client can understand.

Generating Referrals

The importance of personal recommendations (referrals) to CPA firms was evidenced by the responses to another question in our survey, "If you were to change CPA firms, how would you go about finding another one?" Overwhelmingly, respondents stated that they would seek recommendations from friends and/or business associates. Most CPAs acknowledge that referrals are the primary source of new business for their firm. Still, few small CPA firms have adopted standardized procedures for making their referral generation efforts more effective. Most CPAs would probably describe what they do as "seizing an opportunity." However, when referral generation procedures are systematized, more opportunities can be spotted and efforts to obtain referrals can become more productive.

Successful generation of referrals is based on the accomplishment of three essential tasks: selecting appropriate sources of referrals, cultivating these sources, and educating these sources (Denney, 1983). Selecting appropriate sources entails identifying those sources most likely to produce leads on potential clients with needs that can be served well by the small CPA firm. Cultivating the source involves establishing a relationship with the potential referrer so that the CPA feels comfortable in asking for referrals. Educating the source means letting the source know what services the CPA firm offers and what benefits accrue from that using particular firm–i.e., providing reasons for making a referral.

Cultivating a Source

The strategy used to cultivate a source depends on whether it is an internal or external source. Internal sources usually comprise friends, relatives, current clients, and business associates–those persons with whom a relationship has been established before any effort is made to cultivate the source. External sources include other professionals and businesspeople–in the same or different fields.

Internal sources are often the easiest to cultivate, since the nature of the relationship between the CPA and these sources often leads to helping one another in some way. Friends, relatives, and business associates may only need to be reminded to "keep their eyes open" for potential clients among their respective acquaintances and business associates. Often these convenient sources also can take the next step and provide an introduction as well as a referral.

Cultivating external sources can require considerable effort, yet this type of networking is critical to generating new accounts. Important external sources that are sometimes overlooked are professionals and business associates offering the same or similar services. Being in the same business does not necessarily mean that firms are direct competitors. Larger CPA firms, for example, may not find smaller accounts profitable, in which case the small businessperson or professional might be referred to the small CPA firm. CPA and accounting firms located outside the small CPA firm's normal service area may also become a referral source. The small CPA firm can offer the same type of referrals in return.

Businesses and professionals in other fields offer the best opportunity for referrals. Examples of these important sources include bankers, lawyers, insurance agents, and real estate agents. Because of the nature of the services they provide, these sources are often asked to recommend a qualified accounting firm. Accountants, in turn, are also often asked to recommend qualified professionals in other fields. Hence, the basis for establishing reciprocal relationships already exists.

Careful record-keeping is the foundation for an effective referral generation system (Wilson, 1984). As new accounts are added, clients should be asked how they learned of the firm–if they do not volunteer such information. The number and frequency of referrals from each source should be noted, as well as the types of clients referred by each source. These sources then can be used to determine how well the referral system is working and which are the most productive sources. Moreover, such information allows the CPA to acknowledge and thank referrers, on whom the CPA's practice is so dependent.

CONCLUSIONS

Practicing the marketing concept, i.e., adopting a strong client orientation, is fundamental to the success of a CPA firm. A client orientation means understanding–and caring about–clients' needs and wants. It means making the effort to learn about a client's particular problems and to explain how the firm can help solve those problems. It means building and nurturing a relationship with the client. It means attending to clients' psychological as well as accounting needs. Because professional services are provided by people for people, interpersonal skills are as essential as technical competency.

While the larger accounting firm may compete on the basis of prestige and a full range of services, the small CPA firm can more convincingly compete on the basis of "people skills." While many decry the lack of service in service organizations ("Pul-eeze! . . ., 1987), the small CPA firm can easily distinguish itself by its person-alized service and attention. By showing a genuine concern for the clients, CPAs and staff can build lasting relationships–that benefit the firm and clients alike.

REFERENCES

Denney, Robert W., *Marketing Accounting Services*, New York: Van Nostrand Reinhold, 1983.

George, William R. and Paul J. Solomon, "Marketing Strategies for Improving Practice Development," *The Journal of Accountancy*, Vol. 149, No. 2 (February 1980), pp. 79-84.

Parasuraman, A., Valarie A. Zeithaml, and Leonard L. Berry, "A Conceptual Model of Service Quality and Its Implications for Future Research," *Journal of Marketing*, Vol. 49, No. 4 (Fall 1985), pp. 41-50.

"Pul-eeze! Will Somebody Help Me?", *Time*, February 2, 1987, pp. 49-57.

Wilson, Aubrey, *Practice Development for Professional Firms*, London: McGraw-Hill, 1984.

Winston, William J., "Internal Marketing–Key to a Successful Professional Service Marketing Program," *Journal of Professional Services Marketing*, Vol. 1, Nos. 1/2 (Fall/Winter 1985/86), pp. 15-18.

PART THREE:
ADVERTISING

Chapter 13

Accountants' Attitudes Toward Advertising and Their Use of Marketing Tools

Robert E. Stevens
C. William McConkey
David L. Loudon
Paul Dunn

INTRODUCTION

Fifteen years have passed since the famous *Bates v. State Bar of Arizona* (1977) case which brought about significant changes in the legality of advertising by professionals. Professional codes of ethics which specifically banned advertising had to be rewritten to reflect these changes.

Although the *Bates* decision was promulgated in 1977, there has been rather little empirical research on the subject of advertising by professionals such as attorneys, physicians, and dentists. One of the benchmark studies in the field of advertising among professionals was done by Shimp and Dyer (1978) who surveyed 1,400 attorneys in two states (with 485 usable responses) to determine their attitudes and intentions toward advertising approximately one year prior to the *Bates* ruling. The study found that a large majority of

This chapter was first published in *Journal of Professional Services Marketing*, Vol. 10(2) 1993.

respondents were strongly opposed to attorney advertising. Opposition was particularly strong among older lawyers and those practicing in larger, corporate-oriented firms. In addition, most lawyers were also strongly opposed to an "anything goes" advertising approach where all forms of information content (including price) and all available media (including television) are acceptable. Since the *Bates* decision, research on attorneys' attitudes toward advertising has generally found negative perceptions (Smith and Meyer, 1980; Dyer and Shimp, 1980; and Stem, Laudadio, and Israel, 1981).

Some research studies have focused on additional professional groups to gauge differences in their perception of advertising. For example, Darling and Hackett (1978) researched attitudes held by accountants, attorneys, dentists, and physicians toward advertising. Their study found significant differences in these four groups' attitudes regarding professional advertising. Although all of the groups had a negative perception of advertising, accountants and attorneys were more positive about the potential role of advertising in their professions.

Another study focusing on changes in CPAs' attitudes toward advertising between 1976 and 1988 found that accountants were generally more receptive to advertising than they had been 12 years earlier. In addition, less experienced accountants appeared to be more positive toward advertising (Heischmidt and Elfrink, 1991).

Hite and Fraser (1988) conducted two meta-analyses of attitudes toward advertising by professionals (such as accountants) covering ten years of research findings. Results indicate that a rather large attitudinal schism still separates consumers and professionals. While consumers favor increased professional advertising, professionals continue to be reluctant to use it, fearing that negative impacts on image, credibility, and dignity are likely, with little benefits to consumers. However, the authors imply that increased exposure to professional advertising tended to reduce the resistance to it by professionals.

Have attitudes toward advertising by accountants become more favorable? How do such factors as years in practice or type of practice (solo vs. group) influence attitudes? This study was designed to answer these types of questions.

RESEARCH OBJECTIVES

To guide the research, a specific set of objectives was developed. The objectives were:

1. To determine currently held attitudes toward advertising by accountants.
2. To analyze differences in attitudes based on age, practice specialty, and practice type (solo/group), and other practice characteristics.
3. To analyze the use of marketing tools, outside marketing services, budgeting for marketing, and other marketing-related issues.

METHODOLOGY

Data for this study were gathered via questionnaires mailed to a randomly selected sample of accountants located throughout the contiguous 48 states. The mailing list was obtained from a mailing list broker who prepared the sample. One thousand questionnaires were mailed out and 243 were returned yielding a 24.3 percent return rate. Areas of questioning included practice characteristics, personal characteristics, attitudes toward advertising, and their own use of advertising, ad agencies, etc. and marketing expenditures. The practice data included years of practice, solo versus group, area of specialty (if any), geographic area, and annual revenues of their firm.

Attitudinal measures were obtained by using a seven-point agree/disagree scale ranging from (1) strongly disagree to (7) strongly agree to 19 attitudinal statements. The statements were patterned after those used by Shimp and Dyer (1978). These statements covered four areas:

1. Philosophic reasons for and against advertising.
2. Economic issues related to advertising.
3. Issues surrounding the potential impact of accounting services advertising.
4. Issues concerning the implementation of accounting services advertising.

Two analytical approaches were used in the study. First, the percentage and mean responses to each of the attitudinal questions were computed for the purpose of determining the direction of response patterns. Second, respondents were divided into those with favorable and unfavorable attitudes toward advertising and Multiple Discriminant Analysis (MDA) was used to analyze differences between these two groups.

OVERALL FINDINGS

Although the response rate was lower than desired, an analysis of differences between early respondents and late respondents (first 75 versus last 75) revealed no significant differences in attitudes using a t-test at the .05 level of significance. Thus, nonrespondent bias may not have strongly affected the results. Many respondents wrote letters or attached notes to the returned questionnaires to express their views of accounting services advertising. Apparently their interest in the topic is high but overall negative attitudes prevailed as will be discussed later.

Table 1 shows the findings of the attitudinal statements by the percentage of responses. The + /- in parentheses at the end of the statement indicates whether the specific statement was positive (+) or negative (-) toward advertising of accountants' services.

The findings displayed in Table 1 quickly point out the overall negative attitudes held by accountants toward advertising. A consistent pattern of results occurred in all four areas of issues covered in the study. While the overall results revealed negative attitudes there were significant differences in attitudes when accountants were broken down into subgroups of favorable/unfavorable attitudes toward advertising. The favorable/unfavorable groups were established by using the grand means for all respondents on all attitudinal scales and defining the unfavorable as equal to or less than the grand mean and favorable as above the grand mean.

Multiple Discriminant Analysis was employed to determine if the **a priori** defined favorable/unfavorable groups differ with respect to the factors studied and the demographic characteristics. All dimensions were included in the analysis, and each had a chance of entering. A step-wise analysis was used requiring a minimum F

TABLE 1. Percentage Distribution of Responses to Attitude Statements

I. Philosophic Issues

1. The accountant-client relationship is personal and unique, and should not be established as a result of pressures exerted by advertising. (–)

Strongly Agree	Moderately Agree	Slightly Agree	No Opinion	Slightly Disagree	Moderately Disagree	Strongly Disagree
31.5%	18.1%	19.7%	15.0%	7.5%	3.9%	4.3%

2. Existing information sources (i.e., Yellow Pages, association referral services, lists, etc.) provide inadequate information to guide potential clients' accountant selection. (+)

Strongly Agree	Moderately Agree	Slightly Agree	No Opinion	Slightly Disagree	Moderately Disagree	Strongly Disagree
7.5%	3.9%	11.0%	16.9%	16.5%	22.8%	21.3%

II. Economic Issues

Demand:

1. The demand for accountants' services would increase if veterinary service advertising were widely used. (+)

Strongly Agree	Moderately Agree	Slightly Agree	No Opinion	Slightly Disagree	Moderately Disagree	Strongly Disagree
14.2%	19.7%	20.5%	23.2%	12.2%	5.5%	4.7%

Competition:

1. One principal effect of the veterinarian profession's past ethical canon against advertising is to protect established accountants and large firms from competition from young accountants and small firms. (+)

Strongly Agree	Moderately Agree	Slightly Agree	No Opinion	Slightly Disagree	Moderately Disagree	Strongly Disagree
16.5%	15.4%	15.4%	16.1%	10.2%	13.0%	13.4%

2. Ethical codes against advertising exist to maintain and increase the incomes of practicing accountants. (+)

Strongly Agree	Moderately Agree	Slightly Agree	No Opinion	Slightly Disagree	Moderately Disagree	Strongly Disagree
19.3%	19.3%	16.9%	18.5%	13.4%	8.3%	4.3%

TABLE 1 (continued)

3. If accounting service advertising were widely used, the large, established firms would get bigger, while the smaller firms would become even less competitive than they are at present. (−)

Strongly Agree	Moderately Agree	Slightly Agree	No Opinion	Slightly Disagree	Moderately Disagree	Strongly Disagree
12.6%	9.1%	14.2%	22.4%	14.2%	14.2%	13.4%

Employment:

1. Accountant service advertising would help provide positions for thousands of new accountants entering the profession. (+)

Strongly Agree	Moderately Agree	Slightly Agree	No Opinion	Slightly Disagree	Moderately Disagree	Strongly Disagree
28.7%	8.7%	11.4%	37.4%	6.7%	4.3%	2.8%

Prices:

1. Prices of accounting services would decrease if accounting service advertising were widely used. (+)

Strongly Agree	Moderately Agree	Slightly Agree	No Opinion	Slightly Disagree	Moderately Disagree	Strongly Disagree
19.3%	20.9%	21.7%	18.5%	10.6%	4.7%	4.3%

Quality:

1. The quality of accounting services would improve if advertising were widely used. (+)

Strongly Agree	Moderately Agree	Slightly Agree	No Opinion	Slightly Disagree	Moderately Disagree	Strongly Disagree
26.4%	23.6%	18.9%	16.1%	6.7%	5.1%	3.1%

III. Consumer Issues

Facilitative Effects

1. The public would be provided with useful information through the advertising of accountants' services. (+)

Strongly Agree	Moderately Agree	Slightly Agree	No Opinion	Slightly Disagree	Moderately Disagree	Strongly Disagree
15.4%	12.2%	20.1%	24.4%	17.3%	7.9%	2.8%

2. Accounting service advertising would heighten the public's understanding of situations where accounting assistance is needed. (+)

Strongly Agree	Moderately Agree	Slightly Agree	No Opinion	Slightly Disagree	Moderately Disagree	Strongly Disagree
9.1%	11.4%	13.8%	16.9%	24.8%	15.7%	8.3%

3. Accounting service advertising would assist potential clients in knowing which accountants are competent to handle particular accounting problems. (+)

Strongly Agree	Moderately Agree	Slightly Agree	No Opinion	Slightly Disagree	Moderately Disagree	Strongly Disagree

4. The information provided the public through accounting service advertising would enable potential clients to make a more informed selection of accountants. (+)

Strongly Agree	Moderately Agree	Slightly Agree	No Opinion	Slightly Disagree	Moderately Disagree	Strongly Disagree
16.5%	15.0%	17.7%	19.3%	15.7%	9.8%	5.9%

Negative Effects

1. Public confidence in the accounting profession would be impaired by accounting service advertising. (−)

Strongly Agree	Moderately Agree	Slightly Agree	No Opinion	Slightly Disagree	Moderately Disagree	Strongly Disagree
7.1%	10.6%	11.8%	21.7%	18.9%	16.1%	13.8%

2. Advertising of accounting services confuses rather than enlightens potential clients. (−)

Strongly Agree	Moderately Agree	Slightly Agree	No Opinion	Slightly Disagree	Moderately Disagree	Strongly Disagree
7.1%	15.7%	15.0%	30.3%	13.8%	8.3%	9.8%

3. The public would not regard information in accounting service advertisements as credible. (−)

Strongly Agree	Moderately Agree	Slightly Agree	No Opinion	Slightly Disagree	Moderately Disagree	Strongly Disagree
5.1%	7.5%	9.4%	40.6%	19.3%	13.0%	5.1%

4. The advertising of accounting services would tend to intensify client dissatisfaction after services have been rendered. (−)

Strongly Agree	Moderately Agree	Slightly Agree	No Opinion	Slightly Disagree	Moderately Disagree	Strongly Disagree
3.1%	6.7%	10.2%	38.6%	18.1%	16.9%	8.3%

TABLE 1 (continued)

---

5. If accounting service advertising were widely used, it eventually would degenerate into a circus of misleading and deceptive advertisements. (–)

Strongly Agree	Moderately Agree	Slightly Agree	No Opinion	Slightly Disagree	Moderately Disagree	Strongly Disagree
14.2%	16.9%	15.7%	20.1%	9.8%	14.2%	9.1%

6. If advertisement of accounting services were widely used, stringent regulations would have to be imposed, e.g., something like a Truth in Accountants' Advertising Law. (–)

Strongly Agree	Moderately Agree	Slightly Agree	No Opinion	Slightly Disagree	Moderately Disagree	Strongly Disagree
22.4%	18.1%	20.5%	14.6%	7.9%	10.6%	5.9%

value of 1.0 to enter. SPSSX Method = Wilks controlled the entry order.

MDA generates linear functions based on the predictor variables that best discriminate among the groups, and it provides an overall test for significant differences among the groups. If a significant difference is determined, the relative importance of each predictor variable in discrimination among the groups is provided, and the dimensions on which the groups differ can be determined. The discriminant function is validated by first estimating the function on half of the sample and then applying the function to the hold-out sample. Because the actual group memberships are known, the percentage of correct classifications can be computed (Frank, Massey, and Morrison, 1965).

The canonical loadings (the correlation between the predictor variables and the discriminant function coefficients) are used to minimize the potential "weighting" problems caused by multi-collinearity. Furthermore, the loading can be rotated to aid in interpretation (Perreault, Behrman, and Armstrong, 1979). The relative value of the canonical loading for each variable indicates the directional relationship.

Dummy variables were created for each of the demographic characteristics. (For example, if a respondent reported his marital status as single, that category was coded 1. Each of the other categories was then coded 0 for that respondent.) This was done for two reasons. First, virtually all of the demographic characteristics were measured categorically, not continuously–the respondent selected the one age, income, etc., category that described him. Second, this approach provides richer, more descriptive information. For example, instead of merely finding that years of practice is a discriminating variable, the specific length of practice (i.e., 6-10 years) that discriminates is shown.

Table 2 shows the mean attitudinal score for each of the 19 statements used in the study. Higher scores indicate higher levels of agreement with a statement. This table reveals that while most accountants feel advertising would heighten understanding of the use of accounting services, there would be several negative outcomes. These would include: (1) large firms getting bigger, (2) impaired public confidence, and (3) advertising would intensify client dissatisfaction.

The discriminant analysis of respondent characteristics produced

TABLE 2. Mean Scores on Attitudinal Dimensions

Attitudinal Dimensions	Mean Score N=243
1. Relationship personal	5.22
2. Existing information adequate	4.85
3. Increase demand	3.35
4. Protect large firms	3.81
5. Maintain incomes	3.30
6. Large firms get bigger	3.87
7. Provide new positions	3.09
8. Prices would decrease	3.12
9. Quality would improve	2.81
10. Provide useful information	3.51
11. Heighten understanding	4.17
12. Competent accountants	3.29
13. More informed selection	3.56
14. Impair public confidence	3.62
15. Confuses rather than enlightens	3.92
16. Ads not credible	3.79
17. Intensive dissatisfaction	3.56
18. Deceptive	4.27
19. Stringent regulations	4.77

a significant discriminant function (.0001 level). The percentages correctly identified in the analysis and holdout samples were 76.7 and 56.7, respectively, compared with a proportional chance of 50 percent. The canonical loadings and group means are presented in Table 3.

DIFFERENCES AMONG RESPONDENTS

Respondents were analyzed for differences based on age, practice chacteristics, and other criteria. The respondents who were more favorable toward advertising accounting services: (1) were younger, (2) had been in practice a fewer number of years, (3) were more likely to have used an advertising agency, (4) rated yellow page display ads higher, (5) were more likely to have a brochure available for clients, (6) rated radio as a more effective medium, (7) were less likely to rate marketing activities as unproductive, and (8) spent a higher percentage of revenue on marketing.

The findings indicate that the younger accountants are not only more favorable toward advertising but are more likely to spend money for marketing activities. They are also more likely to avail themselves of the services of facilitating marketing organizations such as ad agencies and use promotional tools such as firm brochures.

TABLE 3. Discriminant Analysis of Respondent Characteristics

Characteristic	Canonical Loadings	Group Means	
		Favorable	Unfavorable
Years in practice	.3201	17.7661	23.4783
Age	.1703	49.9839	51.7928
Used Advertising Agent	.1663	.1129	.0290
Used yellow page ads	.2509	.6936	.4783
Use Client Brochure	.2951	.4355	.1739
Radio advertising	.2011	.2097	.0725
Marketing unproductive	.1460	.0807	.1739
Marketing's percent of budget	.2064	1.5323	.7681

Wilks' Lambda = .49505, Chi Square = 83.32, df = 21, sig. = .0000

ACCOUNTANTS' USE OF MARKETING TOOLS

As shown in Table 4, yellow page ads, newspaper ads, brochures, and seminars were the four most frequently used marketing tools. Few accountants reported using TV advertising and billboards but 13.8 percent had used radio advertising.

The ranking of marketing tools is shown in Table 5. Brochures and seminars were ranked as the two most effective techniques. These were followed by newspaper ads and yellow page ads. The higher ranking of seminars compared to their relative use may mean that many firms are plannnig to use seminars in the future as a marketing tool.

Respondents were also asked why they did not engage in more marketing activities. While some were concerned about how they

TABLE 4. Marketing Tools Used

Marketing Tool	Percent Using
Yellow page ads	61.0%
Newspaper ads	37.0
Seminars/other	34.6
Brochures	28.3
Radio	13.8
TV ads	3.1
Billboard	2.0

TABLE 5. Ranking of Marketing Tools

Marketing Tool	Rank
Billboard ads	7
Radio ads	6
TV ads	5
Newspaper ads	4
Brochures	3
Yellow page ads	2
Seminars	1

might be perceived by clients and other accountants, the major concern was the benefit/cost trade-off expressed in both the "costs too much" and the "costs outweigh benefits" responses. In other words, the value of marketing to the firms in terms of increased revenues, status, and position is questionable. The results are shown in Table 6.

MARKETING BUDGETS/PERSONNEL

About 33 percent of the firms responding reported that they made some allocation for marketing expenditures. The median amount was 12 percent of revenues and the highest percent was 18 percent of revenue. This included total expenditures for all marketing activities such as promotion, consulting fees, and marketing personnel.

Many of the firms had part- or full-time marketing personnel in their firms. Part-time personnel were used by 8.3 percent of the firms and 3.5 percent had full-time marketing staffs.

USE OF EXTERNAL MARKETING SERVICES

Respondents were also asked whether they had used external marketing service providers. Their replies are shown in Table 7. Marketing consultants were the most frequently used service provider. While only 2.0 percent reported using a marketing research firm, 10.2 percent stated that they had completed some type of

TABLE 6. Why More Marketing Is not Used

Reason	Percent
Costs too much	52.4%
Costs outweigh benefits	51.6
Looks unprofessional to clients	29.5
No competitive pressure	25.2
Other reasons	20.1
Not enough knowledge of what to do	18.9
Looks unprofessional to other accountants	14.6

TABLE 7. Use of External Marketing Services

Service Provider	Percent Utilizing
Marketing consultant	7.9%
Advertising agency	7.1
Public relations firm	3.1
Marketing research firm	2.0

formal marketing research. Evidently, most of these projects were completed by internal staff or by consultants.

CONCLUSIONS

Although many changes have taken place in professional services marketing over the 15-year period since the *Bates* decision, this study reveals that the majority of accountants still hold negative attitudes toward advertising their services. However, younger accountants are more favorably disposed to advertising and the use of marketing activities than older members of the profession. This would indicate that future generations of accountants may be more open to marketing as a legitimate business function.

It also appears that the demand for marketing services designed specifically for this group should expand in the future. Many accountants do use yellow page advertising, brochures, and seminars to promote their services. Some firms are also using external marketing service providers and some have part-time or full-time marketing personnel.

REFERENCES

Bates v. State Bar of Arizona (1977), 97 S. Ct. 2691, 34 U.S., L.W. 4895.

Dyer, Robert F., and Terence A. Shimp (1980), "Reactions to Legal Advertising," *Journal of Advertising Research,* Volume 20 (April), 43-51.

Frank, Ronald E., William F. Massey, and Donald G. Morrison (1965), "Bias in Multiple Discriminant Analysis," *Journal of Marketing Research*, Volume 2 (August), 250-258.

Heischmidt, Kenneth A, and John Elfrink (1991), "The Changing Attitudes of CPAs Toward Advertising," *Journal of Advertising*, Volume 20 (June), 39-51.

Hite, Robert E., and Cynthia Fraser (1988), "Meta-Analyses of Attitudes Toward Advertising by Professionals," *Journal of Marketing*, Volume 52 (July), 95-105.

Murphy, Jim (1991), "Reader Poll: Marketing Architectural Services," *Progressive Architecture*, (April), 61-63.

Perreault, William D., Jr., Douglas N. Behrman, and Gary M. Armstrong (1979), "Alternative Approaches for Interpretation of Multiple Discriminant Analysis in Marketing Research," *Journal of Business Research*, Volume 7, Number 2, 151-173.

Shimp, Terence and Robert Dyer (1978), "How The Legal Profession Views Legal Services Advertising," *Journal of Marketing*, Volume 41 (July), 74-81.

Chapter 14

A Survey of the Utilization
of Advertising by CPA Firms

Robert E. Hite
Norman O. Schultz

INTRODUCTION

The profession of accounting has faced long-standing prohibitions against the use of advertising, though this has not always been the case. For example, the organized accounting profession in the United States had no prohibitions against advertising until 1922. In that year, the American Institute of Certified Public Accountants' Council, apparently following the examples set by the legal and medical professions, adopted a rule against advertising (Ostlund, 1978). This restriction on accountants in public practice held for 56 years and prohibited all paid advertising.

In 1975, some advertising was allowed by the AICPA. This included press releases concerning changes in partnership status, admissions of new partners, mergers, office relocations, and changes in telephone numbers. In 1976 the AICPA set up a task force to look at the ban against advertising. In 1977 the Supreme Court decision in *Bates v. State Bar of Arizona* stated that a State Bar could not prohibit the advertising of lawyers' services in the printed media. This landmark decision plus the threat of government intervention added to the pressure felt by the accounting profession to change its practices. The Justice Department and the Federal Trade Commis-

This chapter was first published in *Journal of Professional Services Marketing*, Vol. 3(1/2) 1987.

sion were investigating the accounting profession for antitrust violations and anticompetitive practices respectively (Ostlund, 1978).

On March 31, 1978, Rule 502 became effective (Wood and Ball, 1978) which simply stated says, "A member shall not seek to obtain clients by advertising or other forms of solicitation in a manner that is false, misleading or deceptive. The direct uninvited solicitation of a specific potential client is prohibited" (Ostlund, 1978). In March of 1979 the last sentence was struck from the rule (Schwersenz, 1979).

PREVIOUS RESEARCH

Practitioner Attitudes Toward Accountant Advertising

Darling (1977) performed a study of accountants, attorneys, dentists, and physicians and found that all of them had a negative perception of advertising, but lawyers and accountants had a more positive viewpoint than the other professions. Bloom and Loeb (1977), found that three-fourths of the accountant respondents believed the integrity of the CPA profession would be questioned if advertising were permitted. In 1978, the membership of the AICPA was surveyed and the responses were categorized according to whether a member was a public or industrial (private) accountant. Generally public accountants were more conservative and opposed advertising, and industrial accountants accepted the idea. The majority of CPAs felt advertising would not help the accountants' image, but would not harm it either. Public accountants believed prices would increase; private accountants believed they would decline. Services, professional credentials, and specializations were appropriate to advertise, but price and quality of services were inappropriate. Those surveyed believed newspapers and professional magazines were appropriate media. Advertising of tax services and management advisory services were considered allowable, but respondents were divided on advertising auditing services (Sellers and Solomon, 1978).

The *Practicing CPA* conducted a poll of their readers in 1979 and found that CPAs were still reticent about advertising. Of the 731 replies, 7 percent planned to advertise, 31 percent believed advertising was unprofessional, and about 31 percent doubted that advertising paid off (Hanggi, 1980). The Patton Accounting Center and Division of Research conducted a survey which found that the majority of CPA firms believed the pressure to advertise would come mostly from the large firms because of economic resources. The majority of firms reported they would begin to advertise only if other firms started to advertise (Block, 1980).

Traynor (1983/1984) performed a study of CPAs in Pennsylvania regarding their perceptions, attitudes, and use of advertising and found that 23 percent had advertised, only 9 percent of these would continue to advertise, and only 13 percent ranked advertising as important. Sixty-three percent perceived advertising as having a harmful effect upon a professional image. In spite of these results, a majority said they would be likely to advertise in the future.

Consumer Attitudes Toward Accountant Advertising

An early survey of consumers by Shapiro and Bohmbach (1979) concerning professional advertising found that 80 percent believed advertising served a useful purpose. Since advertising was monitored by industry and government, the public was sufficiently protected. The professional regulations were to protect the professional, not the public, according to the consumer respondents.

Corporate financial officers were surveyed nationwide to determine their attitudes toward accountant advertising, and the influence advertising had on purchase (Carver, King, and Label, 1979). Seventy-three percent of the financial officers thought accountants should be allowed to advertise. They believed that advertising was an effective way to communicate services. Eighty percent believed that the quality of accounting services would not decline and only 35 percent felt that prices would increase. Financial executives who had used an accounting firm for less than five years were more favorable toward advertising and could be influenced by ads, and smaller firms were more favorable toward advertising than larger firms (Carver, King, and Label, 1979).

A study of both practitioners and business people in Virginia by Scott and Rudderow (1983) revealed differences of opinion between the two groups. Seventy-one percent of the business people, but only 42 percent of the accountants believed advertising would heighten public awareness of CPAs. The results indicated that accountants had much more restrictive opinions of advertising than business people. Hite (1985) performed a consumer attitudinal study and found that over 75 percent of the respondents believed that it was proper for accountants to advertise, and (if it is done properly) their credibility and dignity would not suffer. Professional magazines and newspapers were found to be the most appropriate media for accountants to advertise. Hite and Bellizzi (1986) found that consumers are now receptive to advertising by accountants, lawyers, and physicians, though lawyers and physicians are held to higher standards than accountants with regard to advertising.

Content and Strategy of Accountant Advertising

One of the first studies of executives to indicate what clients look for in an accountant was done by Wood and Ball (1978). They interviewed 30 representative companies made up of banks, savings and loan associations, retailers, manufacturers, real estate brokers, and service firms. The six most important factors, in order, included technical expertise in the client's field; general technical competence as evidenced by being a CPA; sufficient size to provide back-up when necessary and specialists if needed; reputation based on recommendations of business associates, attorneys, and bankers; ability to get along with clients; and price. A separate survey on individual tax preparation indicated that technical expertise should be emphasized and price and office proximity de-emphasized (Wood and Ball, 1978).

George and Solomon (1980) conducted a survey of executives involved in the selection of accounting firms. This study confirmed some of the findings in the Wood and Ball (1978) study. The results indicated the following:

1. Seventy-eight percent considered location more influential than other factors.
2. Recommendations by other clients and third-party referrals are important.
3. Indication of specialization would influence them.

4. Offerings of additional services were a consideration.
5. Sixty percent believed aggressiveness, which implies an active business and strong client organization, is important.
6. CPA client list and Big Eight Firm status influenced them.
7. Fee estimates would not influence them.
8. Personal friendship was the last consideration.

In 1984 King and Carver did a review of advertising since their 1979 study. The purpose was to determine if CPA advertising was consistent with earlier recommendations which were to advertise industry specializations and a variety of services. Advertising was found to generally fall into one of two categories–direct mailings or published advertisements appearing in newspapers, journals, and magazines. Ads were found in general business and specific industry publications (construction, health care, and banking). Forty-eight percent of the corporate financial officers surveyed had seen published ads.

Based on the previous research cited above, a relative void was found with regard to investigating the promotional strategy of accounting firms. The purpose of this study was to survey accounting firms nationwide to determine the extent to which they reported using publicity and advertising.

RESEARCH OBJECTIVES

The specific objectives of this study were to determine the following (as reported by accounting firms):

1. The extent and methods utilized to gain publicity.
2. The extent to which accounting firms have advertised.
3. The use of advertising media.
4. The message content in advertisements.
5. The advertising components utilized.
6. The advertising objectives.
7. The differences in advertising strategy based on demographic characteristics of the accounting firms.

THE STUDY

The sample utilized for this study was 500 accounting firms which were drawn at random from the AICPA Division of Firms. A self-administered questionnaire was mailed to the firms, and 227 usable responses were returned for a response rate of 45.4 percent. The firms responding to the survey were classified as local firms (84 percent), regional firms (13 percent), and national firms (3 percent). Approximately 96 percent of the firms had five or fewer offices. More than half (56 percent) had one office location. The majority of the firms (99 percent) reported having ten or fewer partners, 53 percent of the practices had five or fewer partners, and 13 percent were sole proprietors. Half the firms (52 percent) reported employing 15 or fewer professionals in the practice.

The majority of the firms responding to the survey provide the following services to their clients: tax planning (97 percent), audit services (85 percent), small business support (84 percent), financial planning (70 percent), and management advisory services (64 percent). The firm's client list was dominated by business (94 percent) as opposed to either individuals, government, or not-for-profit organizations.

The sample was regionally representative with returns from the following areas: Midwest (36 percent), Southeast (22 percent), Northeast (21 percent), Pacific (12 percent), Mountain (12 percent), and Southwest (6 percent).

RESULTS

Use of Publicity by Accounting Firms

The results with regard to obtaining publicity by accounting firms are shown in Table 1. The techniques for gaining publicity in order of reported use are the following: attend social affairs (94 percent), contribute to charity (91 percent), newsletters or technical bulletins (85 percent), seminars (74 percent), press releases (53 percent), submit newsworthy articles to media (52 percent), and media tours (6 percent). Six of the seven techniques for gaining

TABLE 1. Use of Publicity by Accounting Firms

Techniques for Gaining Publicity[a]	NEVER	1 TIME A YEAR	2-3 TIMES A YEAR	4-6 TIMES A YEAR	7-11 TIMES A YEAR	12 TIMES A YEAR (once a month or more)
1. Submit newsworthy articles to media . . .	112 (48.5)	36 (15.6)	52 (22.5)	15 (6.5)	10 (4.3)	6 (2.6)
2. Newsletters or technical bulletins. .	34 (14.8)	10 (4.3)	29 (12.6)	56 (24.3)	13 (5.7)	88 (38.3)
3. Press releases. . . .	109 (46.6)	48 (20.5)	36 (15.4)	21 (9.0)	12 (5.1)	8 (3.4)
4. Seminars.	61 (26.2)	63 (27.0)	77 (33.0)	20 (8.6)	5 (2.1)	7 (3.0)
5. Media Tours.	214 (94.3)	7 (3.1)	4 (1.8)	2 (.9)	–	–
6. Attend Social Events. .	13 (5.6)	6 (2.6)	23 (9.9)	29 (12.4)	30 (12.9)	132 (56.7)
7. Contribute to Charity. .	21 (8.9)	9 (3.8)	33 (14.0)	47 (20.0)	27 (11.5)	98 (41.7)
Has your firm *ever* used advertising?	NO	110 (48.5)		YES	117 (51.5)	

[a]Based on 100% of the surveyed population (N = 227).

publicity were utilized by a majority of the accounting firms who responded to this survey, which indicates the importance of publicity as an element of the promotional mix. Additionally, the accounting firm respondents were asked if their firm had ever used advertising, of which 117 (51.5 percent) had advertised and 110 (48.5 percent) had not. Those who had advertised were asked to continue with the questionnaire and respond to the items related to such activity.

Use of Advertising Media by Accounting Firms

The results pertaining to use of advertising media by accounting firms are shown in Table 2. The media preferences in order of reported use are the following: newspapers (58 percent), specialty advertising (52 percent), direct mailings (50 percent), general business magazines (39 percent), industry journals (23 percent), and technical journals (21 percent). Only four firms (3.5 percent) reported using spot (local) television, and none of the firms used national television or billboards.

TABLE 2. Use of Advertising Media by Accounting Firms

Advertising Media[a]	NEVER	1 TIME A YEAR	2-3 TIMES A YEAR	4-6 TIMES A YEAR	7-11 TIMES A YEAR	12 TIMES A YEAR (once a month or more)
1. Newspaper.	49 (42.2)	13 (11.2)	24 (20.7)	16 (13.8)	3 (2.6)	11 (9.5)
2. Spot (local) television.	109 (96.5)	1 (.9)	3 (2.5)	–	–	–
3. National television. . . .	116 (100.0)	–		–	–	–
4. Radio.	95 (81.9)	4 (3.4)	6 (5.2)	2 (1.7)	3 (2.6)	6 (5.2)
5. General business magazines.	70 (60.9)	10 (8.7)	18 (15.7)	13 (11.3)	1 (.9)	3 (2.6)
6. Technical journals (i.e., Management Accounting).	92 (79.3)	6 (5.2)	7 (6.2)	–	–	3 (2.6)
7. Industry journals (i.e., Oil and Gas). . . .	89 (77.4)	9 (7.8)	9 (7.8)	5 (4.3)	1 (.9)	2 (1.7)
8. Direct Mail.	58 (49.6)	14 (12.0)	24 (20.5)	7 (6.0)	2 (1.7)	12 (10.3)
9. Billboards.	113 (100.0)	–		–	–	–
10. Specialty advertising (business promotional gifts).	55 (47.8)	33 (28.7)	17 (14.8)	7 (6.1)	–	3 (2.6)

[a]Based on the surveyed population who have used advertising (N = 117).

Message Content in Advertising by Accounting Firms

The results involving message content in advertising are shown in Table 3. The items included most often were the following: location (95 percent), services (86 percent), names of accountants (57 percent), special talents/expertise (52 percent), organizational memberships (46 percent) and use of rational appeals (45 percent). The items which were reported to be used least often were fees (3 percent), use of emotional appeals (7 percent), testimonials from clients (9 percent), case histories (10 percent), hours (12 percent) and use of a humor appeal (15 percent).

Use of Advertising Components by Accounting Firms

The results involving the use of advertising components are shown in Table 4. The components in order of reported use were the

TABLE 3. Message Content in Advertising by Accounting Firms

Message Content[a]	NEVER	1 TIME A YEAR	2-3 TIMES A YEAR	4-6 TIMES A YEAR	7-11 TIMES A YEAR	12 TIMES A YEAR (once a month or more)
1. Location (address)	5 (4.5)	17 (15.5)	23 (20.9)	13 (11.8)	6 (5.5)	46 (41.8)
2. Hours	97 (88.2)	3 (2.7)	2 (1.8)	3 (2.7)	–	5 (4.5)
3. Services (i.e., tax, auditing, etc.)	15 (13.8)	16 (14.7)	25 (22.9)	20 (18.3)	3 (2.8)	30 (27.5)
4. Fees	108 (97.3)	1 (.9)	1 (.9)	–	–	1 (.9)
5. Special Talents (expertise)	53 (47.7)	14 (12.6)	16 (14.4)	11 (9.9)	3 (2.7)	14 (12.6)
6. Degree letters/ certifications	76 (69.1)	10 (9.1)	6 (5.5)	7 (6.4)	1 (.9)	10 (9.1)
7. Organizational memberships	59 (54.1)	10 (9.2)	18 (16.5)	8 (7.3)	2 (1.8)	12 (11.0)
8. Names of accountants	47 (42.7)	16 (14.5)	14 (12.7)	11 (10.0)	2 (1.8)	20 (18.2)
9. Testimonials from clients	103 (91.2)	3 (2.7)	6 (5.3)	1 (.9)	–	–
10. Case histories	102 (90.3)	4 (3.5)	3 (2.7)	2 (1.8)	–	2 (1.8)
11. Use emotional appeals	105 (92.9)	2 (1.8)	1 (.9)	1 (.9)	–	4 (3.5)
12. Use rational appeals	61 (54.4)	7 (6.3)	11 (9.8)	13 (11.6)	1 (.9)	19 (17.0)
13. Use a persuasive appeal	76 (67.9)	4 (3.6)	10 (8.9)	12 (10.7)	–	10 (8.9)
14. Use a humor appeal	96 (85.0)	6 (5.3)	4 (3.5)	4 (3.5)	–	3 (2.7)
15. Use a risk management appeal	91 (82.0)	2 (1.8)	7 (6.3)	7 (6.3)	–	4 (3.6)

[a]Based on the surveyed population who have used advertising (N = 117).

following: headline (82 percent), short body copy (71 percent), trademark/logo (67 percent), subhead (67 percent), medium body copy (40 percent) illustration/picture (36 percent), long body copy (25 percent), and slogan (16 percent).

Advertising Objectives of Accounting Firms

The results involving objectives of advertising by accounting firms are shown in Table 5. The objectives reported most often were to increase awareness (97 percent), enhance the firm's image (92 percent), increase tax planning business (87 percent), cultivate

TABLE 4. Use of Advertising Components by Accounting Firms

Advertising Components[a]	NEVER	1 TIME A YEAR	2-3 TIMES A YEAR	4-6 TIMES A YEAR	7-11 TIMES A YEAR	12 TIMES A YEAR (once a month or more)
1. Headline.........	31 (28.2)	14 (12.7)	25 (22.7)	14 (12.7)	4 (3.6)	22 (20.0)
2. Subhead (print smaller than the headline but larger than the body copy)..........	36 (33.3)	19 (17.6)	19 (17.6)	13 (12.0)	5 (4.6)	16 (14.8)
3. Illustration (picture)..........	70 (63.6)	8 (7.3)	18 (16.4)	6 (5.5)	–	8 (7.3)
4. Short body copy (1 paragraph or less)....	32 (29.4)	17 (15.6)	23 (21.1)	18 (16.5)	7 (6.4)	12 (11.0)
5. Medium body copy (2-3 paragraphs).....	65 (59.6)	13 (11.9)	13 (11.9)	12 (11.0)	1 (.9)	5 (4.6)
6. Long body copy (over 3 paragraphs)...	79 (75.2)	8 (7.6)	6 (5.7)	3 (2.9)	–	9 (8.6)
7. Trademark (logo)....	36 (33.0)	12 (11.0)	17 (15.6)	11 (10.1)	4 (3.7)	29 (26.6)
8. Slogan (i.e., The Tax Specialists)......	91 (83.5)	–	4 (3.7)	5 (4.6)	–	9 (8.3)

[a]Based on the surveyed population who have used advertising (N = 117).

public relations (83 percent), increase management advisory services (60 percent).

Cross-Tabulations of Advertising Objectives by Media

Cross-tabulations of advertising objectives by advertising media which were significant (at the .10 level or lower) are shown in Table 6. These provide an indication of which media are utilized in order to accomplish a particular advertising objective. Direct mail was utilized by firms who sought to increase tax planning and information systems, provide information, sell in-house materials, and publicize specialties and firm members. Technical journals were used by firms who wanted to provide information, attract new employees, sell in-house materials, and publicize specialties. General business publications were used by firms who wanted to announce personnel changes, attract new employees, and publicize specialties. Newspapers were used by those who desired to announce personnel changes

TABLE 5. Advertising Objectives of Accounting Firms

Advertising Objectives[a]	NEVER	1 TIME A YEAR	2-3 TIMES A YEAR	4-6 TIMES A YEAR	7-11 TIMES A YEAR	12 TIMES A YEAR (once a month or more)
1. To increase auditing business.	41 (36.6)	17 (15.2)	24 (21.4)	11 (9.8)	1 (.9)	18 (16.1)
2. To increase tax planning business.	15 (13.3)	16 (14.2)	27 (23.9)	19 (16.8)	4 (3.5)	32 (28.3)
3. To increase management advisory services.	25 (22.3)	17 (15.2)	26 (23.2)	13 (11.6)	5 (4.5)	26 (23.2)
4. To increase information systems advisory services.	44 (39.6)	13 (11.7)	18 (16.2)	13 (11.7)	4 (3.6)	19 (17.1)
5. To increase awareness of the firm.	3 (2.6)	16 (14.0)	25 (21.9)	22 (19.3)	4 (3.5)	44 (38.6)
6. To provide information (i.e., tax tips).	31 (27.7)	7 (6.3)	22 (19.6)	19 (17.0)	2 (1.8)	31 (27.7)
7. To announce changes in personnel.	53 (46.9)	16 (14.2)	27 (23.9)	10 (8.8)	3 (2.7)	4 (3.5)
8. To cultivate public relations (i.e., publicity).	18 (16.5)	13 (11.9)	27 (24.8)	20 (18.3)	4 (3.7)	27 (24.8)
9. To attract new employees.	66 (60.0)	18 (16.4)	13 (11.8)	9 (8.2)	–	4 (3.6)
10. To enhance the firm's image (reputation).	9 (8.1)	14 (12.6)	28 (25.2)	20 (18.0)	4 (3.6)	36 (32.4)
11. To license or sell manuals, training programs or software (in-house developed audit, tax, or management aids).	95 (85.6)	5 (4.5)	4 (3.6)	2 (1.8)	1 (.9)	4 (3.6)
12. To publicize specialization (i.e., tax planning).	57 (51.4)	9 (8.1)	17 (15.3)	10 (9.0)	4 (3.6)	14 (12.6)
13. To publicize location.	51 (46.4)	18 (16.4)	10 (9.1)	12 (10.9)	1 (.9)	18 (16.4)
14. To publicize members of the firm.	58 (51.8)	17 (15.2)	18 (16.1)	4 (3.6)	3 (2.7)	12 (10.7)

[a]Based on the surveyed population who have used advertising (N = 117).

TABLE 6. Significant Cross-Tabulations of Advertising Objectives by Advertising Media

Advertising Objectives	Advertising Media					
	NEWSPAPER	GENERAL BUSINESS PUBLICATIONS	TECHNICAL JOURNALS	INDUSTRY JOURNALS	DIRECT MAIL	SPECIALTY ADVERTISING
1. Increase auditing business				.05		
2. Increase tax planning business					.02	.06
3. Increase information systems					.004	
4. Provide information			.03		.0007	
5. Announce personnel changes	.01	.05				
6. Public relations	.01					
7. Attract new employees		.08	.006			
8. Sell in-house materials			.03		.02	
9. Publicize specialities		.07	.07		.006	
10. Publicize firm members					.04	

and improve public relations. Industry journals were used by those firms who sought to increase auditing business, and specialty advertising was correlated with increasing tax planning business.

Cross-Tabulations of Accounting Specialties by Media

Table 7 shows that general business publications were used by firms with specialities in financial planning, general management, specialized industry and MAS. Technical journals were used by those in general management, specialized industry, and MAS, while specialty advertising was correlated with auditing and specialized industry.

Cross-Tabulations of Advertising Objectives by Accounting Specialties

Table 8 indicates that accounting firms with an MAS specialty sought to enhance the firm's image, increase information systems

TABLE 7. Significant Cross-Tabulations of Accounting Specialties by Advertising Media

Accounting Specialties	Advertising Media				
	RADIO	GENERAL BUSINESS PUBLICATIONS	TECHNICAL JOURNALS	INDUSTRY JOURNALS	SPECIALTY ADVERTISING
1. Auditing					.05
2. Financial Planning		.003			
3. Government	.07				
4. Specialized industry		.08	.02		.05
5. MAS		.09	.04	.07	
6. General management		.0003	.0007		

TABLE 8. Significant Cross-Tabulations of Advertising Objectives by Accounting Specialties

Advertising Objectives	Accounting Specialties					
	TAX	FINANCIAL PLANNING	SPECIALIZED INDUSTRY	SMALL BUSINESS	MAS	GENERAL MANAGEMENT
1. Increase tax planning				.03		
2. Increase MAS					.009	.04
3. Increase information systems					.005	.003
4. Provide information						.04
5. Public relations					.08	
6. Attract new employees	.05				.04	.009
7. Enhance firm's image					.0001	
8. Sell in-house materials			.05			
9. Publicize specialties		.10	.009		.05	.01
10. Publicize firm members					.02	

and MAS, publicize specialties and firm members, and attract new employees. Firms with a general management specialty sought to increase information systems and MAS, publicize specialties, provide information, and attract new employees.

DISCUSSION

The results indicate that accounting firms are actively seeking publicity and have well-developed programs for doing so. This was expected as gaining publicity was the only promotional tool that CPA firms could utilize from 1922 until the late 1970s. Though accounting firms are now permitted to advertise, publicity is likely to remain the lead element in the promotional mix for most accounting firms.

With regard to advertising, the results of this study showed that 51.5 percent of the accounting firms surveyed have used some type of advertising. This was greater than expected based on previous research and indicates a growth in such activity in recent years. Newspapers, specialty advertising, and direct mailings were the media vehicles utilized to the greatest extent, followed by general business magazines, industry journals, and technical journals. Only four firms reported using spot television, and none indicated the use of national television or billboards. As expected, the media strategy employed by accounting firms is relatively conservative. Since many firms which compete with CPA firms (i.e., financial planners, tax preparers, business consulting firms, etc.) have been using television extensively, it is likely that CPA firms will utilize television to a greater extent in the future.

Based on the results involving message content, it appears that accounting firms are providing proper information (location, services, names of accountants, and special talents/expertise when they advertise. There would appear to be untapped potential to utilize case histories and successful clients more often in the future. Such advertising provides a dual benefit: positive information to potential clients and publicity for present clients. With regard to advertising components; headlines, short body copy, trademark/logo, and subhead were reported to be used most often. While this result appears favorable, opportunities exist for some accounting firms to improve. Though 67 percent indicated the use of a trademark/logo, it is recommended that all accounting firms consider the benefits of doing so. A distinctive logo can be used in all advertising, thereby providing continuity between advertisements and a more clearly defined image. The logo can also be used on letterhead stationary, business cards, signs, etc., and thus tie-in with advertising (and publicity when the logo may be utilized). When a distinctive logo is developed, it should be trademarked in order to afford protection against replication. Additionally, while the use of an illustration/picture was reported by 36 percent of the accounting firms, it would appear that more firms could benefit by considering the power of an illustration to gain attention.

The advertising objectives reported most often by the accounting firms surveyed were to increase awareness, enhance the firm's image, increase tax planning business, and cultivate public relations. These objectives are appropriate, and the goal of such advertising should generally be to provide information rather than persuasion.

In conclusion, a well conceived advertising program may provide benefits to potential clients and an accounting firm simultaneously. Consumers desire the information provided to aid in the choice process and discover what services are available. An accounting firm can utilize advertising to enhance the image of their professionals, the firms, and cultivate public relations. The public can be informed regarding the value, availability, and special kinds of services (i.e., customer consultation, timely service, unique training, etc.) provided by a specific firm. Thus an advertising program provides an accounting firm with the opportunity to grow by informing potential clients about special capabilities, and at the same time provide a service to the public.

REFERENCES

Bates v. State Bar of Arizona (1977), 97 S. Ct. 2691, 2699, 2700.

Block, Max (1980), "Any Limits to 'Marketing' CPA Services?" *CPA Journal*, 50 (August), 35-40.

Bloom, Paul N. and Stephen E. Loeb (1977), "If Public Accountants Are Allowed to Advertise," *MSU Business Topics*, 25 (Summer), 57-64.

Carver, Robert M., Jr., Thomas E. King, and Wayne A. Label (1979), "Attitudes toward Advertising by Accountants," *Financial Executive*, 47 (October), 27-32.

Darling, John R. (1977), "Attitudes toward Advertising by Accountants," *Journal of Accountancy*, 143 (February), 48-53.

George, William R. and Paul J. Solomon (1980), "Marketing Strategies for Improving Practice Development," *Journal of Accountancy*, 149 (February), 79-88.

Hanggi, Gerald A., Jr. (1980), "Media Advertising as a Practice Development Tool," *Journal of Accountancy*, 149 (January), 54-58.

Hite, Robert E. (1985), "Consumers' Attitudes toward Accountants with Regard to Advertising Professional Services," *Developments in Marketing Science*, 8 (May), 321-326.

Hite, Robert E. and Joseph A. Bellizzi (1986), "Consumers' Attitudes Toward Accountants, Lawyers, and Physicians with Respect to Advertising Professional Services," *Journal of Advertising Research*, 26 (June/July), 45-54.

Ostlund, A. Clayton (1978), "Advertising–In The Public Interest?" *Journal of Accountancy*, 145 (January), 59-63.

Schwersenz, Jack (1979), "Marketing Your Services," *CPA Journal*, 49 (October), 11-15.

Scott, Richard A. and Donna H. Rudderow (1983), "Advertising by Accountants: How Clients and Practitioners Feel About It," *Practical Accountant*, 16 (April), 71-76.

Sellers, James H. and Paul J. Solomon (1978), "CPA Advertising: Opinions of the Profession," *Journal of Accountancy*, 145 (February), 70-76.

Shapiro, Leo J. and Dwight Bohmbach (1979), "Much Ado About Nothing," *Advertising Age*, 50 (December), 4-5.

Traynor, Kenneth (1983/1984), "Accountant Advertising: Perceptions, Attitudes, and Behaviors," *Journal of Advertising Research*, 23 (December/January), 35-40.

Wood, Thomas D. and Donald A. Ball (1978), "New Rule 502 and Effective Advertising by CPAs," *Journal of Accountancy*, 145 (June), 65-70.

Chapter 15

False, Misleading, or Deceptive Advertising by CPA Firms: Opinion of Practicing Accountants

Jim Grant

INTRODUCTION

Promotion of one's own business has been around since the first days of a surplus and exchange of goods and service. But, most of the promotion by professional groups was fairly subtle until recent times. The right club, social interacting, a nice location, referrals and, most importantly, the delivery of quality goods and/or services were the primary tools used to attract business. However, since the *Bates v. the State Bar of Arizona*[1] and various current decrees, advertising has become a prevalent, if not fully accepted, tool in the professions. While the Federal Trade Commission encourages the use of advertising, it has not precluded the use of guidelines by professional associations. The AICPA issues guidelines under rule 502 for accountants and attempts to police deceptive or misleading advertising. The rule specifically states "a member shall not seek to obtain clients by advertising or other forms of solicitation in a manner that is false, misleading, or deceptive."

How effective do practicing accountants feel the efforts have been in eliminating deceptive and misleading advertising? This chapter addresses the issue of misleading accountant advertising.

This chapter was first published in *Journal of Professional Services Marketing*, Vol. 4(2) 1989.

DECEPTIVE ADVERTISING

When is an advertisement deceptive? If a person tells an outright lie, almost everybody would classify the action as deceptive. On the other hand, the lack of release of pertinent or relevant information, or the release of correct but irrelevant information may not be classified as a deception. For example, a soap marketer may advertise that its brand has more green crystals without telling the public that the green crystals are an inactive ingredient. The reader often makes the logical jump and believes that the more green crystals, the more cleaning power. The green crystals are obviously put in the product to mislead the prospective customer, yet some individual may not feel the green crystals are deceptive. Personal ethics and values result in fairly wide disagreement as to what is deceptive or misleading.

Other product deceptions might include: comparative advertising on irrelevant facts or features, price cuts of previously inflated prices, selling lesser quality products or service as high quality, describing something as new, improved, or on sale when it is the same old offering, bait and switch, indicating a specialty without the expertise, and a host of others. People can be misled either very subtly or by direct lies. In any case, the prospect is left in the same deceived position. They are without the complete satisfaction that the full disclosure may have provided.

Why should the accountant be concerned with deception in advertising? First, if there is a direct falsehood or even slight intent to mislead, the image of the whole field suffers accordingly. Those consumers that recognize the deception tell others about it. Those consumers that do not recognize the deception may use the service and become dissatisfied. If the deception is highly successful and profitable, it may even tempt others to copy the deceptive approach.

Advertising already suffers from an image problem. Five reasons for the negative image are:

A. A few direct factual false statements.
B. Readers' failure to distinguish between fact and value judgements or trade puffery.
C. Misinterpretation or inferred meanings by readers that were unintended by the advertiser.

D. Contradiction of competing brands and service advertising either related, implied, or inferred.

E. Much advertising attempts to make significance out of trivial unimportant products.[2]

Because of these image problems, advertising associations adopted internal copy codes of ethics as far back as the 1920s which still exist today.[3]

The Federal Trade Commission, which has broad legal authority to police and enforce "deceptive acts or practices" in an extremely wide range of commercial activities, has devoted the major proportion of its efforts to tangible goods rather than services in the past. The FTC's primary tool is the cease-and-desist order and recently the use of corrective advertising requirements in cases of unfair advantage gained by deception or misleading information. In addition, the FTC issues guidelines, trade practice rules, special statutes, and standard rules for advertising.

The FTC is concerned with any type of deception, but some of the main areas of interest are: guarantees and warranties; premiums; contests, lotteries, and sweepstakes; and testimonials and endorsements. The use of deceptive pricing is another major problem area which the FTC finds difficult and troublesome. The use of words and phrases which the consuming public has learned to look for as an indicator of a price reduction (i.e., "close-out" or "clearance") must be truly a reduced price.[4]

STUDY

A mail survey to 500 nationally distributed practicing CPAs in 1984 resulted in a rather low response rate and only 84 usable questionnaires. Because the questions dealt with advertising by CPA firms, which is still not fully accepted and somewhat controversial to some accountants, the lower response level was expected. The total questionnaire was designed to measure the impact of advertising since the 1979 AICPA ruling which opened up CPA firms to use advertising.

This chapter is concerned more specifically with one question. What, if any, false, misleading, or deceptive advertising have the respondents noticed by CPA firms? Out of the 84 respondents, 51 completed the deceptive advertising questions by indicating the specific type of deception. The individual subjectiveness in evaluation of what is deceptive eliminated some responses. Those who simply said they had seen deceptive advertising without stating the type were not counted. The study did not attempt to break down the deceptions by a particular media.

FINDINGS

The complaints were broken down into five categories. By far, the biggest problem area as seen by the accountants was misleading statements as to the expertise of the respective firms. Over half of the responses indicated an exaggeration or overstatement as to what the firm is really capable of adequately supplying. The table displays the percentage of responses and number by issues.

Deceptive Percentages Reported

	Number	Percent
Lack of Expertise	29	57%
False Information About Taxes	11	21%
Selective Reporting of Surveys	6	12%
Small Firms Using "Big Names"	4	8%
Misleading Prices	1	2%

The second area of concern was false or misleading information about possible or actual taxes, savings, and shelters. Basically, this covers a variety of statements in the advertisements indicating the person using the services of respective firms will benefit from reduced taxes paid on income and other taxed items. One-fifth of the respondents identified the tax saving statements as a problem for the profession.

Approximately ten percent of the respondents complained about large firms using unfair or misleading advertising. At the same time, about ten percent of the complaints were against small firms attempting to sound like big firms by using "big names." Those complaining about the small firms apparently felt the credentials of the small firms were questionable to have such big-sounding names. The names might lead one to believe the firm was statewide or even a national firm while, in fact, the firm might only employ one or two personnel. On the other side, the large firms were cited for using surveys which suggested they provide better service than the smaller firms.

Only one person said he had observed false, misleading, or deceptive CPA advertising concerning the price of services offered and delivered. No indication was made as to the type of price deception, whether hidden costs, add-on services, or simply understating prices.

In total, while approximately 60 percent of those responding listed some type of deception, the complaints against those who advertise seem to be largely highly subjective value judgements as to whether or not there is falsehood, deception, or misrepresentation. With the exception of the tax savings comment, and the one price comment, it is only one person's opinion versus another as to the degree of expertise, quality of service, or promotion of an image which is acceptable. The key governing factor must still be: if the service delivered meets or exceeds the established guidelines and standards of association and, secondly, if the customer is satisfied that he received just value for the service purchased.

The tax savings can also be looked at subjectively. If one is comparing accounting services of one firm against the same accounting services of another firm, then given the exact application of accepted and standard practices of accounting there should be absolutely no tax advantage of using any CPA over another. On the other hand, if one is simply looking at using a CPA versus the average individual's knowledge concerning tax loss and reporting requirements, the particular CPA, or any CPA, can probably save the client money by taking all the deductions available and planning cash flows to the best advantage.

CONCLUSION AND SUMMARY

A wide range of actions can be interpreted as deception, misleading, or even false or fraudulent. The judgement of the individual evaluation is certainly a consideration as to whether or not he is misled. Even with a consensual validation of objective measures, there are degrees of deception ranging from the withholding of information to the complete lie.

Accountant advertising has increased substantially since 1979 as more and more code restrictions were adjusted to reflect legal changes. The FTC is keeping a watchful eye on professional advertising as it always has with more tangible goods.

The respondents in our survey indicated deception exists, but upon closer inspection most of the reported deception appears to be a value judgement by the responding accountants. Very little direct deception, if any, can be found in accounting advertising. In fact, with the increases in lawsuits against all manner of professions, it would be even more unlikely today for a professional to take a chance with a false or misleading advertisement. The accounting profession interprets the 502 rule to prohibit creating false or unjustified expectations of favorable results and self-laudatory statements not based on verifiable facts.[5]

In total, the accounting profession does not seem to have much to fear in the way of a damaged reputation because of false, deceptive, or misleading advertisement as indicated by their membership that responded to the questionnaire. But, with the non-response level being so substantial, one can only speculate as to whether the non-responding accountants are happy or unhappy with the promotions used by their colleagues. The majority of respondents believed the advertisements were deceptive, but the value judgement interpretations of deceptions might lead almost any product or service advertisement to be classified as deceptive.

NOTES

1. *Bates v. State Bar of Arizona*, 97 S. Ct. 2691.

2. Kottman, E. John, "Truth and the Image of Advertising," *Journal of Marketing*, American Marketing Association, Chicago, Vol. 33 (October 1969), pp. 64-75.

3. See *Printers Ink*, May 26, 1932, p. 52, and Pease, Otis A., "Advertising Ethics" in *Advertising's Role in Society*, edited by Wright, John S. and Mertes, John E., New York: West Publishing Company, 1974, pp. 271-277.

4. Burton, Philip Ward, *Advertising Copywriting*, Fourth Edition, Columbus, Ohio: Grid Publishing, Inc., 1978.

5. AICPA Staff, "Ethics Feature Advertising: What Forms of Advertising Are Permissible Under the Ethics Code?" *Journal of Accounting*, November 1986, pp. 98-100.

Chapter 16

Advertising by Accountants:
Attitudes and Practice

Sherman Folland
Eileen Peacock
Sandra Pelfrey

The professional proscription against accountant advertising was formally rescinded with the 1978 revision of the Code of Professional Ethics. The present, near the end of the first decade of advertising, is an appropriate time to assess the effects of this policy change. For the new policy to have effects, a necessary first step is that accounting firms adopt advertising to a significant extent. The adoption decision in turn depends on the circumstances, attitudes, and perceptions of the accountant decision maker. Despite the importance of advertising to the profession, there have been relatively few studies of the nexus of accountant opinion and practice. Too often the literature relies on means and correlates of scattered individual items from a variety of surveys.

The present research assesses the nature of accountant opinion on advertising through the generation of reliable scales of the underlying attitude factors. It then investigates the relationship of attitudes with age and other accountant characteristics. Finally, we investigate whether these attitudes affect advertising practice.

Section I provides perspectives for the present study from legal history and empirical marketing research. Section II describes the data used for this study. Section III presents factor analysis results and reliability tests for the generated scales. Section IV investigates

This chapter was first published in *Journal of Professional Services Marketing*, Vol. 6(2) 1991.

the relationship of accountant age and other characteristics to these attitude scales. Section V examines the relationship of the attitude scales to advertising practices. A discussion and conclusion follows in Section VI.

PERSPECTIVES

Legal History

Accountants, especially accountants in public practice, are bound by the Code of Professional Conduct.[1] Prior to the revisions of 1978, the Code proscribed the solicitation of clients, which explicitly included a proscription against advertising. The pre-1978 Code stated:

> Solicitation to obtain clients is prohibited under the Rules of Conduct because it tends to lessen the professional independence towards clients which is essential to the best interests of the public . . . Advertising, which is a form of solicitation is prohibited . . . Promotional practices such as solicitation and advertising, tend to indicate a dominant interest in profit . . .

The Code, explicitly or through formal interpretations, extended its proscriptions to ads in newspapers, television, radio, magazines, and direct mail that is unsolicited by the client (Cashin, [1971]).

The wording of the Code cast accountancy as a self-policing profession concerned primarily with the quality of the accountant-client relationship and, if secondarily, with the image of the profession. The wording reflects a legal environment in which the professions were accustomed to be self-regulating and exempt from the intrusions of government and the courts common to other lines of business. This environment changed substantially with the 1975 U. S. Supreme Court decision in *Goldfarb v. The Virginia State Bar* (1975), which declared that the learned professions were nevertheless subject to antitrust law. Shortly thereafter, the U. S. Supreme Court, in *Bates and O'Steen v. State Bar of Arizona* (1977), ruled, on freedom of speech grounds, that it is unconstitutional to prohibit certain forms of advertising in the legal profession. The accounting profession responded to the *Bates* decision the following year; in the Referendum January 30, 1978, the AICPA proposed that its rules be changed to read:

> A member shall not seek to obtain clients by advertising or other forms of solicitation in a manner that is false, misleading, or deceptive.

The wording of the amendment, in addition, cited advertising as possibly helpful to "enable CPAs to inform the public of their services in areas in which non-CPA competitors are already advertising" and to "facilitate new CPAs making their services known to potential clients." The amendment passed by a two-thirds majority of the membership.

Empirical Marketing Research

Considering the potentially important effects of accountant advertising on the profession and the public, there has been relatively little research on accountant attitudes and practices. Bussom and Darling (1978) surveyed four professions in several large cities finding accountants to be unfavorable toward advertising and pessimistic about its effects. A follow-up study by Darling and Bergiel (1983) found that accountants in these same cities had become substantially more favorable toward advertising.

More recently, Traynor (1984) sampled Pennsylvania CPAs on selected attitude items and practices. Most viewed advertising as harmful and 80 percent considered it an unnecessary activity. Traynor reported that a relationship existed between accountant age and their response to individual survey items. Younger accountants were less concerned about the effect of advertising on the accountant's public image and younger accountants and accountants from larger firms were more likely to advertise.

These studies are suggestive, but, they do not investigate the underlying nature of accountant opposition toward advertising. Also, there has been no multivariate examination of the relationship of accountant characteristics to attitudes. Finally, this literature has not examined the ultimate question regarding accountant attitudes, that is, are these attitudes related to actual practice?[2] It is the purpose of the present chapter to address these issues.

THE DATA

The data were generated from responses to a survey instrument of our devising. The questionnaire solicited demographics, advertising practices and plans, and responses to Likert-type scale items reflecting attitudes and perceptions regarding advertising. To aid in comparability, 10 attitude items from the Bussom and Darling (1978) survey were included.

A systematic sample was generated by selecting every *i*th case after a random start from an alphabetically sorted address list maintained by the Michigan Association of Certified Public Accountants. The sample was confined to those CPAs who maintain a Michigan address of practice. The first mailing was sent in July of 1987 with follow-ups sent in August and September. This effort generated 341 useable, completed questionnaires for a response rate of 39 percent.

To test for nonresponse bias, we conducted a telephone survey of a systematic sample of nonrespondents. We continued sampling until 40 of the nonrespondents were reached. Based on the Chi-square statistic, the differences between respondents and nonrespondents over activity status, form of practice (local vs. regional/national), partner status, age group, and sex, were not significant at the 95 percent level of confidence. The two groups did, however, differ on advertising behavior in that a significantly larger percentage of respondents' firms were advertisers. This fact warrants caution in attempts to base estimates of population mean advertising rates on unadjusted sample means. Such estimates are not the purpose of the present chapter where oversampling of advertisers is arguably useful. To the present point, respondent nonadvertisers did not differ in characteristics from nonrespondent nonadvertisers (based on Chi-square tests), similarly for advertisers in both samples.

ATTITUDES AND PERCEPTIONS

The first issue of identifying the underlying factors representing accountant attitudes on advertising was approached through factor analysis. Factor analysis of the 13 Likert scale items revealed the factor structure presented in Table 1. Five factors, accounting for 65 percent of the variance in the original 13 variables, were extracted.

These factors were semantically identified as: a general factor related to opinions about the benefits and helpfulness of advertising to both the accountant and the customer (GENERAL FAVORABILITY); attitudes toward the legal control of advertising (LEGAL CONTROL); the effect of advertising on the professional image of quality service (EFFECTS ON IMAGE); the effect of advertising on price (EFFECTS ON PRICE); and concerns about the accuracy of the content of advertising in this field (CONTENT).

Alpha reliability coefficients were calculated for the group of variables identified with each factor. Alpha coefficients for the first three factors indicate that these are the strongest factors. The remaining price and content factors, however, make sense intuitively as underlying factors and are also pursued in the subsequent analysis.

The results of the factor analysis in Table 1 were used to generate values for five scales.[3] The resultant scales are devised so that a score of one represents extreme unfavorability toward advertising (or pessimism about its effects) and a score of five indicates extreme favorability (optimism). The mean scale values indicate that the accountants sampled tend to be unfavorable toward advertising across the board, although the third scale value is close to a neutral value of three (see Table 2).

ON THE RELATIONSHIP OF AGE TO ACCOUNTANT ATTITUDES

Theoretical Considerations

Given its relative newness to the accounting profession, advertising by accountants represents a technological innovation. The diffusion of an innovation "is a complex social phenomenon which clearly involves both economic and noneconomic factors" (Warner, 1974). Loosely following Rogers and Shoemaker's (1971) and Rogers' (1983) theory, a key role is played by channels of communication. These channels transmit technical information as well as ideas about the attractiveness of the innovation.

In the case of the age relationship, age probably plays a dual role.

TABLE 1. Factor Analysis of Attitude and Perception Variables

Attitude and Perception Items	Factor 1: GENERAL	Factor 2: LEGAL CONTROL	Factor Loadings** Factor 3: IMAGE	Factor 4: PRICE	Factor 5: CONTENT
Advertising is a valuable way to communicate to consumers	.64				
Advertising helps consumers make intelligent choice of firm	.76				
Control of advertising lessens competition among accountants	.52	.49			
Advertising my services is beneficial to me personally	.65				
Overall accountant advertising will benefit the average consumer	.79				
Accountant advertising should be allowed without restriction		.79			
AICPA restrictions on advertising are necessary to protect consumer*		.80			
Advertising will adversely affect the public image of accounting*			.62		
Advertising by accountants will tend to lower average service quality*			.74		

Factor Loadings**

Attitude and Perception Items	Factor 1: GENERAL	Factor 2: LEGAL CONTROL	Factor 3: IMAGE	Factor 4: PRICE	Factor 5: CONTENT
Advertising usually increases the price of the service advertised*				.66	
Accountant advertising will tend to lower fees in accounting				.83	
There is no correlation between advertising level and accounting ability*					.88
Difficult to advertise competence or quality in my profession*					.53
Percent of Variance Explained	20.3	13.9	11.4	10.2	10.1
Eigenvalue	2.63	1.81	1.48	1.33	1.31
Alpha Coefficient	.74	.61	.68	.38	.34

*Indicates scale with polarity reversed.

**Coefficients less than .4 are suppressed.

TABLE 2. Scale Values on Advertising Attitudes and Perceptions

Scale	Mean*	Std. Deviation
General favorability to advertising	2.62	0.83
Legal control issues	2.41	0.97
Effects on professional image	2.96	0.97
Effects on price	2.39	0.81
Concerns about ad content	2.15	1.00

*A score of 1 indicates the most unfavorable/pessimistic response possible, 3 is a neutral response, and 5 represents the most favorable/optimistic response possible.

First, younger accountants, and youth in general are probably more receptive to new ideas such as advertising. Accountants who joined the profession in the past decade or two probably received more favorable communications about the role of advertising than those which were prominent during the era when advertising was prohibited. Second, younger accountants who are establishing a sole practice or a new local partnership are likely to find advertising an important tool in communicating the availability of services to a prospective clientele. Thus both economic and social factors suggest that the younger accountant will be more favorable toward advertising and more likely to adopt advertising given the decision-making authority.

The relationship of professional age and attitudes toward advertising has been reported for other professions (Braun and Braun, [1985]; Ebert [1985]; McChesney [1985]; Folland, Parameswaran, and Darling [1989]). It has also been reported by Traynor (1984) for the accounting profession. It is of some interest to test Traynor's report in a context in which reliability tested scales of opinion have been identified and also in a context in which other perhaps confounding variables have been identified.

Correlates of Advertising Attitudes Under MANOVA

The next step taken in the study was to assess the relationship of accountant characteristics to their scores on the five attitude scales. This issue was pursued by multivariate analysis of variance. The results are reported in Table 3 where the five scales are used as the dependent variables and five personal or firm characteristics appear as main effects. These main effect variables are defined as follows: SMSA equals one if the accountant's firm address is located in a metropolitan statistical area, zero else; FEMALE equals one if the accountant respondent is female; FIRMTYPE represents four categories in which the firm is either (1) sole practitioner, (2) multipractitioner firm serving a single local market area, (3) regional firm, or (4) national firm; PARTNER equals one if the accountant is a partner in his firm; and finally AGEGROUP describes four age categories (1) age 34 or less, (2) age 35 to 44 years, (3) age 45 to 54 years, and (4) age 55 or older.

The data presented in Table 3 show without a doubt that the strongest effect is for the age of the accountant respondent. Mean scores for each age group (not shown) are consistent. As theory suggests, younger accountants are more favorable toward advertising on each issue represented by the five scales, and this relationship is statistically significant for three of the five scales and strongly significant overall. Interestingly, group means also show that female respondents are less favorable toward advertising, although in most cases the effect is not significant at conventional levels.

ATTITUDES AND PRACTICE

The ultimate question of interest is whether and to what extent attitudes and perceptions of accountants are related to advertising practice. Our data set, by measuring both attitudes and the past year's advertising practices, permits an investigation of this issue.

The fulfillment of attitudes in practice requires that the accountant have some decision-making authority within the firm. Favor-

TABLE 3. Multivariate Analysis of Variance: Dependent Variables Are the Scales

Dependent Variable	Sources of Variation	DF	Type III SS	F	P-value
General Favorability	Main Effects				
	SMSA	1,168	0.00393	0.01	0.938
	FEMALE	1,168	1.38989	2.14	0.145
	FIRMTYPE	3,168	1.95825	1.01	0.391
	PARTNER	1,168	2.01197	3.10	0.080
	AGEGROUP	3,168	6.49696	3.34	0.021
Legal Control	Main Effects				
	SMSA	1,168	0.68904	0.69	0.406
	FEMALE	1,168	1.49877	1.51	0.221
	FIRMTYPE	3,168	0.37027	0.12	0.946
	PARTNER	1,168	1.34223	1.35	0.247
	AGEGROUP	3,168	4.30045	1.44	0.232
Image	Main Effects				
	SMSA	1,168	3.14547	4.09	0.045
	FEMALE	1,168	3.25155	4.63	0.038
	FIRMTYPE	3,168	8.54010	3.70	0.013
	PARTNER	1,168	0.76468	0.99	0.320
	AGEGROUP	3,168	7.22794	3.13	0.027
Price	Main Effects				
	SMSA	1,168	0.35421	0.53	0.467
	FEMALE	1,168	0.12429	0.19	0.666
	FIRMTYPE	3,168	1.24540	0.62	0.600
	PARTNER	1,168	0.43778	0.66	0.419
	AGEGROUP	3,168	9.89813	4.95	0.003
Content	Main Effects				
	SMSA	1,168	0.55708	0.60	0.442
	FEMALE	1,168	0.62863	0.67	0.414
	FIRMTYPE	3,168	3.41938	1.22	0.305
	PARTNER	1,168	0.05212	0.06	0.814
	AGEGROUP	3,168	1.74063	0.62	0.603

Overall	Main Effects	Wilks' Lambda	F	P-value
	SMSA	0.96307	1.257	0.285
	FEMALE	0.97078	0.987	0.427
	FIRMTYPE	0.86521	1.627	0.063
	PARTNER	0.95187	1.658	0.148
	AGEGROUP	0.80811	2.424	0.002

ability toward advertising by a younger nonpartner in a national firm would not likely be relevant to the firm's decision mechanism.[4] Thus to investigate the fulfillment issue, we include only those observations where the accountant is a sole practitioner or a partner in a local firm.

We begin this investigation with a simple comparison of the differences in the mean scale values between advertisers and nonadvertisers. These results are shown in Table 4. Advertisers are clearly more favorable toward advertising than nonadvertisers on each scale, and this effect is significant at the 1 percent level for the cases of the general factor and the image issue.

The question of the relationship of attitudes to behavior, however, is better investigated in a multivariate context. To this end we model the probability that a given accountant (sole owner or local firm partner) will advertise based on the accountant's measured scale values. For this purpose, logit is the appropriate technique in that it avoids the problem of heteroscedasticity and also ensures that the estimated probabilities fall within the zero-one interval. The natural hypothesis is that each of the five scales contributes positively to the probability of advertising (ADVTSD) and to the probability that the accountant will add to the level of advertising during the coming year (ADDAD).

TABLE 4. Attitude Differences Between Advertisers and Nonadvertisers

Variable	Mean for Advertisers	Mean for Nonadvertisers	t-value
GENERAL FAVORABILITY	3.02	2.38	4.28***
LEGAL CONTROL	2.52	2.19	1.81**
IMAGE	3.42	2.68	4.37***
PRICE	2.47	2.31	1.14
CONTENT	2.28	1.99	1.34*

Note: A score of 1 indicates the most unfavorable/pessimistic about advertising; a score of 5 indicates the most favorable/optimistic response possible. * = significant at the 10% level; ** = significant at the 5% level; *** = significant at the 1% level—each in a one-tail test.

The logit results are presented in Table 5. The general factor is significantly related to both the probability of advertising and the probability that the accountant will increase the level of advertising. This is the strongest of the attitude predictors of advertising behavior.

The image scale also significantly affects advertising though it is not quite significant at the 5 percent level for plans. Price, Content, and Legal Control are each insignificant.

DISCUSSION AND CONCLUSIONS

Some informal discussion of the previous sections may help to add flesh to the numerical results. In reconsidering these results, it is as interesting to note what is not statistically significant as well as what is statistically significant. Consider the price factor first. The survey items that make up our price factor are really empirical

TABLE 5. Logit Equations

Dependent Variables

Independent Variable	ADVTSD	Asymp. t value	ADDAD	Asymp. t value
General Favorability	0.7522	1.86**	0.7961	1.95**
Legal Control	−0.2976	0.93	−0.2402	0.74
Image	0.7072	2.20**	0.4965	1.57*
Price	0.3445	0.98	0.3807	1.09
Content	0.1447	0.57	0.2297	0.90
Intercept	−5.7049	3.86***	−5.6514	3.84***
Model Chi-square	15.21**		13.97**	

ADVTSD = one if the accountant advertised during the past year in newspapers, radio, TV, magazines, or direct mail, else zero.
ADDAD = one if the accountant planned to increase the amount of advertising during the coming year, else zero.
* = significant at the 10% level; ** = significant at the 5% level; *** = significant at the 1% level—each in a one-tail test.

economic research questions: does advertising raise or lower the price of services in general and in the accounting profession in particular? Most of the accountants surveyed take the pessimistic view, by which we mean the view that advertising does not lower prices and in fact may inflate them. Interestingly, the younger accountants are more optimistic.

This parallels what has been going on in economic research. In the 1970s, Phillip Nelson (1970, 1974) published two influential theoretical articles that argued that advertising is essentially information. Armed with more information, market forces tend to drive prices downward. During this time, influential empirical work also appeared reporting evidence that advertising has in fact lowered prices in some services, notably optometry (Benham, [1972]; Feldman and Begun, [1978]). Although the issue is still disputed, the optimistic view is now widely accepted among academics. Clearly, younger accountants were trained in schools of business administration during a time when research-based communications regarding the role of advertising were much more favorable.

Despite this trend toward optimism, it is quite understandable that accountant opinions on the price issue does not affect the decision to advertise. "Optimism" in our sense means optimism on the marketwide effects of advertising in benefiting the average consumer by lowering average prices. Regardless of the accountant's belief about this broad social science issue, his decision to advertise more plausibly is determined by perceptions of advertising effects on his own practice and his own clients.

The role of the content issue is similar though less clear. Accountants in general tend to find advertising to be a questionable vehicle for conveying accurate and meaningful information about this professional service. Again younger accountants are more favorable toward advertising's potential or actual content but this trend is not statistically significant. Despite the lack of statistical significance, this age relationship makes sense, especially if one considers that the function of advertising is somewhat different for the younger CPAs. The younger CPAs are more likely to be in the process of establishing a practice. Here advertising is quite competent to play its role of communicating the availability, location, and type of services provided. The lack of significance may reflect the low alpha score for this factor, rather than the importance of ad content per se.

The results for the legal control factor probably reflect the fact that the items underlying this factor are the least evaluative of the survey questions. A respondent who feels that accountant advertising should be subject to legal controls may mean only minor prohibitions on false or misleading advertising or instead may prefer substantial limitations. It is not so surprising that this factor is not significantly related to accountant age nor to advertising practice.

What then does matter for the decision to advertise? We find two significant factors: a general factor, and the specific image factor. It is of interest to review the survey items that make up these factors. The key items in the general factor all appear to relate to the perceived benefits of advertising to the client as well as to the accountant advertiser. These items refer specifically to the "helpfulness" of advertising and the "benefits" of it. This factor is significantly related to age suggesting as well that advertising practice will continue to grow among accountants as these currently younger accountants pass through the age cohorts.

Finally, the image factor is significantly related to advertising practice and thus remains a key issue. Many accountants still worry about their own image of professionalism as well as that of the profession as a whole. It is interesting to recall that the question of image was an issue in the original AICPA prohibitions against advertising.

In conclusion, the present study is an attempt to fill gaps in the literature on accountant advertising and professional advertising in general. Too often this literature has examined responses to individual survey items without attention to the identification of underlying factors, multivariate analysis of the correlates of attitudes, and investigation of the fulfillment of attitudes in practice. Nevertheless, one of our central sets of findings, that four of five advertising attitude factors are related to age, is confirmation in a more rigorous framework of a conclusion that has been widely accepted. Younger accountants not only evaluate advertising more favorably in a personal sense, but they are also more optimistic on the empirical issues of advertising's effects. More importantly, we investigate empirically which of these attitude factors are closely related to advertising behavior. Our results of this point make clear that attitudes do matter for practice. That is, advertising practice is amenable to increased understanding by accountants of the potential benefits of advertising as information for both the professional services advertiser and the client. Together, these results suggest both that accountant acceptance of advertising and advertising practice by accountants will continue to grow.

NOTES

1. The name of the Code was formally changed in January 1988; prior to this time it was termed the Code of Professional Ethics and Interpretive Opinions.

2. Despite the opposition to advertising among accountants, the public has been receptive. Hite and Bellizza (1986) reported that consumers have a favorable attitude toward accountant advertising. Similarly, Carver et al. (1979) found that 73 percent of financial analysts surveyed believed that public accounting firms should be allowed to advertise and most responded that cost and quality of services would not be adversely affected by advertising.

3. The scales in each case are a weighted average of the polarity-adjusted item scores with the weights defined as the factor loading divided by the sum of the factor loadings.

4. If there were any relationship in such a case, it may merely reflect the effect of experience with advertising on attitudes.

REFERENCES

Bates and O'Steen v. State Bar of Arizona, 433 U. S. 350 (1977).

Benham, Lee, "The Effects of Advertising on the Price of Eyeglasses," *Journal of Law and Economics*, Vol. 15, October 1972, pp. 337-352.

Braun, Irwin, and Marilyn Braun, "Advertising Health Care Professionals: Problems, Solutions and Benefits," in *Advertising by Health Care Professionals in the 80's*, (Washington, DC: Federal Trade Commission, December 1985).

Bussom, Robert S. and John R. Darling, "Medical Fee and Service Advertising, A Response from Physicians," *Medical Care*, Vol. 16, No. 2, February 1978, pp. 110-121.

Cady, John F., *Drugs on the Market*, (Lexington, MA: Lexington Books, 1975).

Carver, Robert M., Thomas E. King, and Wayne A. Label, "Attitudes Toward Advertising by Accountants," *Financial Executive*, October 1979, pp. 27-32.

Cashin, James S., *Handbook for Auditors*, (New York: McGraw-Hill, 1971), pp. 4-1 to 4-28.

Code of Professional Ethics and Interpretive Opinions, (New York: AICPA, 1970).

Code of Professional Ethics and Interpretive Opinions, (New York: AICPA, 1978).

Darling, John R., and Blaise J. Bergiel, "Health Care Advertising: A Comparative Analysis," *Journal of Health Care Marketing*, Vol. 3, No. 1, Winter 1983, pp. 21-28.

Ebert, Robert, "Developments in Professional Advertising and Steps the Professions Can Take to Limit Deception," in *Advertising by Health Care Professionals in the 80's*, (Washington, DC: Federal Trade Commission, December 1985).

Feldman, Roger, and James W. Begun, "Effects of Advertising: Lessons from Optometry," *Journal of Human Resources*, Vol. 13 Supplement, 1978, pp. 247-262.

Folland, Sherman, Ravi Parameswaran, and John Darling, "On the Nature of Physicians' Opposition to Advertising," *Journal of Advertising*, Vol. 18, No. 1, 1989, pp. 4-12.

Goldfarb v. The Virginia State Bar, 421 U. S. 773 (1975).

Hite, R. E. and J. A. Bellizza, "Consumers' Attitudes Toward Accountants, Lawyers, and Physicians with Respect to Advertising Professional Services," *Journal of Advertising Research*, June/July 1986, pp. 45-54.

McChesney, Fred S., "The Law and Economics of Professional Advertising: An Overview," in *Advertising by Health Care Professionals in the 80's*, (Washington, DC: Federal Trade Commission, December 1985).

Nelson, Phillip, "Information and Consumer Behavior," *Journal of Political Economy*, Vol. 78, March/April 1970, pp. 311-329.

Nelson, Phillip, "Advertising as Information," *Journal of Political Economy*, Vol. 82, July/August 1974, pp. 729-754.

Rogers, E.M., *Diffusion of Innovations*, (New York: The Free Press, 1983).

Rogers, E.M., and F.F. Shoemaker, *Communications of Innovations: A Cross-cultural Approach*, (New York: The Free Press, 1971).

Traynor, Kenneth, "Accountant Advertising: Perceptions, Attitudes, and Behaviors," *Journal of Advertising Research*, Vol. 23, No. 6, 1984, pp. 35-40.

Warner, Kenneth, "The Need for Some Innovative Concepts of Innovation: An Examination of Research on the Diffusion of Innovations," *Policy Sciences*, Vol. 5, 1974, pp. 433.

Chapter 17

The Changing Face
of Accounting Advertising

James H. Thompson
L. Murphy Smith
Robert E. Jordan

INTRODUCTION

Advertising by accountants has been permitted for a decade. Advertising is now generally accepted despite early concerns about professional propriety. For example, the AICPA Board of Directors approved an advertising program for national media at its April 7-8, 1988 meeting. To what extent are practitioners using advertisements and for what purpose are the ads being used? That question is the subject of this study.

In 1978 the American Institute of Certified Public Accountants (AICPA) rescinded its longstanding ban on advertising. The following year it also lifted the ban on direct solicitation. These changes in policy were prompted by inquiries and rulings emanating from the United States Justice Department. The Justice Department actions were precipitated by the 1975 U.S. Supreme Court ruling in *Goldfarb v. Virginia State Bar*. In this case, the Court ruled that "learned professions" were not exempt from antitrust legislation. Later that same year, the Federal Trade Commission (FTC) registered a complaint against the American Medical Association (AMA) and two Connecticut medical societies, alleging that they

This chapter was first published in *Journal of Professional Services Marketing*, Vol. 6(2) 1991.

had "adopted, disseminated, and enforced ethical restrictions on physician advertising" (FTC Decisions, 1979).

In response to the Justice Department concerns and actions, the AICPA decided to permit advertising. William L. Trombetta, Deputy Attorney General for the Antitrust Section/Division of Criminal Justice in New Jersey, expressed the Justice Department position:

> Anticompetitive conduct, such as group boycotts, arbitrary and unreasonable licensing requirements, barriers to entry and exclusionary practices, price-fixing, restraints on advertising, stifling of innovative delivery systems, and restrictions on professional productivity, has resulted in federal and state anti-trust-enforcement agencies directing their attention to those aspects of professional services that are predominantly commercial in nature.[1]

As far as the Justice Department was concerned, removing restraints on advertising would benefit the public. Their rationale was that advertising would increase competition and that competition among professionals would lead to lower prices, higher quality, and increased productivity.

Some accountants have also held positive expectations for advertising. This viewpoint has been expressed as follows:

> Factual advertising is an indispensable source of the information needed for the efficient functioning of the economy and for the intelligent consumption choices of individuals. Therefore, public interest demands that advertising supply this information. The good of the accounting profession itself depends on the efficient functioning of the economy. Therefore, advertising by accountants will work for the common good of the accounting profession and the economy.[2]

Because of advertising, the accounting profession can expand the market for products and services by providing the purchasers of accounting services with better information. Better information should lead to more effective consumer decisions, bringing increasing rewards to the providers of the desired products and services.

Other accounting professionals, however, have expressed a negative perspective: that increased competition brought about through advertising would be to the long-term public detriment. According to Walter W. Regel, both the accounting profession and the public were likely to suffer if accounting firms became more aggressive advertisers.[3] Regel (1984) expressed the concern that competition would lead to a decrease in audit quality. In addition, the Big Eight accounting firms would likely pursue small business engagements that have traditionally belonged to regional firms. Moreover, Regel believed that not only would the public image of the profession suffer because of advertising, but that the results of advertising–lower quality audits and decreased competition in the long run–could bring increased governmental regulation in order to protect the smaller firms.

A decade has now passed since the advertising ban was lifted. What type of ads are most often used? To what extent has the accounting profession used this marketing tool? To gain some insight into its effect on the accounting profession, this chapter analyzes advertising of the Big Eight CPA firms in selected professional journals.

RESEARCH METHOD

Twelve journals were selected as a basis for investigating the advertising philosophy of Big Eight accounting firms. Table 1 identifies these journals. Each issue of these journals during 1980, 1983, and 1986 was surveyed for display ads. To keep the size of the project manageable, this study considers only Big Eight display advertising.

An attempt was made to survey additional industries for Big Eight advertising. Real estate, manufacturing, and retailing journals were examined, but few ads were found. Some industry journals, for example, *Industrial Development Site Selection Handbook*–a real estate journal– contained various forms of advertising; however, no ads by Big Eight accounting firms appeared.

As each issue of the selected journal was surveyed, a record of advertisement size, frequency, purpose, and target market was recorded. In order to compare the size of ads among journals, ads

TABLE 1. Journals Surveyed

Journal Name	Issues per Year	Target Market
ABA Banking Journal	12	Banking
Bank Administration (*Magazine of Bank Administration* prior to March 1986)	12	Banking
Financial Executive	12	General Business
Fortune	26	General Business
Healthcare Financial Management (*Hospital Financial Management* prior to June 1982)	12	Healthcare
Hospitals	12	Healthcare
Journal of Accountancy	12	Public Accounting
The CPA Journal	12	Public Accounting
The Internal Auditor	6	Private Accounting
Management Accounting	12	Private Accounting
Pension World	12	Insurance
Risk Management[a]	12	Insurance

[a]The 1980 issues of *Risk Management* were unavailable. The 1981 issues were used as a substitute under the assumption that since there were no ads in 1981 there would be no ads in 1980.

were classified into one of five size categories: one-fourth page or less; more than one-fourth page, but less than one-half page; more than one-half page, but less than a full page; a full page; and multi-page ad size.

The frequency of advertising is a count of advertising occurrence, disregarding any differences in size. Accordingly, a one-half page ad and a multiple page ad were both counted as one occurrence.

Each ad was classified into one of eight categories according to the purpose of the advertising. These categories are training programs (solicitation for enrollment in education programs), time-sharing or software (solicitation for sale of computer time-sharing or computer programs), executive search services, management advisory services, employee recruitment, tax services, audit services, or general image advertising.

The target market of each ad was inferred from the industry associated with the journal in which the advertisement occurred. The target markets were identified as: public accounting, private accounting, healthcare, banking, insurance, and general business. Table 1 identifies the target market associated with each journal considered in this study.

ADVERTISING PROFILE

In the early 1980s the accounting profession was not in agreement on the effect that advertising would have on the profession and the public. Perhaps there still is no consensus, but an analysis of advertising that is placed by an individual firm provides insight into the value which that particular firm places on advertising. A trend of increased advertising indicates that a firm considers the ads valuable, whereas a decreasing trend indicates a lack of perceived value. Increased advertising does not determine the "good" of advertising–only that advertising has value in maintaining or increasing an accounting practice.

In addition, if an individual firm focuses its advertising toward a particular industry, some accountants contend that increased efficiency is the result (Smith and Smith, 1984). When a firm establishes a trend of increased advertising within a specific industry, it indicates that the firm has been successful in marketing its products and services. An informed customer purchases those products and services that have the greatest marginal utility to him. Marketing success is evidence that one firm's products and services are meeting informed customers' needs more effectively than its competitors.

Although complete assessment of the effect of advertising on the accounting profession cannot be made, some insight into its effect on the accounting profession can be established by examining advertising trends. This study considers advertising in selected journals in 1980, 1983, and 1986 as a basis for investigating the advertising philosophy of each Big Eight accounting firm. To facilitate this investigation, advertisements of each Big Eight firm found in selected journals during the years under study are compared according to advertisement size, frequency, purpose, and target market.

Size of Ads

A comparison of ad size by firm for the years of 1980, 1983, and 1986 is shown in Figure 1. The trend in advertising size is toward larger ads. The trend toward larger ads appears to be associated with the purpose of the advertisement (see Figure 2). Since 1980, the amount of advertising placed for the purpose of employee recruitment has decreased, while ads placed for management advisory services have increased. Employee recruitment ads historically are small ads, while ads for management advisory services tend to be full-page ads.

When average ad size for the different advertising purposes is examined as shown in Figure 2, the most frequent use of smaller ads occurs in employee recruitment. Of the 44 ads placed for employee recruitment, only nine exceeded one-half page. Ads for most other purposes tend to utilize mostly full-page ads with an occasional use of a multi-page ad.

Frequency of Ads

The frequency of Big Eight advertising surveyed in this study varies greatly among firms as shown in Figure 3. Touche Ross placed the fewest advertisements in the journals that were examined. The firm placed five full-page ads in 1986 issues of *Healthcare Financial Management* for management advisory services and three smaller ads in 1983 for employee recruitment in the *Journal of Accountancy* and *The CPA Journal*.

At the other end of the spectrum, Ernst & Whinney; Peat, Marwick, Main; and Deloitte, Haskins & Sells placed numerous ads. A large percentage of Ernst & Whinney's and Peat, Marwick, Main's advertising is targeted toward the healthcare industry, while Deloitte, Haskins & Sells' advertising has been broader in both target market and purpose.

As Figure 3 shows, Arthur Young had a relatively high frequency of advertising in 1980. The bulk of this advertising was small ads for employee recruitment placed in public accounting journals. The number of ads placed by the Big Eight firms overall has generally increased. Table 2 shows the frequency of ads placed by the Big Eight firms in the different advertisement purpose categories.

Advertising Purpose

The purpose for which firms advertise also varies. As Figure 4 shows, the most frequently occurring ads were computer-related.

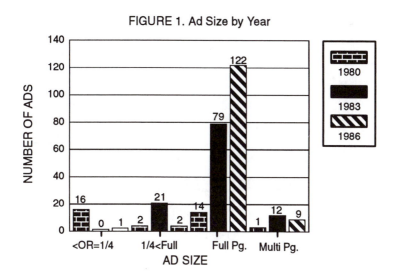

FIGURE 1. Ad Size by Year

FIGURE 2. Ad Size by Purpose

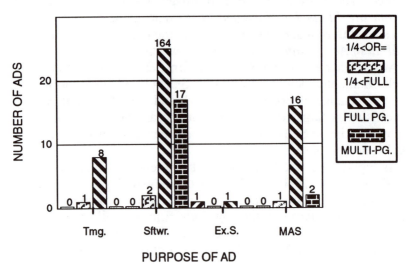

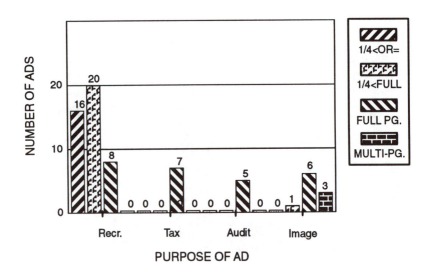

FIGURE 3. Frequency by Firm by Year

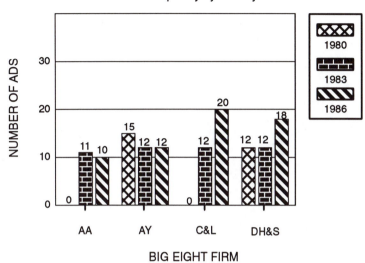

TABLE 2. Advertising Frequency by Purpose/Firms (Total Ads 1980, 1983, and 1986)

Advertisement Purpose	—Accounting Firms—								
	AA	AY	C&L	DH&S	E&W	PMM	PW	TR	TOTAL
Training Programs	—	1	—	—	—	8	—	—	9
Time-Sharing or Software	20	—	27	23	50	37	26	—	183
Executive Search Services	—	—	—	—	1	1	—	—	2
Management Advisory Services	—	—	—	5	4	5	—	5	19
Employee Recruitment	—	33	5	1	—	2	—	3	44
Tax Services	—	—	—	7	—	—	—	—	7
Audit Services	—	—	—	5	—	—	—	—	5
General Image	1	5	—	1	1	2	—	—	10
Total Advertising	21	39	32	42	56	55	26	8	279

FIGURE 4. Purpose of Ads by Year

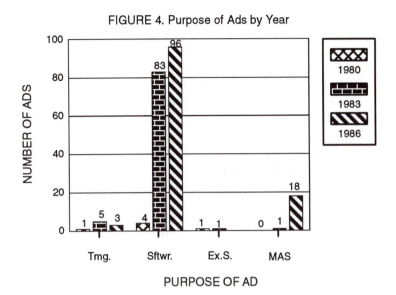

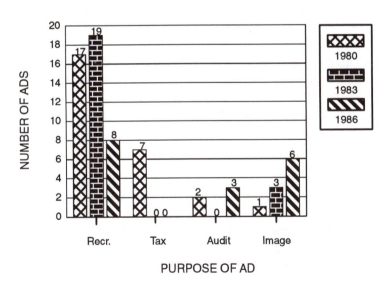

These ads have shifted from main-frame, time-sharing ads in 1980 to micro-computer software programs in 1983 and 1986. The least frequent ads have been for audit services. Advertisements for both software programs and management advisory services are increasing over the time period surveyed. Although the greatest increase in the number of ads occurred in the computer software area, the increase in the number for management advisory services was also substantial. There were no ads in 1980, only one in 1983, but 18 ads in 1986.

Only one firm–Deloitte, Haskins & Sells–has placed direct advertisement for audit services or tax practice in the journals examined. For audit services, two full-page ads appeared in the 1980 issues of *Fortune*, and three full-page ads appeared in the 1986 issues of *The Internal Auditor.* None of the audit service ads identified rates or used terms to imply audit cost-savings. For their tax practice, Deloitte, Haskins & Sells placed seven ads in the 1980 issues of *Fortune*.

Even though an increasing number of ads are placed for the purpose of software sales, the personal contact necessary to service software programs can serve as a door-opener to expand an audit practice, tax practice, or management advisory service. Bruce W. Marcus stated:

> The one thing we all learned the hard way is that the tools of marketing–advertising, public relations, direct mail, etc.–may sell products. They don't sell services.
> Only people sell service.[4]

Target Market

Just as size, frequency, and purpose have varied among the Big Eight advertisements examined in this study, the target market of the individual firms also varied. Table 3 shows the diversity of advertising focus among firms. The number of ads varies significantly depending upon the target market of the ad. The frequency of ads placed by the Big Eight firms is greatest in the healthcare market. The lowest frequency of ads is in the insurance market.

TABLE 3. Big Eight Ads Classified by Firm and Target Market

Firm	Target Market	Ad Frequency 1980	1983	1986
Arthur Andersen	Public Accounting	—	—	10
	Private Accounting	—	—	—
	Healthcare	—	10	—
	Banking	—	1	—
	Insurance	—	—	—
	General Business	—	—	—
Arthur Young	Public Accounting	15	11	7
	Private Accounting	—	1	—
	Healthcare	—	—	—
	Banking	—	—	—
	Insurance	—	—	—
	General Business	—	—	5
Coopers & Lybrand	Public Accounting	—	5	9
	Private Accounting	—	1	—
	Healthcare	—	6	10
	Banking	—	—	—
	Insurance	—	—	1
	General Business	—	—	—
Deloitte, Haskins & Sells	Public Accounting	1	—	—
	Private Accounting	—	—	3
	Healthcare	—	5	4
	Banking	—	7	11
	Insurance	—	—	—
	General Business	11	—	—
Ernst & Whinney	Public Accounting	—	—	3
	Private Accounting	—	—	—
	Healthcare	1	21	26
	Banking	—	—	—
	Insurance	—	—	2
	General Business	—	—	3
Peat, Marwick, Main	Public Accounting	1	2	—
	Private Accounting	—	3	3
	Healthcare	4	22	13
	Banking	—	—	6
	Insurance	—	—	—
	General Business	—	1	—
Price Waterhouse	Public Accounting	—	—	3
	Private Accounting	—	—	—
	Healthcare	—	13	10
	Banking	—	—	—
	Insurance	—	—	—
	General Business	—	—	—
Touche Ross	Public Accounting	—	3	—
	Private Accounting	—	—	—
	Healthcare	—	—	5
	Banking	—	—	—
	Insurance	—	—	—
	General Business	—	—	—
Total		33	112	134

FINDINGS

The advertising profile shows a great degree of diversity among the Big Eight firms regarding the nature and amount of display advertising. One of the early fears of lifting the ban on advertising was that professional image would be damaged. The Big Eight firms apparently have different philosophies concerning the effect of advertising upon their professional image.

If the Big Eight firms were rated for advertising aggressiveness, Deloitte, Haskins & Sells might be considered the most aggressive advertiser based upon advertising diversity–both in purpose and target markets–and frequency. In a study by King and Carver, Deloitte, Haskins & Sells had slightly higher name recall resulting from published ads than did other Big Eight firms.[5] The least aggressive advertiser, based upon the same criteria, might be Touche Ross. The other Big Eight firms would be ranked along a continuum between these two firms.

A second fear was that advertising would lead to price-competitive, lower quality audits. It appears that this fear can be set aside. There is very little advertising for audit services over the three-year period, and the trend suggests less in the future. An examination of the ads which have been placed for audit services contains no reference to service rates or cost-savings. Advertising for any purpose, however, could lead to new audit engagements, but the bulk of advertising is for things other than services (e.g., software and employee recruitment).

A third fear was that the Big Eight accounting firms would pursue small engagements that have traditionally belonged to the smaller regional CPA firms. Based on the results of this study, Big Eight firms appear to pursue small business vigorously when the proper conditions exist. For example, the healthcare industry is the object of a great deal of advertising effort. Other areas, however, receive little attention. The healthcare industry has a well-defined group of financial managers with specific management problems. Third party reimbursement and cost control in an increasingly difficult cost control environment are management problems which the Big Eight have addressed with computer programs and management advisory services. The industries that receive little attention do not have a well-defined group of financial managers or specific management needs. Elizabeth Willson has stated:

> While the Big Eight are courting small business as never before, they remain selective as to what kind of small client they want. A Big Eight firm might take a chance on a start-up, especially a high technology business with strong growth potential, while declining an account with a much more established business that is unlikely to grow into a substantial customer.[6]

CONCLUSION

Only as time passes will the effect of increased advertising be known to the profession and the public. Based upon the trend of Big Eight advertising examined in this study, advertising is a widely used marketing tool by the Big Eight. The trend is toward increased advertising. The present trends in advertising indicate that advertising of products–such as computer programs–is perceived by firms to be increasingly valuable. Additionally, advertising aiming at specific target markets is increasing. Advertisements are serving a useful purpose in the profession by making people aware of accounting products and services. These ads enable firms to formally communicate pertinent information that prior to lifting the ban could only be communicated informally.

NOTES

1. William L. Trombetta, "Should the Professions Go Competitive?" *Business* (May-June 1981):35-41.

2. L. Murphy Smith and Katherine T. Smith, "Advertising for Today's Accountant: Contribution or Clutter?" *The National Public Accountant* (July 1984):22-25.

3. Walter W. Regel, "Advertising and Direct Solicitation by CPAs: Assets or Liabilities," quoted in News, *CA Magazine* (October 1984):40-41.

4. Bruce W. Marcus, "Marketing in a Competitive Environment," *New Accountant* (March 1988):6-9.

5. Thomas E. King and M. Robert Carver, Jr., "CPA Advertising: How Successful Has it Been?" *Financial Executive* (September 1984):34-42.

6. Elizabeth Willson, "Red Carpet Treatment–Why the Big Eight Are Courting Small Business," *CFO* (February 1986):40-45.

Chapter 18

Attitudes Toward the Advertising by Lawyers, Doctors, and CPAs

Gene E. Burton

PROFESSIONALS EXPERIENCE HARD TIMES

Ask a professional how things are going, and you are apt to hear a response that dwells on hard times. Indeed, for many professionals, the "good ole' days" are over. The professional, who was once the community's only lawyer, doctor, or accountant, needed only to follow the advice, "(1) hang up your shingle and you'll get new clients from walk-in traffic; (2) take a handful of your colleagues to lunch and you may get a few referrals; (3) join civic and social groups to get your name into the community. Then, as your referral base grows, your established clients will send enough new business to build a profitable practice."[18]

Make no mistake about it, those "good ole' days" *are* over, and "Lawyers are driving cabs, dentists are drilling in corporate storefronts and some med students are $100,000 in debt."[2]

This new era of professional service problems has resulted from a number of factors, namely a glut of service providers, new forms of competition, mounting costs, a loss of control, and the legal-commercialization of the professions.

THE LEGAL-COMMERCIALIZATION OF THE PROFESSIONS

The American Medical Association (AMA) has been a long-time opponent of medical advertising on the grounds that it is unprofes-

This chapter was first published in *Journal of Professional Services Marketing*, Vol. 8(1) 1991.

sional and diminishes the status of medical professionals. Not only did the AMA ban advertising but its code of ethics used to regulate the size of the letters on a doctor's office sign.[25] The American Bar Association (ABA) declared advertising to be unprofessional in its first code of ethics in 1908.[24] Following the lead of the AMA and ABA, The American Institute of Certified Public Accountants (AICPA) established a ban on CPA advertising in 1922.[17]

This ban on professional advertising was removed by a series of enforcement agency and court decisions, principally *Bigelow v. Virginia* in 1975 and *Bates v. Arizona* in 1977. These rulings established advertising as a form of free speech that is protected by the First Amendment of the U.S. Constitution and which cannot be universally prohibited.[9] Thus, the door was opened for professionals to advertise their services and, as professions proceeded to use more and more advertising, their attitudes toward the use of advertising also seemed to change.

ATTITUDES OF DOCTORS

The attitudes of doctors with respect to their use of advertising were found to be greatly improved during the decade from 1978 to 1988. A 1978 AMA study found that only 8 percent of its members approved of medical advertising. However, by 1983, 17 percent of the AMA approved of their advertising. By 1986, 9 percent of AMA members had used advertising, and 15 percent planned to use it in the future. Furthermore, the study found that advertising was more prominent among young practitioners, among prepayment contractors, and among the larger group practices.[7]

A 1983 survey of physicians found that 46 percent of the physicians surveyed saw little value in advertising to the consumers, while 26 percent felt that physician ads are likely to be untruthful, and 27 percent believed that physicians who advertise will charge more for their services.[16] Many doctors resent the implications of the new marketing thrust, protesting that a "doctor is not detergent."[21] A spokesperson for the AMA noted that "Lots of physicians still associate advertising with quackery. Some doctors don't want to even list their names in the yellow pages."[13] This rather negative attitude toward medical advertising is compounded by the fact that, throughout the medical profession, there is a poor understanding of the basic principles of marketing, with most practitioners believing that marketing is "selling."[14]

ATTITUDES OF LAWYERS

In 1981, a survey found that only 10 percent of attorneys had used advertising in spite of the *Bates* decision that allowed attorneys to avail themselves of this marketing device.[14] However, since then, the number of lawyers who advertise has been increasing,[11] although most attorneys still believe that advertising is unprofessional and tends to tarnish their professional image.[15]

ATTITUDES OF CPAs

A survey of CPAs found that, in 1979, despite the opportunities and forces for the use of advertising, only 7 percent of the responding CPAs had made plans to use advertising, and 31 percent still believed that CPA advertising was unprofessional.[8] Then, in 1982, another survey found that 23 percent of the responding CPAs had used advertising. Over 63 percent of the CPAs expressed a belief that advertising would have a harmful impact on their public image. Also, 80 percent of the sample felt that paid advertising was not necessary. Of those that had used advertising, 52 percent had used newspapers, 26 percent had used direct mail, 21 percent had used magazines, 15 percent had used point-of-purchase materials, 5 percent had used radio, and 5 percent had used television. One more positive result was the finding that 53 percent indicated that there was at least a 50-50 chance that they would advertise in the future.[21]

CONSUMER ATTITUDES

Just as professionals have generally held to the traditional belief that advertising their services was unprofessional, the consuming public has typically found such advertising to be both appropriate and helpful to the consumer. For instance, a 1980 study found that attorneys held a most negative and unprofessional attitude toward the advertising of legal services, while consumers held a significantly more positive opinion of legal service advertising.[6] Another 1980 survey reported that consumers had a positive attitude toward the advertising of legal services by attorneys, believing that those ads contained valuable information, especially regarding specialties and prices.[20]

A 1983 survey of physicians reported that 46 percent of the physicians surveyed saw little value in advertising to the consumers, 26 percent felt that physician ads are likely to be untruthful, and 27 percent believed that physicians who advertise will charge more for their services. That same report found that consumers felt that it was acceptable for physicians to advertise their services.[16] Another 1983 study reported that consumers have a more positive attitude toward dental advertising than dentists.[19] A 1984 report notes that executive consumers of CPA services have a positive reaction to CPA ads, noting that such advertising has an impact on the choice of CPA firms by helping consumers become more aware of specializations and the variety of services offered.[12]

In 1986, another survey found that consumers have a more positive attitude toward the advertising of accountants, lawyers, and physicians than the professionals have. The study noted that the professionals seem oversensitive about the danger of tarnishing their public images with advertising.[9] Finally, a 1988 survey reported that consumers were more positive in their opinions about dental advertising than the dentists. Specifically, consumers believed that dental advertising was proper and would not diminish the dignity or public image of the dentists.[10]

THE CONTINUING CONTROVERSY

Because many professionals continue to hold to the belief that advertising is unprofessional and would tarnish their public image, the overall acceptance of advertising as a legitimate tool for managing a professional practice is impaired. The controversy regarding the pros and cons of advertising professional services center around eight issues: (1) the impact of advertising on consumer demand; (2) the impact of advertising as a barrier to market entry and as an advantage for the larger providers that can afford bigger advertising budgets; (3) the impact of advertising on employment opportunities for professionals; (4) the impact of advertising on prices charged to consumers; (5) the impact of advertising on service quality; (6) the impact of advertising on consumer awareness of service needs; (7) the impact of advertising as an aid to consumers in choosing service providers; and (8) the impact of advertising on consumer expectations, leading to ultimate consumer dissatisfaction.[1,3,5,6,14,15,18,20]

THE INVESTIGATION

This study was designed to measure and compare the attitudes of professionals and consumers toward the advertising of the professional services of the CPA. Specifically, three categories of professional advertising were investigated: (1) legal advertising; (2) physician advertising; and (3) CPA advertising. A survey was administered in California to six random samples: (1) lawyers; (2) physicians; (3) CPAs; (4) consumers of legal services; (5) consumers of physician services; and (6) consumers of CPA services. The instrument investigated the controversial issues outlined earlier by collecting attitudinal responses on a 7-point Likert scale ranging from 1 (strongly disapprove) to 7 (strongly approve).

The Results of the Investigation

The survey collected usable responses from 179 lawyers, 64 physicians, 86 CPAs, 82 legal consumers, 103 physician consumers, and 92 CPA consumers. A summary of the key findings are as follows.

ADVERTISING BEHAVIOR AND INTENTIONS

Table 1 compares the responses by the three professional groups with respect to their past, present, and future advertising behavior.

TABLE 1. Advertising Behavior/Intention Comparisons

	LAWYERS (n = 179)		PHYSICIANS (n = 64)		CPAS (n = 86)	
	YES	NO	YES	NO	YES	NO
Have advertised in the past (%)	22	78	22	78	100>	0
Will advertise in the future (%)	35*	65	45*@	55	100>	0

> = Significantly Higher Than The Other Two Groups

* = Significant Shift From Action To Intention

@ = Physician Intention Is Significantly Higher Than Lawyer

(p < .05)

It is interesting to note that all CPA respondents have advertised in the past and intend to continue to do so in the future. It is also interesting to note that 22 percent of both the lawyer sample and the physician sample have advertised in the past. For the future, both of these groups show a significant increase over past behavior, as 35 percent of the lawyers and 45 percent of the physicians report that they will probably advertise in the future. It should also be noted that the 45 percent future advertising projection for the physicians is significantly higher than the 35 percent projection for the lawyers.

ATTITUDES OF THE PROFESSIONALS

Table 2 compares the response means reflecting the advertising attitudes of the three professional samples. Overall, the lawyers reported a significantly low opinion of advertising in general, while the physicians reported the most positive attitude toward advertising in general. With respect to their own advertising, the CPAs reported a significantly positive attitude. The lawyers are significantly more convinced that their advertising is unprofessional.

Lawyers reflected significantly negative attitudes toward the potential for their advertising to increase employment opportunities for lawyers, to improve the quality of their services, to improve consumer awareness of their legal needs, and to help consumers choose a lawyer.

Physicians reported significantly strong opinions that their advertising would increase the demand for their services, increase the employment opportunities for physicians, aid the larger providers with the big ad budgets, raise the prices charged for their services, and create consumer dissatisfaction by raising their expectations to unreasonable levels.

CPAs have a significantly strong conviction that their advertising will aid consumer awareness of their CPA needs.

Table 3 contains the comparisons of the response means of the three consumer groups–legal service consumers, physician service consumers, and CPA service consumers.

Consumers reflect a significantly more positive attitude toward CPA advertising and are convinced that it has a significantly positive impact on CPA employment, CPA service quality, consumer

TABLE 2. t-Test Comparisons of Response Means Between Lawyers, Physicians, and CPAs

FACTOR	LAWYERS (n = 179)	PHYSICIANS (n = 64)	CPAS (n = 86)
Approve of advertising, in general	3.4302<	4.6719	4.4565
Approve of _____ advertising	2.4022	2.5156	3.9767>
_____ advertising is unprofessional	4.5307>	4.0781	4.2791
Believe that _____ advertising will:			
Increase consumer demand	3.6816	4.4375>	3.4565
Aid larger providers	3.3799<	5.1250>	4.6977
Increase employment opportunities for ___	3.5251	3.8438>	3.4186
Increase prices	3.7263	5.1563>	3.8488
Improve service quality	1.9609<	2.5625	2.6395
Benefit consumer awareness	2.8380<	3.4063	3.8372>
Aid consumer choice of provider	2.1732<	2.9219	3.0349
Cause consumer dissatisfaction	4.9106	5.3906>	4.6977

> = Significantly higher than the other two samples

< = Significantly lower than the other two samples

(p < .05)

TABLE 3. t-Test Comparisons of Consumer Attitudes Toward Advertising by Lawyers, Physicians, and CPAs

FACTOR	LAWYERS (n = 82)	PHYSICIANS (n = 103)	CPAS (n = 92)
Approve of advertising, in general	5.6098	5.5114	5.5880
Approve of _____ advertising	4.1951	3.5627<	4.7114>
_____ advertising is unprofessional	3.0244<	3.5422	3.7721
Believe that _____ advertising will:			
Increase consumer demand	3.8171	3.4326<	3.9975
Aid larger providers	4.2439	4.1881	5.7109>
Increase employment opportunities for _____	4.3415	3.0019<	4.0663
Increase prices	3.5366	5.3472>	3.7922
Improve service quality	3.2683	3.2889	3.4278
Benefit consumer awareness	4.1463	4.3886	4.8860>
Aid consumer choice of provider	3.5976<	4.6022	5.0226>
Cause consumer dissatisfaction	4.0854	4.0263	4.0163

> = Significantly higher than the other two samples
< = Significantly lower than the other two samples
(p < .05)

awareness of CPA service needs, and on consumer choice of CPA service providers.

Consumers have a significantly negative attitude toward physician advertising and its capacity to increase consumer demand or to provide additional employment opportunities for physicians.

Finally, consumers reflect a significantly negative reaction to the notion that legal advertising is unprofessional and feel that it is significantly weak at helping the consumer choose a provider of legal service.

SUMMARY

This California survey finds that all of the CPA respondents have used advertising and will continue to advertise. Lawyers and physicians, on the other hand, have been slow to avail themselves of this marketing tool, as only 22 percent of these two samples indicate that they have advertised in the past. However, that advertising rate should increase, as 35 percent of the lawyers and 45 percent of the physicians report that they will probably advertise in the future.

The acceptance of advertising by the CPAs is reflected in their positive attitudes toward advertising and its potential for good in the marketplace. Furthermore, this positive attitude is generally shared by the CPAs and their consumers.

Physicians have a fairly positive attitude with respect to their advertising, but hold strong beliefs that their advertising may have some negative consequences, such as raising the prices charged for their services. Consumers agree that physician advertising has the strongest potential for raising prices and, thus, have a significantly negative attitude toward physician advertising.

Lawyers, unlike the CPAs and physicians, tend to cling to the traditional belief that their advertising is unprofessional and has few redeeming qualities, a position that is completely opposite of that taken by their consumers.

Thus, it would seem that CPA advertising has been right on target and has created strongly positive attitudes on the part of the CPAs and their consumers. Lawyer advertising has been fairly well received by the consuming public but not by attorneys, themselves. Thus, the legal profession needs to focus on an educational program to raise the attitudinal level of attorneys regarding the potential for good that their advertising has to offer, especially with respect to informational advertising that will aid the consumer on choosing a provider of legal services. Finally, the physicians report a reasonably positive attitude toward their advertising, which is also reflected in their intentions to significantly increase their ad campaigns. However, since that positive attitude is clearly not shared with their consumers, the physicians should consider moving more slowly into the advertising arena and should shift their advertising to themes addressing the negative attitudes held by the public regarding the negative consequences perceived to result from physician advertising.

REFERENCES

1. *Bates v. State Bar of Arizona*, 433 U.S. 350.

2. Berkowitz, Eric. "Health Care Marketing: Issues for Future Development," in Donnelly, J. and W. George (eds.), *Marketing of Services* (Chicago: American Marketing Association, 1981), 151-154.

3. Burton, Gene and Jeff Dorough. "A Survey of Lawyer Attitudes Toward the Advertising of Legal Services," *Proceedings: Annual Joint Conference Of The Institute For Management Science and The Operations Research Society of America*. Washington, D.C., April 1988.

4. Cebrzynski, Gregg. "Marketing, Tradition Clash In Health Care," *Marketing News*. November 8, 1985, 1-30.

5. Darling, John and Blaise Bergiel. "Health Care Advertising: A Comparative Analysis," *Journal of Health Care Marketing*. Winter 1983, 21-28.

6. Dyer, Robert and Terence Shimp. "Reactions to Legal Advertising," *Journal of Advertising Research*. April 10, 1980, 43-51.

7. Folland, Sherman. "Advertising By Physicians: Behavior and Attitudes," *Medical Care*. April 1987, 311-326.

8. Hanggi, George, Jr. "Medical Advertising As A Practice Development Tool," *The Journal of Accountancy*. February 1980, 54-56.

9. Hite, Robert and Joseph Bellizzi. "Consumers' Attitudes Toward Accountants, Lawyers, and Physicians With Respect To Advertising Professional Services," *Journal of Advertising Research*. June/July 1986, 45-54.

10. Hite, Robert, Joseph Bellizzi, and David Andrus. "Consumer Versus Dentist Attitudes Toward Dental Services Advertising," *Journal for Health Care Management*. March 1988, 30-38.

11. "Kentucky Lawyer Sees Win In Big Ad Cases," *Marketing News*. August 14, 1987, 16.

12. King, Thomas and M. Robert Carver, Jr. "CPA Advertising: How Successful Has It Been?" *Financial Executive*. September 1984, 34-36.

13. Kleinfield, N. R. "A Push to Market Health Care," *The New York Times*. April 16, 1984, 34.

14. "Law Poll: Advertising Attracting Neither Participants Nor Supporters," *American Bar Association Journal*. December 1981, 1618-1619.

15. Linenberger, P. and G. Murdock. "Legal Service Advertising: Wyoming Attorney Attitudes Compared With Consumer Attitudes," *Land and Water Law Review*. 17, 1982, 209-240.

16. Marks, Ronald and Bob Ahuja. "Situations Impact Peoples' Views of Ads for Doctors," *Demographics*. December 9, 1983, 28-33.

17. Ostlund, A. Clayton. "Advertising–In The Public Interest?" *The Journal of Accountancy*. January 1978, 59-63.

18. Ryder, T. "Direct Marketing Is The Key To Professional Success," *Direct Marketing*. September 1985, 24-31.

19. Shapiro, Irwin and Robert Majewski. "Should Dentists Advertise?" *Journal of Advertising Research*. June/July 1983, 33-37.

20. Shimp, T. and R. Dyer. "How The Legal Profession Views Legal Service Advertising," *Journal of Marketing*. July 1978, 74-81.

21. Simon, Murray. "Doctor Not a Laundry Detergent," *Marketing News*. May 10, 1985, 2.

22. Smith, Robert and Tiffany Meyer. "Attorney Advertising: A Consumer Perspective," *Journal of Marketing*. Spring 1980, 56-64.

23. Solomon, Paul and William George. "Marketing Professional Accounting Services: Traditional Marketing May Not Work," *Proceedings: 14th Annual Meeting of the American Institute for Decision Sciences*. San Francisco, November 1982, 54-56.

24. Traynor, M. and A. Mathias. "The Impact of TV Advertising Versus Word of Mouth on the Image of Lawyers: A Projective Experiment," *Journal of Advertising*. April 1983, 42-49.

25. Tyndal, Katie. "Doctors Drum Up Business Success," *Insight*. September 29, 1986, 12-13.

PART FOUR:

MARKETING TOOLS AND STRATEGIES

Chapter 19

Strategic Marketing Planning
for the Development
of the Small Accounting Practice

Troy A. Festervand
Scott J. Vitell
R. Eric Reidenbach

INTRODUCTION

The services provided by accounting firms traditionally have consisted of such activities as income tax preparation, the conduct of financial audits, and generation of financial statements. However, recent years have witnessed a significant departure from the traditional product offering. In response to market demands, accounting firms have expanded the scope of their services dramatically to include an assortment of business services. For example, when the Olympic Organizing Committee decided to finish the 1984 Summer Games in the black (something that had never before been accomplished), they hired a consultant to (1) help develop a comprehensive five-year plan, (2) conceive the largest ticketing system ever attempted, (3) create ideas for an integrated telecommunications network and (4) design the first automated electronic Olympic identification and accreditation system (Wantuck 1984). The consultant hired was a 90-year-old public accounting firm, Arthur Young & Company. The outcome, a $150 million surplus!

This chapter was first published in *Journal of Professional Services Marketing*, Vol. 3(3/4) 1988.

Accountants have long been considered valued advisors to business and government. That esteem is even more apparent today as evidenced by a recent survey of business executives which found that 64 percent of the executives surveyed used their independent accountants as their major advisor over bankers, attorneys, secured lenders, and independent consultants (Smith 1984). In essence, few managers and investors will make a key strategic decision without checking to see if it makes sense to their accountant. Furthermore, indications are that more and more firms will look to accounting firms to play an even greater role in the operation of their firm and/or organization (Boland 1983).

The stimuli behind this role expansion appears to be a combination of factors (Wantuck 1984). First, there is a scarcity of new audit contracts which have long been the major profit center of accounting firms. This, in turn, is the result of fewer firms going public, mergers, and increased competition.

Other factors underlying this product/role revolution are the needs and opportunities presented by the market. For example, as businesses have grown, the character of their needs has also changed. Firms are now seeking assistance in such matters as executive compensation, corporate health care cost containment, management recruitment, and strategic marketing, to name only a few. Furthermore, many of these firms not only prefer their accounting firm to provide assistance in these areas; they require it. Call it a form of "one-stop shopping."

With different degrees of responsiveness, accounting firms have recognized that the provision of these new services is simultaneously an insurance policy and a profit opportunity. In providing these management services, accounting firms not only increase their client retention rate, but increase the likelihood that their client will remain a viable enterprise. This, in turn, better guarantees the firm a continued stream of income and profitability, which is enhanced even more because of the higher than average margin associated with nonaccounting related services (Scherschel 1982).

In response to these changes, most large accounting firms have expanded their service offering. For example, Arthur Andersen offers services in three broad areas: tax and management information consulting, accounting, and auditing. Another Big Eight member,

Coopers & Lybrand, offers the same basic services, but divides them into auditing, tax and financial planning, management consulting services, actuarial, benefits, and compensation consulting. Other firms (e.g., Deloitte, Haskins & Sells, Peat, Marwick, Mitchell and Co., and Price Waterhouse & Co.) offer a similar assortment of client services, of which, management consulting/advisory services are increasingly important.

In explaining the growth of these services, Malcolm Myers, managing partner of Coopers & Lybrand's management consulting group, noted that the market for their services usually consists of those who have recently gone into business or purchased a business which is not performing well. He also noted that the reception of potential clients to their consulting services depends upon clear communications (Myers 1985). "It is of the utmost importance that we understand each individual client's problems and needs and that the client, in turn, understands how Coopers & Lybrand is proposing to solve their problem(s)."

In analyzing the expanding product mix of these firms, as well as their underlying philosophy, an increasing sensitivity to the needs of customers can be recognized. While this strategy of product line expansion is responsive to market demands and represents a significant growth/profit opportunity for large accounting firms, an obvious question appears to be whether or not such a strategy is also appropriate for small accounting firms who may not have the resources to develop such a product offering? What marketing opportunities, alternatives, and strategies are available to them?

The purpose of this chapter is to identify and describe four distinct types of growth opportunities which are available to the small accounting firm. These market opportunities are depicted in Figure 1 and include the following strategies: (1) Market Penetration; (2) Market Development; (3) Product Development; and (4) Diversification.

REQUISITES FOR GROWTH

Prior to beginning a discussion of these growth alternatives, it should be pointed out that there are two requisite ingredients associated with these strategies. These ingredients are (1) the availability of adequate resources for expansion and (2) management's

FIGURE 1. Growth/Opportunity Matrix

	PRESENT PRODUCTS	NEW PRODUCTS
PRESENT MARKETS	MARKET PENETRATION	PRODUCT DEVELOPMENT
NEW MARKETS	MARKET DEVELOPMENT	DIVERSIFICATION

ability to develop and implement a new marketing strategy (Cravens, Hills, and Woodruff 1987). If these resources are in place, then any or all of the growth strategies are equally available to both small and large accounting firms. Conversely, if these resources are not available, then the firm should look elsewhere for performance/ profit opportunities.

While excess capacity may exist for many small accounting firms, the development and implementation of a marketing strategy has been the source of much difficulty in the past. This may be explained by the fact that in many instances, accounting firms are simply not sure of what marketing encompasses (Denney 1981). According to Gotlieb and Conner (1983), there are four basic elements of marketing:

1. The "product line" or the group of services which the CPA firm is offering.
2. The "promotional mix" or the combination of personal selling, advertising, and sales promotion which the CPA firm will use to communicate the firm's messages to actual and potential clients.
3. The "price strategy" or the manner in which the firm determines the price to charge for its services. The price charged clients may be based upon cost incurred, competition, the CPA firm's perception of client reaction to price, or some combination of the above.
4. The "distribution system" which includes the location of the CPA firm's office and the physical appearance of the office. In

addition, it includes the manner in which accounting services are dispersed both at the CPA firm's office and at the client's facility.

In order for accounting firms, especially small firms, to take fullest advantage of growth opportunities, they must become more marketing oriented. In so doing, these firms must not only recognize and accept the importance of marketing as a business tool, but develop and implement marketing strategies which are reflective of and responsive to the market's needs and are compatible with the firm's resources and objectives.

MARKET PENETRATION

As can be seen in Figure 1, a market penetration strategy involves marketing existing products to existing markets. Since market penetration is the equivalent of a firm's market share, such a strategy seeks to increase a firm's share of the relevant market(s) it currently serves with an established product offering via a more aggressive marketing effort. A penetration strategy is particularly desirable for the small accounting firm because it generally represents the least costly and risky approach to growth.

Three alternative methods are available for achieving greater market penetration. First, the small firm may try to increase the volume and/or frequency of services it currently provides to its existing customer base. Second, it may try to provide other established services currently available to other clients, but not provided to all clients. Finally, the firm may increase its market share by attracting competitors' customers or current nonusers.

Increase Usage

If the small accounting firm is to enhance its market share by increasing the customer's use of existing services, it must first demonstrate the benefits of such to the client. For example, a small accounting firm has been providing annual retail sales analyses to a client who uses the information to evaluate the performance of individual product lines and make product retention/deletion decisions. However, if the client were provided with more frequent and timely sales information, it could more than offset the additional cost of such by adjusting inventory and inventory levels, using available floor space more effectively or taking markdowns in a more expedient manner.

Extend Services

While the product line of most small accounting firms consists of a set of basic or core services, all of these services may not be provided to all clients. Further, because of the focal position occupied by the firm, it often is able to evaluate the client's problem(s) and propose appropriate recommendations. In some instances, these recommendations may involve the utilization of other core services not currently used by the client. In still other instances, it may be that the firm simply has to inform existing clients about the availability of other services and have them adopted.

New Accounts

From a marketing perspective, the most aggressive route to follow in generating additional business is to attract new accounts. These accounts currently may be nonusers of accounting services or clients of another firm. In either instance, the attraction of these accounts may be achieved via more aggressive marketing efforts. These efforts include the use of such well-established marketing tools as advertising, direct solicitation, public and social appearances, and referrals.

Following the U. S. Supreme Court's decision in the now famous *Bates* case (*Bates v. the State Bar of Arizona* 1977), most state and professional organizations, including the AICPA, altered their by-laws to allow marketing activities. While the response to this change generally has varied across areas, markets, and professions, recent years have witnessed a significant growth in the frequency and nature of professional services marketing (Kessler 1980; Traynor 1983). Therefore, while the purpose of this chapter is not to advance a particular position with regard to the practice of professional services advertising, it would be naive to ignore the existence of such. As such, in addition to newspaper advertisements, other advertising alternatives include yellow page listings, sponsorships, published information (e.g., "tax tips"), and published documents (Kotler and Conner 1981).

To most people, the term direct solicitation conjures up negative connotations. However, if professionally conducted, this tool not only can be extremely effective, but be perceived as totally professional. The key question is what form(s) does or should direct solicitation take? While "cold calls" and telemarketing are widely recognized techniques in some circles, in this instance, professionally prepared direct correspondence may be most desirable. Using the firm's stationary, a letter can be drafted and mailed to a number of potential clients. The letter may introduce and describe available services, propose a follow-up meeting, or inform the reader of the benefits to be enjoyed as a result of the use of certain services. Regardless of content or purpose, the correspondence must exhibit the level of professionalism the would-be client expects.

Visibility and word-of-mouth communication are two of the most effective marketing tools available in any profession. This is true regardless of a firm's size, location, or experience. Whether at social, public, or professional functions, visibility and image are two factors which are critical to business development (Hilliard 1983). In most instances, this exposure must be cultivated. Consequently, it is imperative for the accountant in the small firm to assume an aggressive role relative to public speaking, participation, and interaction in order to communicate an image of professionalism, knowledge, and fairness (Kotler and Conner 1980).

MARKET DEVELOPMENT

Another strategy for expanding a small accounting firm's business is market development. With this strategy, the service needs of new markets are met using core or existing services. For many firms, this extension of existing products into new markets is particularly attractive because it paradoxically allows the firm to potentially achieve substantial profits while incurring little product development cost and/or risk.

A key requirement of the market development strategy is the segmentation of the total market into distinct consumer or industry groups. Market segmentation may be accomplished using a number of alternative means. For example, the small accounting firm may find they can effectively segment the market for their services using such variables as SIC codes, product(s) sold, market(s) served, etc. It should also be recognized that it may be desirable, if not necessary, to employ two or more segmentation criteria in order to arrive at a meaningful breakdown of the different types of customers which potentially may be served (McCarthy and Perreault 1984).

Once segmented, the financial and/or management services needs of each group should be examined and compared to those currently provided. In some instances, the needs of the new market(s) will be so unique that satisfying them would require the development of an array of totally new services. In other instances, service needs will be similar to those currently provided, needing only cosmetic changes and an appropriate marketing mix.

For some firms, this exercise may also prove to be rewarding in another way. It would not be surprising to find that some small accounting firms do not know what market(s) they currently are serving with what product(s). In segmenting the total market, the small accounting firm not only answers these questions, but may determine that they are not addressing the needs of some market(s) at all, despite the fact that to do so would require only a slight modification in existing services or simply marketing what is currently available.

PRODUCT DEVELOPMENT

Another strategy available to the small accounting firm is that of product development. This growth alternative involves the development of new services which in turn, are marketed to existing clients. The advantages of a product development strategy include a reduction in dependence on one line of products and the potential of benefiting from established marketing practices. The disadvantage of this strategy is its continued reliance on existing markets.

In pursuing a product development strategy, a key question which the small accounting firm must answer involves the area(s) of new product development. Consistent with current trends, many firms, both large and small, are adding management consulting and advisory services. The reasons for doing so are twofold. First, the market is receptive to virtually all forms of management services because of their need to better compete in an increasing complex business environment. Second, the provision of these services represents a significant profit opportunity.

Despite its obvious appeal, a product development strategy may be perceived by the small firm as being unrealistic. Where large accounting firms simply add a management services group, small firms often lack the resources to do so. Therefore, they do not pursue this growth alternative. However, if the small firm contracts these services rather than develops them, the associated costs are variable as opposed to fixed. The prospect of adding a complete assortment of management services now becomes not only affordable, but strategically advantageous.

In considering this tactic, the small accounting firm also should be cognizant of the fact that it potentially may become a virtual clearing-house for consultants of all types. This caveat strongly suggests that considerable discretion should be exercised in the selection of consultants since it is the reputation of the firm that is at stake.

DIVERSIFICATION

Finally, diversification is the provision of new services to new markets. Where the market penetration strategy potentially is the least risky and costly growth alternative, diversification potentially is the riskiest and costliest strategy. However, this strategy may be desirable if existing products are providing negligible growth and significant growth/profit opportunities are sought.

Three alternative forms of diversification are available to the small accounting firm. These include (1) Concentric Diversification, (2) Horizontal Diversification, (3) Conglomerate Diversification.

Concentric Diversification. Concentric diversification involves the acquisition or development of services that offer synergies with existing products, but are directed toward new markets. For the small accounting firm, these are products that are tangentially related to existing services. Examples of such products might include tax services, financial planning, and capital asset management services.

Horizontal Diversification. This form of diversification involves new products which are technically unrelated to existing products, but which might appeal to either existing or new markets. Examples of such might include estate planning and investment portfolio management services. These services increasingly are being demanded by myriad market segments, but heretofore have been available only from specialized sources.

Conglomerate Diversification. Conglomerate diversification involves the offering of new services that are totally unrelated to existing products, to totally new markets. This is the purest form of diversification and, in all likelihood, represents the least opportunity for small accounting firms because of its inherently greater level of risk and cost. It remains a growth possibility if a significant amount of excess capacity exists and the firm does not expect an acceptable level of growth from established products operating in established markets. Examples of conglomerate diversification include project management and development, entrepreneurial pursuits, and joint venturing.

SUMMARY AND CONCLUSIONS

Many growth opportunities are available to the small accounting firm. Despite intense competition and what may appear to be limited resources, growth may be achieved by pursuing any of four distinct growth alternatives. These include (1) Market Penetration, (2) Market Development, (3) Product Development, and (4) Diversification.

While these alternatives are not likely to be equally available or attractive to all small firms, each possesses some benefit(s) which make it desirable as a growth strategy. In some instances, it may be that an existing customer base demands a greater variety of services, while in other instances, new markets and/or new service opportunities are the determining factors.

Regardless of the growth strategy pursued, it should be recognized that the small accounting firm can compete effectively. Further, the same opportunities which presently are being pursued by larger firms, also are available to the small firm. Foremost among these service opportunities are management consulting and advisory services.

Finally, the small firm must recognize that regardless of the growth strategy espoused, effective marketing is a requisite ingredient. This chapter has outlined some of the ways in which marketing can be used to facilitate the achievement of the growth objective.

REFERENCES

Bates v. the State Bar of Arizona (1977), 97 S. Ct. 2691, 2699, 2700.

Boland, Richard J. "A Positive View of Management Advisory Services and the Public Well-Being," *Journal of Business Strategy* (Summer 1983), pp. 81-86.

Cravens, David W., Hills, Gerald E., and Woodruff, Robert B. *Marketing Management*, Homewood, IL: Richard D. Irwin, Inc. (1987), pp. 34-37.

"CPA's Ranked First as Outside Consultants to Small, Private Companies," *Journal of Accountancy* 157 (January 1983), pp. 22-24.

Denney, Robert W. "How to Develop and Implement a Marketing Plan for Your Firm," *The Practical Accountant* (July 1981), pp. 18-29.

Gotlieb, Jerry B. and Schwartz, Bill N. "How a CPA Firm Can Analyze the Market for Its Services," *The Ohio CPA Journal* (Summer 1983), pp. 11-15.

Hilliard, Robert A. "Marketing a Knowledge Base: PR's Role in Positioning Today's Accounting and Consulting Firm," *Public Relations Quarterly* (Spring 1983), pp. 13-18.

Kessler, Ellen T. "Advertising Accountant Services: How Effective Has It Been," *The Practical Accountant* (July 1980), pp. 37-42.

Kotler, Philip and Conner, Richard A. "Basic Stategies for Marketing Professional Services," *The Practical Accountant* (July 1980), pp. 24-25.

Kotler, Philip and Conner, Richard A. "The Three Marketing Approaches," *The Practical Accountant* (July 1981), pp. 28-29.

McCarthy, E. Jerome and Perreault, William D., Jr. *Basic Marketing, A Managerial Approach*, 8th Edition, Edited by Gilbert A. Churchill, Jr., Homewood, IL: Richard D. Irwin, Inc. (1984).

Myers, Malcolm, Managing Partner of the Management Consulting Group of Coopers & Lybrand, a private correspondence (1985).

Scherschel, Patricia M. "The Powerful Unseen Hand of the Accountant," *U. S. News and World Report* (April 19, 1982), pp. 50-52.

Traynor, Kenneth. "Accountant Advertising: Perceptions, Attitudes, and Behaviors," *Journal of Accountancy*, 23 (December 1983), pp. 35-40.

Wantuck, Mary Margaret. "Accountants' Roles are Multiplying," *Nation's Business* (November 1984), pp. 54-56.

Chapter 20

The Use of Marketing Plans and Advertising Among Accounting Firms: Is This Profession a Viable Candidate for Marketing?

Thomas G. Hodge
Michael H. Brown
James R. Lumpkin

INTRODUCTION

The accounting profession has experienced many significant changes in recent years. Certain of these changes have received a skeptical reception by the profession. Perhaps the change that was viewed with the greatest skepticism by the profession occurred in 1978. As a result of action by the Federal Trade Commission (FTC), the American Institute of Certified Public Accountants (AICPA) revised its Code of Professional Ethics to allow advertising and solicitation.

Although the ban on advertising was removed, initially most CPAs were reluctant to advertise. Some CPAs felt advertising was unprofessional and refused to advertise. Those CPAs who were not opposed to advertising took a wait-and-see approach, possibly to see how the public, clients, and fellow practitioners would react to advertisements.

This chapter was first published in *Journal of Professional Services Marketing*, Vol. 6(1) 1990.

More than a decade has passed since the Code of Ethics was revised to allow CPAs to advertise. How has the accounting profession responded to its freedom to use advertising? Since the benefits of written marketing plans are frequently espoused, do CPA firms have written marketing plans (Helgeson and Birrer 1986)? In the future, how much emphasis will be placed on marketing by CPA firms? What are the current attitudes of CPAs toward advertising? What types of advertising media have been used by CPAs? How do CPAs perceive the effectiveness of various forms of advertising media? This study attempts to answer these questions. The findings of this study should provide useful information for practicing CPAs, since this information is derived from fellow practitioners. In addition, it will assess the role that marketing and marketing professionals will play in the future of the accounting profession.

ATTITUDES TOWARD ADVERTISING

Empirical research in the area of advertising of accounting services has been limited. Most of the articles are descriptive and generally consist of information on "how to" use advertising in practice development. These articles do provide insight concerning the various forms of advertising which are being utilized by CPA firms.

In a study conducted before the 1978 Code of Ethics change, Arndt and Hanks (1978) found 79 percent of the responding CPAs approved of institutional advertising by state societies and 87 percent approved of institutional advertising by the AICPA. Only 30 percent approved of advertising by individual CPA firms. Eighty-four percent of the respondents felt advertising by individual firms should be limited to services only.

However, Sellers and Solomon (1978) had previously found a majority of the respondents felt advertising would not have an adverse effect on the professional image of CPAs. In addition, a majority felt advertising could be conducted in a professionally tasteful manner and advertising could improve the consumer's awareness of accounting services.

In a study by Scott and Rudderow (1983), 52 percent of the accountants agreed advertising was inconsistent with professionalism, while only 23 percent of the businesspeople agreed.

Flesher and Carpenter (1984) found only a small percentage of CPAs were using advertising media forms other than the yellow pages. Almost 55 percent were currently using the yellow pages. However, 20 percent indicated they may use newspaper advertising, 19 percent indicated they may use professional magazines, and 25 percent indicated they may use direct mail in the future.

MARKETING PLANS AND THE ACCOUNTING FIRM

Helgeson and Birrer (1986) suggest marketing plans can contribute to the success of accounting firms. They recommend a marketing plan which includes a mission statement, target markets, a determination of the firm's market position, and a determination of the service mix. A mission statement is used to define the firm's reason for being. By targeting markets to serve, an accounting firm's resources (i.e., technical skills of the staff, size of the firm) can be utilized in a more efficient and effective manner. The service mix consists of variables such as services provided, fees charged, location of facilities, and form and content of communications with clients. Service mix variables are combined to achieve the target market and market positioning objectives. As an added benefit, the process of preparing a marketing plan forces the accounting firm to take an objective, detailed look at its strengths and weaknesses.

OBJECTIVES OF THE STUDY

The espoused benefits to be derived from utilizing a marketing plan are many. Do accounting firms believe a marketing plan is beneficial? This study will attempt to answer this question by determining the extent to which marketing plans are currently being utilized by accounting firms, and CPAs' attitudes toward them.

Early studies revealed a majority of CPAs were against the use of advertising. This study will determine if CPAs' attitudes toward advertising have changed. The study will also attempt to determine the degree of utilization and perceived effectiveness of various advertising media forms.

METHODOLOGY

A self-administered questionnaire was mailed to the managing partners of 224 local and regional accounting firms. Sixteen cities with populations exceeding 100,000 were selected for the study.[1] A sample of 14 firms was then randomly selected from the Certified Public Accountants section of the telephone yellow pages of each city. A total of 83 usable responses was received by the cut-off date, representing a 37 percent response rate.

Of the 83 respondent firms, 24 are sole practitioners, 48 firms have 2 to 5 partners, and 11 firms have more than 5 partners. The firms have been in practice: (1) sole practitioners, 10 for 1 to 5 years, 6 for 5 to 10 years, and 8 for more than 10 years; (2) partnerships with 2 to 5 partners, 11 for 1 to 2 years, 10 for 2 to 5 years, 7 for 5 to 10 years, and 30 for more than 10 years; (3) partnerships with more than 5 partners, all 11 have been in business more than 10 years.

This study did not include all accounting firms in the United States in the sample population, consequently the results of this study must be generalized with caution. Past studies have often used the AICPA Membership Directory which suffers from a similar deficiency, since not all accounting firms are members of the AICPA. In fact, this study found only 41 percent of the accounting firms surveyed were members of the AICPA. The use of the telephone yellow pages excluded firms from our sample population that did not have a listing. We believe the number of firms without a listing in the telephone yellow pages is relatively small.

RESULTS

Marketing Plans

Of the firms responding, only 13 percent (11) have written marketing plans. Of the firms that have written marketing plans 64 percent (7) have mission statements, 91 percent (10) specify target markets, 27 percent (3) determine market positioning, and 36 percent (4) specify service mix. Based on these findings the use of written marketing plans is not widespread among accounting firms. Of the firms that use written marketing plans, market positioning and service mix are not used as extensively as mission statements and target markets. Possibly this process is evolving and the use of market positioning and service mix will be forthcoming.

Attitudes Toward Marketing and Marketing Plans

To provide additional insight, several attitudinal questions concerning written marketing plans were posed to the sample. Table 1 lists the eight statements that were presented to the respondents and the response distribution.

When asked if firms should have a written marketing plan, 78 percent of the respondents agreed. Although a majority of the respondents believe written marketing plans are needed by accounting firms, only 13 percent of the firms have them. An analysis of the demographic information revealed 5 percent of the 21 firms in business from 1 to 5 years, 14 percent of the 28 firms in business from 5 to 15 years and 18 percent of the 34 firms in business 15 or more years have written marketing plans. Of the 59 firms with fewer than 4 partners only 3 percent have written marketing plans; whereas, 15 percent of the 11 firms with 4 to 5 partners, 38 percent of the 8 firms with 6 to 10 partners, 50 percent of the 2 firms with 11 to 15 partners, and the 1 firm with over 15 partners have marketing plans. Possibly, small firms are reluctant to commit their limited resources, and newly organized firms are reluctant to commit their time to the development of a plan. Age of the managing partners was also a significant factor, since 19 percent of the 54 firms with managing partners between 25 and 45 years of age, and only 2 percent of the 29 firms with managing partners over 45 had marketing plans. Firms in business more than 5 years, with more than 5 partners, and with managing partners between the age of 25 and 45 years of age are more likely to have written marketing plans.

Since a majority of the firms surveyed believe accounting firms should have written marketing plans, how important do the 83 respondents consider certain components that are normally a part of these plans? When asked if accounting firms should have a written mission statement, 90 percent of the respondents agreed. When

TABLE 1. Respondents' Attitudes Toward Marketing (By Percentage of Respondents)

Statement	Agree or Strongly Agree	Slightly Agree	Disagree or Strongly Disagree	Slightly Disagree
1. Accounting firms should have a written marketing plan.	49%	29%	7%	15%
2. Accounting firms should have a written mission statement.	59	31	1	9
3. Accounting firms should target their markets and not try to serve all sizes and types of clients.	66	19	10	5
4. Accounting firms should decide how they want clients to view their firm and then work to create and maintain that image.	81	16	1	2
5. Marketing is nothing more than advertising and solicitation.	30	12	33	25
6. Marketing will assume a role of increasing importance in the future plans of your firm.	66	23	5	6
7. Accounting firms should provide partners and staff with training in basic selling concepts.	66	22	6	6
8. Accounting firms should use professional marketing consultants to develop a marketing plan.	15	36	29	20

asked if accounting firms should target their markets, again 90 percent of the respondents agreed. When asked if accounting firms should decide how they want clients to view their firm and then work to create and maintain that image, 97 percent agreed. Based on the response to these questions, strong support for the components of written marketing plans exist among the respondents surveyed.

A vital first step in the development of a written marketing plan requires that the accounting firm develop an understanding of what marketing encompasses. Marketing is often erroneously viewed as consisting solely of advertising; whereas, advertising is merely one of the tools that can be used to accomplish the goals of a marketing plan.

To determine if CPAs are aware of the difference between marketing and advertising, the respondents were presented with the following statement, "Marketing is nothing more than advertising." Since 42 percent of the respondents agreed with this statement, many CPAs need to develop a better understanding of what marketing actually encompasses.

As competition between accounting firms increases, marketing could play an important role in the future of many firms. When presented with the following statement, "Marketing will assume a role of increasing importance in the future plans of your firm," 89 percent of the respondents agreed. Apparently most accounting firms realize marketing is important for growth in their firms. However, many CPAs may not be fully aware of the benefits to be obtained from a marketing plan.

Accounting firm partners and staff often obtain clients based on face-to-face contact and communications with prospective clients. Eighty-eight percent of the respondents agree that accounting firms should provide partners and staff with training in basic selling concepts. The concept of personal contact with prospective clients is not new. In fact, CPAs have been using this practice development approach for many years. The willingness of accounting firms to advocate the use of training in basic selling concepts may be indicative of the changing attitudes of CPAs toward marketing.

Accounting firms will likely need to engage professional marketing consultants to train the partners and staff in the concepts of marketing and to assist the firm in developing a written marketing plan. When asked if accounting firms should use professional marketing consultants to develop a marketing plan, 51 percent of the respondents agreed. Based on age, 59 percent of the 17 respondents between 25 and 35 years of age agreed, while only 11 percent of the 9 respondents over 55 agreed. As previously mentioned, a total of 78 percent of the respondents agreed that CPA firms should have written marketing plans. Apparently many of these firms believe they can develop the marketing plans without the benefit of marketing consultants.

Advertising

The Arndt and Hanks (1976) study revealed 70 percent of the CPAs surveyed were against advertising by CPAs. Have the attitudes of CPAs concerning the use of advertising by CPA firms changed? Only 39 percent of the respondents to this study believe CPA firms should *not* advertise. The attitudes of CPAs toward advertising by accounting firms have changed significantly since 1978.

The future environment of public accounting will certainly be more competitive. In recent years, the auditing market has matured due to fewer companies going public. In addition, increased merger and acquisition activity has resulted in a reduction in the total number of audit clients. As the auditing market decreases in size, the consulting market is seen as a high-growth market. The use of advertising could increase as competition for new and existing markets heightens. Since 96 percent of the respondents agree the use of advertising will increase as the level of competition increases, advertising now appears to be a fact of life in the public accounting profession. These findings again emphasize the need for a written marketing plan in which advertising can be utilized as one of the tools in the overall plan.

CONCLUSIONS

A majority of the CPAs responding to this study recognize the need for a written marketing plan. Many of these CPAs may need additional information concerning what a written marketing plan encompasses and how it can be used to improve the growth potential of their firm.

Advertising is only one of the tools used to accomplish the objectives specified in a marketing plan. A majority of the CPAs surveyed believe the use of advertising by accounting firms will increase in the future. Firms that devote the required resources to the development of a written marketing plan may find their advertising efforts produce results. As competition between accounting firms increases, the firms that experience the greatest growth and prosperity will be the firms that most effectively and efficiently market their services. The first step in this process is to develop an understanding of marketing concepts, and how these concepts can be applied to improve the growth potential of the accounting firm.

There appears to be a real opportunity for marketers (either in-house departments or through consultants) to help accounting firms develop the marketing expertise that will be required for competitiveness in the future. A large percentage of the firms realize the need for marketing plans but have not yet incorporated them into their organizational structure. The time appears ripe for a marketing orientation to enter the accounting profession. The larger, more established firms will seemingly lead the way but with the younger accountants being more receptive to marketing consultants.

NOTE

1. The following 16 cities were selected for use in this study: Shreveport, LA; Mobile, AL; Biloxi, MS; Houston, TX; Baton Rouge, LA;, Little Rock, AR; Kansas City, MO; Louisville, KY; Atlanta, GA; St. Louis, MO; New Orleans, LA; Memphis, TN; Jackson, MS.

REFERENCES

Arndt, Terry L. and George F. Hanks (1978), "Advertising–Yes/No: The Opinions Behind the Vote," *The Woman CPA*, (April), 19-21.

Flesher, Dale L. and Floyd W. Carpenter (1984), "Attitudes of CPAs Toward Practice Development Activities," *The Virginia Accountant*, (June), 24-32.

Helgeson, James G. and G. Eddy Birrer (1986), "Marketing Plans for Accounting Firms," *Journal of Accountancy*, (September), 115.

Scott, Richard A. and Donna H. Rudderow (1983), "Advertising by Accountants: How Clients and Practitioners Feel About It," *The Practical Accountant*, (April), 71-76.

Sellers, James H. and Paul J. Solomon (1978), "CPA Advertising: Opinions of the Profession," *The Journal of Accountancy*, (February), 10.

Chapter 21

Consumer-Oriented Financial Statements: The Changing Role of the CPA

Sandra L. Schmidt
Robert H. Sanborn

INTRODUCTION

Audit business for public accounting firms has reached the maturity stage in the product life cycle. Increasingly, public accounting firms are forced to look beyond the audit market to new product areas such as management, consulting, tax, and electronic data processing (EDP) for growth and increased profits. Audit business, however, continues to generate well over 50 percent of most major accounting firms' revenues, and thus, in order for these firms to remain competitive as new products are introduced, they must also look for new products within the audit segment in order to drive that part of the business into a new and profitable phase of development.

The boom period for public accounting firms came in the 1960s and 1970s when audits became required by law for many companies. Today, however, the marketplace is saturated with auditors, and future areas for expansion are shrinking. With restrictions on advertising, solicitation and promotion having been dropped, the audit marketplace has become an increasingly competitive one. Large CPA firms can no longer open their doors and expect business to come streaming through. Rather, as stated by Donald Aronson, Director of

This chapter was first published in *Journal of Professional Services Marketing*, Vol. 3(1/2) 1987.

Marketing for Arthur Young, "If you wanted to grow in the audit business, you had to attract someone else's client and chances were that someone would do the same" ("Evaluating . . . ," 1985). The audit, then, has become more like a commodity, with firms seeking, in many instances, the lowest price. Accounting firms, unable to differentiate their own audit services from those of other firms, are forced to lower prices in order to be competitive. The danger, however, is that audits are not a commodity item, and, if accounting firms are unable to differentiate their services and convince the marketplace that there can be specific benefits gained from different firms and products, then accounting firms may experience a decreased profitability in their primary product. As prices are cut in order to attract new clients, profits must decrease or expenses must be cut. During the last ten years, accounting firms have successfully reduced expenses by increasing the efficiency of their audit staff and streamlining the audit process. At some point, however, decreased expenses will only decrease the quality of the audit, and firms will have to decide between profitability and the quality of the opinion they render. Therefore, although the audit function is the largest contributor to accounting firms' profits, it is often viewed as a commodity, and thus exposes the profession to the possibility of future audit failures.

MARKET-DRIVEN ORIENTATION

In order to provide a more profitable and more sound audit function, accounting firms must change from a product-driven to a market-oriented profession by developing a marketing orientation. Accountants, until recently, have lagged far behind other professionals in looking outward to their market in order to develop ways of meeting the needs of that market. Perhaps this is because accountants are in the unique position of being hired by and receiving payment from management, but being liable to external third parties who perceive the audit report as free information. Instead of presenting the audit function as a commodity, thought must be given to the possibility of differentiating the audit by adapting it to changing needs in the marketplace. The recent advent of advertising within the profession is only one small part of a firm's overall marketing orientation. Accounting firms must examine all of the marketer's "4 P's"–product, price, place, and promotion–in order to create the marketing mix to best satisfy the needs of the target market. At present, accounting firms have only overtly made use of promotion (and then only in the form of advertising) to help market their audit functions. Price, then, becomes the primary differentiating variable when firms perceive that they are dealing with a commodity item. In order for accounting firms to remain competitive and move their audit business into a new stage of profitability, they must look to the "outside world" for the specific needs of their target market, and then use these needs to develop a product which differentiates itself from others. As Roxanne Coady, Partner, Seidman and Seidman ("Evaluating. . . .," 1985, p. 39), writes: "We are still at the stage where we, being the product developers, are just coming around to telling the marketers what to sell. We are just coming around to letting the marketers tell us what services are needed but are not in existence."

Thus, accounting firms must become more market-driven by examining needs in the marketplace in order to develop products that best satisfy those needs. In developing new products within the audit segment, accounting firms must consider the external users' needs as well as the political/legal environment when attempting to differentiate their products through innovation. There has been a great deal of press lately on audit failures, such as in the case of Penn Square Bank of Oklahoma City, Continental Illinois Bank, and ESM, Inc. In the wake of these failures, more and more shareholders of companies in bankruptcy are suing accounting firms for malpractice. The result has been an increased awareness of accounting firms' liability to investors, decreased confidence in the opinions provided by the accounting firms, and a loss of confidence throughout the accounting industry. Many experts predict that major changes must be made in accounting practices if public credibility in independent auditors is to be maintained ("Accounting . . . , 1985). Rep. John Dingell (D-Michigan) has created a commission to examine accounting practices, self-regulation, and the role of the SEC in governing the accounting industry. According to Dingell, the annual review of a company's financial statement by outside accountants is an important protection for investors; and, when companies audited by these outside accountants fail shortly after receiving an unqualified rating, there is something fundamentally wrong with the system–it is no longer protecting the investor.

THE ENVIRONMENT

These hearings have produced adverse publicity for the accounting firm, and they may also lead to legislation which further complicates the audit process. New regulations may take the form of stiffer corporate disclosure and financial reporting requirements for firms and a more adversarial role for the accountant. Obviously there is a problem with some of the recent audits, and, as a result, change may soon come to the profession. These changes should not be viewed as a series of trials to be borne, but rather as a series of new opportunities. Whatever the form of legislation, whether by action of Congress, the SEC, or by the AICPA, accounting firms must be poised to take advantage of any new product opportunities offered by a change in the audit procedure. Thus, accounting firms must look to develop a new audit product which better examines company records and/or provides the public with an increased amount of information (Berton, 1986).

One major part of the legal/political environment, then, is the public investor's right to information. The AICPA, SEC, and Congress all exist to provide the investor with guarantees that his or her investment dollar is being put into a viable product by an audited firm. At present, however, the audit function may not be meeting all the needs of the investor. Recent audit failures indicate that the accounting profession may not be currently fulfilling the role of "public watchdog" as described by Supreme Court Justice Warren Burger in his guidelines for the industry ("Accounting . . . ," 1985). Dating back to John F. Kennedy's "Consumer Bill of Rights," Congress has increasingly upheld the right of the consumer to be provided with adequate information on the product he or she is buying. Recent legislation in the banking, automotive, and insurance fields has consistently reemphasized the consumer's right to know. And, just as a consumer must be sure that the automobile he or she is buying is well-built and safe, so too must the investor be sure that the company he or she is investing in is "reasonably fit, suitable and safe, and that the representation [of that company] is reasonably sufficient, suitable and accurate" (Minow, 1984). The investor, merely a more sophisticated consumer, has the need to know that the company in which he or she invests is a sound and ongoing concern. The search for additional sources of information has led to the increased development of financial advisory services, and an expansion of older services such as the Standard and Poors Bond rating. Investor's needs have also led them to place more reliance on the audit report. Problems with the increased usage of the audited report by investors fall within three categories–inaccurate or incomprehensible auditing procedures, a differential in what investors perceive as the essence of an audited statement and the role of the CPA, and investor inability to reasonably interpret the audited financial statements.

INFORMATION GAP

Inaccuracies or oversights discovered in the auditing process have already been discussed and are the subject of the Dingell committee investigation. Beyond this, however, there are other areas in which the investor's need for information is not being adequately met by information provided by a company's accounting firm. One area of confusion involves the difference between those functions the public thinks auditors perform and those functions auditors actually do perform. "The audit may be entirely competent, even though the business later fails," asserts Newton N. Minow, a Chicago lawyer who was a member of the internal quality review board of Arthur Andersen and Company from 1974 through 1983 (Berton, 1985). Thus, many investors read more into the audit than actually exists. Therefore, although Mr. Minow's statement may be true, both investors and the court system are placing the accounting firm in a position of responsibility for events that take place within the firm after it has been audited. The accounting function exists to provide information to those in the market who place capital at risk. If this information is being misinterpreted, then a problem exists. Further compounding the problem is the degree to which CPAs themselves differ in the perceptions of their responsibilities. Are accountants responsible merely for asserting that general acceptable accounting practices have been followed, or are they responsible in a more general sense to the public for the revelation of other information which may be important to a potential investor in the company? Many investors put their trust in an accounting firm's opinion as evidence that the company audited is a sound business investment. Obviously, given the gap between what accountants see as their role and how many investors interpret the financial audit, something must change in the marketplace in order to create a more efficient and more easily understood flow of information between investor and borrower, while at the same time providing the investor with the necessary information guaranteed him or her as a consumer. Accounting firms, then, can either educate the public through a promotional campaign on just what an audit statement means, or they can develop a new audit product which better fulfills investor expectations and provides the consumer with more comprehensible information (Lizzio, 1985).

Not only must investors be provided with accurate and adequate information on potential investments, but they must also be able to understand this information. Audited statements are of no use to the average investor if they cannot be interpreted. Instead, this inability to adequately examine the audited statements increases the investor's "blind faith" dependence on the auditing firm. Witnesses heard by the Dingell commission, however, repeatedly emphasized the widespread degree to which information is being hidden from the public under a cover of accounting gobbledygook that few laymen can understand. Thus, even though the audited statements might be entirely sound, the public desire for information is not being met if those statements cannot be interpreted by the average investor. Again, accounting firms can choose to modify their disclosure procedures in order to better meet investors' needs for information in order to fill the expectation gap. Any modification in accounting procedure, then, suggests a potential product change of which these firms should be aware.

THE FUTURE:
CONSUMER-ORIENTED FINANCIAL STATEMENTS

Given the maturity of the audit market, legal pressures to change the audit procedure, and a current lack of sufficient information available to the consumer, accounting firms must develop a new product to meet these changing needs in the marketplace and move the audit function out of the maturity stage and into a new and profitable business segment. One possible innovation within the audit market is the development of "Consumer-Oriented Financial Statements." Instead of merely stating that a company's financial statements comply with generally accepted accounting practices, auditors could instead build upon this by providing investors with a brief interpretation of these statements, a contingency scenario if appropriate, and any other information that may be pertinent.

> Instead of trying to dodge its responsibilities, the accounting profession should take a harder line with some of its clients; not sticking to the narrow confines of "professional standards," but trying to perceive its job in terms of what the public needs and will take court action to pursue. It should recognize that an intense battle for clients that now includes widespread fee discounts may be eroding its professionalism in the eyes of the public and its critics. (Berton, 1985)

Under this approach, investor information needs would be much more effectively met–there would no longer be a gap between what investors *perceive* to be and what actually *is* the essence of the audit statement, and investors would be much more able to understand the contents of the audited statements if they were provided with an explanation of its contents. This, too, would provide accounting firms with the opportunity to check their findings.

If, for example, a specialist in the banking industry is brought in to interpret an audit on a given bank, the accounting firm is twice as sure that the audit is complete and sound. The interpretation of a firm's financial statements also requires a high level of expertise in many different industry areas. This type of expertise must be developed by accounting firms in order to retain a competitive advantage, and, by having experts interpret the financial statements, accounting firms can move much more easily into other roles such as management consulting for their clients. Given the job of interpreting financial statements, accounting firms would also be more able to afford the risk of auditing entrepreneurial and high-tech firms–a risk that, given the recent litigation boom, has forced many firms out of these areas.

In providing the "double check" on statements, in developing expertise on the industry and in being able to qualify statements with additional insight and information, accounting firms can audit these types of firms at a reduced risk of malpractice litigation. The ability to qualify statements with an interpretation, finally, is one possibility being suggested to reduce the CPA's liability. Although the statements may be in order, accountants are increasingly being held responsible for management fraud and omissions. If CPAs provide an interpretation of the financial statements, they will be much better able to express qualifications that may affect the future of the business.

Firms, too, may enjoy increased benefits through the use of investor-oriented statements. In including an interpretation of its financial statements, a firm is able to provide potential investors with more comprehensive and more easily understood information. This, in turn, creates a more efficient marketplace as investor information cost is reduced, and the flow of funds from surplus to deficit spending units is thus facilitated by a more fluid marketplace. Firms competing for investment dollars can differentiate themselves from other firms seeking the same dollars by enabling the investor to obtain an interpreted statement. In weighing investment alternatives, the investor will be much more able to make an informed decision if he or she has complete, understandable, and easily obtainable information. The presence of this information will, in turn, enable the investor to be more confident of his or her decision, thus increasing the possibility that he or she will invest in the given company. Thus, although there is little at present to differentiate a company's annual report from that of its competitor, investor-oriented financial statements, added to the annual report, can become a valuable tool in helping many companies gain access to capital markets.

Finally, given the evolving legal environment surrounding the accounting profession, investor-oriented financial statements may be one answer to the inevitable changes that are about to take place within the industry. Many experts agree that, in the wake of recent investigations by the SEC and by Congress, there will be some fundamental changes in the way accounting firms will be expected to approach an audit. Newton Minow (1984) reports that, "One possibility is the modification of the accountant's report to reflect greater tentativeness about the conclusion." CPA interpretations of financial statements will allow just this sort of latitude for accountants to express opinions not previously allowable in the "cut-and-dried" financial statements of the past. Results of the Dingell commission investigation, too, will likely lead to reforms in the audit process which would go nicely with the user-oriented statements. According to Berton and Ingersoll (1985), findings of the Dingell commission may well force tougher corporate disclosure rules and financial reporting requirements aimed at "giving the public enough advance warning about the deteriorating finances of banks and other companies." Investor-oriented statements are just the type of open document providing more information to the investor and greater insight into situations that may lead to a business failure. Finally, the SEC seems ready to force companies to disclose more information in their annual reports. *Forbes*, March 12, 1983, reports, "Now the SEC is saying firms must put previously non-public information in annual reports if it could affect stock prices. In short, the SEC now punishes the sin of omission as well as the sin of commission." The SEC is cracking down on audit failures, and interpreted statements may, in fact, become a very routine part of the information disclosure procedure. Both the SEC and Congress are set to require more rigid audit standards, and thus, in light of tougher standards, the evolution of investor-oriented statements seems less a revolution and more a pragmatic and not too costly solution to a worsening problem.

Accounting firms are in need of a differentiated audit product. Consumers are not, at present, getting adequate investment information, and both Congress and the SEC are tightening controls in an effort to produce a more reliable audit procedure. Evolution of investor-oriented financial statements can be used to strengthen the value of the audit process, to provide consumers with more complete and more easily understood information, to meet new SEC and Congressional guidelines, and to provide firms with a differentiated product more marketable to the average consumer.

REFERENCES

"Accounting Industry Practices Said in Need of Major Reform," *Washington Post*, February 21, 1985.

Berton, Lee, "Rewriting the Rules: Jerry Sullivan Leads Effort to Increase Auditor's Responsibility," *Wall Street Journal*, December 17, 1986.

_____ . "Investors Call CPAs to Accounts," *Wall Street Journal*, January 28, 1985.

Berton, Lee and Bruce Ingersoll, "Rep. Dingell to Take Aim at Accountants: SEC In Hearings on Professions's Role as Watchdog," *Wall Street Journal*, February 19, 1985.

"Evaluating the Services of Professional Accounting Firms," *Corporate Accounting*, January 1985.

Minow, Newton N., "Accountants' Liability and the Litigation Explosion," *Journal of Accountancy*, September, 1984.

"Truth in Packaging," *Forbes*, March 12, 1983.

Chapter 22

Six Ps for Four Characteristics:
A Complete Positioning Strategy
for the Professional Services Firm
(CPA Firm Example)

Brien Ellis
Jeannie S. Mosher

INTRODUCTION

Professional service firms are faced with considerations that are unique as compared to product marketers. First, many professionals are still adjusting to the change in regulations and standards set by their respective associations since the late 1970s when many of the restrictions on advertising were lifted. Second, marketing is often not considered necessary or professional by groups such as Certified Public Accountants (CPAs), doctors, or lawyers. Third, many professionals do not understand marketing which further limits its use (Honeycutt and Marts 1990). Zeithaml, Parasuraman, and Berry (1985) in a large-scale study confirmed that service firms are also faced with the problems of intangibility (services are not physical), inseparability (services are produced and consumed at the same time), perishability (time cannot be saved), and heterogeneity (fluctuations in quality of service exist due to personnel differences).

Although some research has been done on positioning of professional service firms (e.g., George and Wheiler 1986, Hensel 1988,

This chapter was first published in *Journal of Professional Services Marketing*, Vol. 9(1) 1993.

Honeycutt and Marts 1990), few empirical studies have been done. Even more has been written on how specific variables in the marketing mix affect business (e.g., Hite and Fraser 1988, Ferguson and Higgins 1989, Gray 1989); however, little research has been done on how to develop a complete positioning strategy for the professional service firm. Furthermore, while much has been written on the unique problems faced by service marketers, no one, to date, has effectively integrated, tested, and combined problems and tactics into the development of an overall positioning strategy. This study empirically examines 109 CPA firms to determine what types of marketing tactics they currently use.

The purpose of this study is to show how marketing can be used to help a professional service firm establish a position in the minds of consumers while maintaining acceptable professional standards. Specifically, the objectives of this study are: (1) to identify how much marketing is used by accounting firms, (2) to demonstrate how the concept of positioning can be used to improve the marketing and overall service of CPA firms, (3) to describe how CPAs currently position themselves in the marketplace, (4) to offer recommendations to CPA firms and other professional service firms on how better to market their services by establishing the correct position in the minds of their clients in light of the inherent difficulties of intangibility, heterogeneity, perishability, and inseparability, and (5) to demonstrate how the addition of people and presentation to the marketing mix can effectively counter service problems.

BACKGROUND

The service sector has grown to 60 percent of the United States Gross National Product. Service firms comprise 30 percent of the 500 largest firms (Tootelian and Gaedeke 1990). CPA firms provide an interesting example in the service sector because of the size of the industry, the nature of the business, and the importance of the service to consumers. There are approximately 45,000 CPA firms competing in the United States (AICPA 1991). In today's low growth and highly competitive markets, accounting firms need to include not only the traditional strategies of attracting new clients but they also need to focus on retaining existing clients when developing marketing strategies (George and Wheiler 1986). The amount of growth and prosperity of accounting firms currently depends on how effectively and efficiently they market their services (Hodge, Brown, and Lumpkin 1990).

CPAs are distinguished from other accountants by stringent state licensing requirements, including a college degree or its equivalent and certain experience requirements. In addition to meeting the profession's technical requirements, CPAs are governed by a strict code of professional ethics.

The services provided by the accounting profession are essential in today's complex and competitive environment. CPAs not only perform well-known tax services to individuals and businesses, but they also act as advisors to individuals, businesses, financial institutions, nonprofit organizations, and government agencies on a wide range of finance-related matters. Specialized expertise is often needed to achieve the quality of management essential to the survival and growth of businesses (Tootelian and Gaedeke 1990). In addition to tax and management advisory services, CPAs also provide audit services required for all publicly owned companies. Thus, the accounting profession has far-reaching effects on the American public.

LITERATURE REVIEW

Marketing a professional service firm requires establishing a position or creating an image in the minds of the consumer that can overcome the problems associated with the unique characteristics of services. The intangibility of the products offered by accounting firms (e.g., tax preparation, management consulting, financial audits, etc.) makes it difficult for consumers to grasp what they will receive if they purchase the service. According to McDougall and Snetsinger (1990) intangible services are particularly vulnerable to challenges by competitors who are doing a better job of positioning. The inseparability of production and consumption often results in inefficiencies of the accountant's time, since both the accountant and the client must often be present at certain times. Difficulty also arises in demonstrating what the results of the service will be since the services must be sold first, and then produced and consumed simultaneously (Regan 1963). Perishability involves the time factor which is extremely critical in the billing process of professionals. Any unscheduled time for the accountant results in lost revenue. The heterogeneity of accounting services results in the potential for high variability in the performance of the services since they are often performed by different accountants at different times. Fluctuations in quality often depend on how much experience the accountants have.

Although the idea of positioning a firm is not new, it has become increasingly popular. Ries and Trout (1986) describe positioning as conditioning the mind of the prospect where the firm and product or service are perceived in a particular way. Positioning involves changing key marketing variables in order to secure a worthwhile position with respect to the client's perceptions (for example, the big six accounting firms position themselves to target large corporations to attain sizeable audit and consulting engagements). Since service firms have several unique characteristics, a professional service firm must go beyond the traditional four Ps of the marketing mix in order to understand and utilize effectively the concept of positioning. A useful extension of the marketing mix is the six Ps of retail positioning (Mason and Mayer 1987). The six Ps involve the four traditional marketing mix elements of place, price, product, and promotion, along with people and presentation, both particularly applicable to services.

The people and presentation elements are added to prevent the omission of key tactical decisions and to provide specific direction for the service firm. The presentation of the firm is concerned with the appearance of the office (e.g., furniture, office decor) and any tangible cues that depict the image of the firm (e.g., stationery, logo) or the finished product of the service (i.e., report covers). The people element includes all employees and their characteristics. Because services are labor intensive (Zeithaml, Parasuraman, and Berry 1985), the people component is necessary in the design of a service positioning mix. Creating a successful strategic position requires the personality and expertise of the people employed by the firm and the presentation of the firm to be consistent with the image conveyed in the other promotion variables.

Figure 1 combines the unique characteristics of service firms with the six Ps of the positioning mix. While some of the marketing

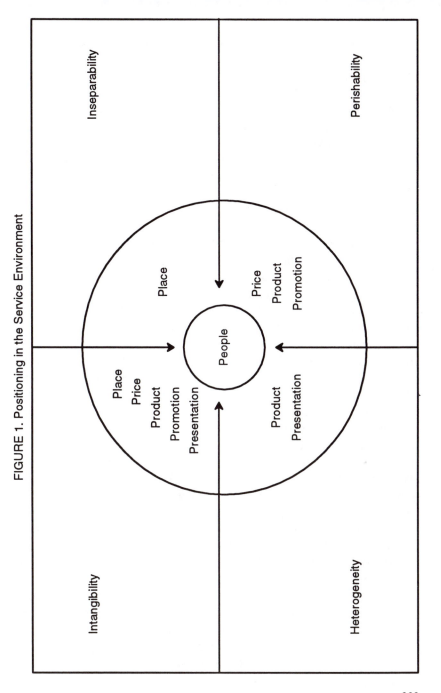

FIGURE 1. Positioning in the Service Environment

mix elements relate to more than one characteristic, for the professional service firm, the people element becomes the "core" element of the mix because it relates to all four of the characteristics.

Positioning the professional service firm in the minds of prospective clients involves selecting target markets that have needs matching the expertise employed by the firm and communicating how selected services can benefit potential clients (Hensel 1988). Research by Hodge, Brown, and Lumpkin (1990) found that mission statements and target markets are used more extensively than market positioning and service mix. However, respondents to their study agreed that accounting firms should decide how they want clients to view their firm and then work to create and maintain that image.

Because of the continued complexity and changes in tax laws and accounting standards, it is important for CPAs to specialize. As Van Doren and Smith (1987) concluded in a recent article, "the time of being all things to all people is past for professionals" (p. 71). This specialization should lead to market segmentation. Those CPA firms that segment their market in some way most often use the type of service offered (e.g., tax, audit) rather than the type of client and industry sector (e.g., manufacturing, real estate) as their basis for segmentation (O'Donohoe, Diamantopoulos, and Lane 1989).

Since accounting firms offer intangible products, pricing of their services not only affects the level of demand but is also an indicator to clients of the quality and value of the services offered (George and Wheiler 1986). Ferguson and Higgins (1989) found that consumers consider other information, such as image, to be more important than price when establishing perceived quality of an accounting service.

Professionals continue to set fees based primarily on the cost of the service, indicating that professionals perceive their market from a production view rather than from the customer's view (Honeycutt and Marts 1990). Zeithaml, Parasuraman, and Berry (1985) suggested that the popularity of cost-oriented pricing is that costs may not be covered if prices are based on what competition charges (competition-oriented pricing) or what the market is willing to pay (demand-oriented pricing). However, the true art in pricing is for the price to be a quantitative reflection of value to the customer. Thus, cost becomes the floor level in pricing and the competitive price, the ceiling (Corey 1978).

Little research has been done on how the location of the firm has affected business; however, several key points have been established. George and Wheiler (1986) have identified location and accessibility of the accounting personnel as critical issues to clients because of the inseparability of production and consumption. In a study by Honeycutt and Marts (1990), over half of the firms surveyed decorated their offices with their clients in mind and 43 percent located close to primary accounts.

O'Donohoe, Diamantopoulos, and Lane (1989) found that promotional tools such as brochures, circulars, seminars, and press releases are considered more important than advertising. Face-to-face contact by partners and staff of public accounting firms with prospective clients is another promotional tool often used by accounting firms to obtain new clients (Hodge, Brown, and Lumpkin 1990).

Honeycutt and Marts (1990) found that most CPA firms use the yellow pages to advertise their services. They also found that most firms advertising and promoting their services are not segmenting the market to target their prospective clients with needed services. Research by Gray (1989) on the content of CPA firm advertisements in the yellow pages found that a haphazard and unfocused approach is suggested by many, indicating no clear advertising objectives. However, with each additional year of advertising, attitudes of both professionals and consumers have become more favorable (Hite and Fraser 1988).

The people component of the positioning mix is particularly important for the professional accounting firm because of the degree of contact and trust between the accountant and the client. Employee attitude and appearance, as well as the process by which the service is delivered, are critical in promoting the firm's services to counter the problem of inseparability of production and consumption (George and Wheiler 1986). Given the importance of this core element of services, relatively little research has been done to determine how accounting firms use people in their positioning strategy.

Intangibility of accounting services requires special attention to be directed toward how the firm is presented to clients. Tangible cues such as office decor and management reports help to facilitate performance and communication of services being offered (George and Wheiler 1986). The presentation element can also be used to help the client associate with the intangible nature of the service through the use of a logo and/or slogan, such as, the Prudential Insurance slogan, "get a piece of the rock" (Donnelly 1980).

METHODOLOGY

In order to accomplish the objectives of the study, a self-administered questionnaire was developed. The questionnaire contained four sections: (1) general business information, (2) target market information, (3) questions regarding the use and understanding of marketing, and (4) the positioning strategy of the firm. Specific items for the questionnaire were developed based on industry and marketing literature. The items were refined through a series of personal interviews with several CPAs. A final pretest of the survey resulted in only minor modifications to the original instrument.

The sample for the study was developed through means of a systematic random sample of CPAs in Kentucky who are members of the Kentucky Society of Certified Public Accountants. A total of 326 surveys were mailed out, 18 were returned because of an incorrect address or because the firms were no longer in business, thus reducing the sampling frame to 308. Within six weeks, 109 questionnaires were returned for a response rate of 35.4 percent. All respondents were assured of confidentiality and offered an executive summary of the results. The sample represented a mix of small, medium, and large firms. Thirty-four percent of the firms surveyed had less than $100,000 in annual billings; 43 percent had billings of over $100,000, but less than $500,000; and the remaining 23 percent had billings greater than $500,000.

RESULTS

The findings of the study indicate that most CPAs do not use much marketing. Only 9 percent of the firms surveyed have a formal marketing plan, and firms spend only an average of 1.5 percent of billings on marketing. However, 40 percent of the firms surveyed indicated they spend no money on marketing. Additionally, only 10 percent of firms use periodic client surveys to measure customer satisfaction.

The target market decision has been identified as the most important choice made in marketing since all other marketing variables are dependent upon a firm's target market selection (Corey 1978). However, most of the firms responding to our survey appear to have very broad and poorly defined targets. Most of the firms offer tax services, yet few specialize in specific industries or businesses. Furthermore, even fewer (20 percent) employ different people for each specialty. These results seem to indicate a general lack of a well-defined target market. The results of the target market variable as well as for each component of the positioning mix are shown in Table 1.

The product measure for this study consisted of the types of services offered by the firm. Two types of services dominate the list. Virtually all firms offer tax services and over 70 percent offer small business related services. Surprisingly, less than half offer auditing and management consulting services. Also, only 29 percent offer financial planning services. These results indicate that tax services are the "bread and butter" of a CPA firm. However, there may be considerable opportunity to overcome the perishability problem by specializing in a second or third service to differentiate their services from other CPA firms. Tax services may be necessary, but likely not sufficient for success. Simply put, unscheduled time outside of tax season must be addressed in the strategy of the firm.

The CPAs in this study base their prices primarily upon the cost of the job; the competition's prices are a distant second. Also, little importance is given to the customer's ability to pay, and about 70 percent of respondents bill at the same rate for each service offered. However, CPAs are somewhat split in their opinions regarding adjustment of prices and services according to the clients' needs and ability to pay. The above results tend to suggest a lack of a cohesive pricing strategy by CPAs. This problem may well be a function of a cost-oriented philosophy acquired in their rigorous training. However, a complete pricing strategy must take into account not only cost, but also the competition and the customers.

The results of advertising and promotion reinforce what has been

TABLE 1. Results

Variable

Products-Target Markets

Type of Clients Targeted	Percent
Individuals/Executives/Professionals	85
Small Businesses/Emerging Companies	82
Corporations/Ptnshps/Estates/Trusts	73
Construction	42
Non-profit	29
Medical/Health Care	28
Real Estate	26
Manufacturing	24

Type of Service Offered	Percent
Tax	97
Small Business Related Services	73
Auditing	48
Management Consulting Services	45
Financial Planning	29

Price

Consideration in Setting Fees	Mean	Rank
Cost of Job	1.31	1
Competition	2.54	2
Customer Ability to Pay	2.67	3
Fixed Costs	2.85	4

% Agree	% Disagree	
Adj Prices According to Client Needs	44	28
Adj Svcs According to Clt Abil to Pay	42	42
Bills Same Rate for Each Service	69	20

Promotion/Advertising

Practice Development	Mean	Rank
Civic Group Participation	2.17	1
Newsletters	2.25	2
Seminars	2.83	3
Public Speaking	3.14	4
Advertising	3.80	5
Publishing Articles	4.61	6

	Percent
Firm Uses an Ad Agency	1
% of Annual Revenue Alloc to Adv	1.5

Advertising Media Used	Mean	Rank
Yellow Pages	2.06	1
Professional Bus Cards	2.08	2
Direct Mail	2.18	3
Newspaper	2.71	4
Radio	4.42	5
Magazine	4.55	6
Television	5.65	7

Advertising Emphasis*	Percent
Specific Services	44
Years of Experience	33
Location	28
Targeted Audience	26
Professional Memberships	23
Size of Firm	17
Business Hours	10

Place

Imp in Choosing Location	Mean	Rank
Proximity to Clients	2.42	1
Appearance	2.58	2
Size	2.81	3
Rent or Mortgage	2.93	4
Parking	3.53	5

Presentation

Office Decor*	Percent
Chosen with Clients in Mind	43
Professionally Done	34
Chosen with Employees in Mind	34
Purely Functional	33
Not Planned	17

Use of Logo	Percent
Firm Has Logo	28
Logo was Professionally Designed	51

People — Percent

Firm Uses Diff. People for Each Specialty	Percent
Firm Uses Diff. People for Each Specialty	20

Hiring Criteria	Mean	Rank
Experience	1.98	1
Expertise	2.23	2
Personality	2.30	3
Background	2.46	4

*Total may not add up to 100 since more than one could be chosen.

stated in the literature. The results of this study confirm that word-of-mouth is the most widely used promotional tool. Civic group participation is the most important promotion, and business cards the most important form of advertising. Both of these activities are a form of word-of-mouth advertising. However, CPAs perceive yellow page ads to be as important as business cards, and direct mail to be almost as important. Another interesting finding is that the respondents perceive advertising as the fifth most important form of promotion following civic group participation, newsletters, seminars, and public speaking. Furthermore, only one firm of the 109 respondents uses an advertising agency.

Several points emerge from the above results. First, most CPAs do not regard advertising as important. Second, mass media advertising is the least important of all. Third, a combination of word-of-mouth forms of promotion supported by yellow page advertising and direct mail is the most widely chosen strategy. Finally, when firms do advertise, there is a definite lack of emphasis. Few firms emphasize such crucial factors as location and professional membership. Most firms choose to emphasize their services offered and years of experience.

The place variable was measured by having respondents rank the reasons why they chose their particular location. The results indicate that at least four factors are important in the choice of a location. Being close to the clients was the number one reason given, although considerable importance was also attributed to the appearance, size, and cost of the office. Parking was not considered an important factor. These results indicate the firms attempt to overcome the inseparability problem inherent in service firms.

The presentation component was measured through a series of "yes" or "no" responses to questions regarding the firm's office decor and logo. No clear-cut pattern emerged as to how or why a particular decor was chosen. However, the most startling result of the presentation measure was that only 28 percent of the firms surveyed had a logo. Given the intangibility of the business, the lack of a clear presentation to help shape the identity of the firm is a dangerous omission.

No clear pattern emerged from this study regarding how people are selected for the firm. Experience was the most important criterion used in hiring; but expertise, personality, and background were all closely bunched in the rankings. These results indicate the value of considering several factors when hiring associates, but the lack of a well-defined hiring strategy.

RECOMMENDATIONS

Service firms can use a variety of simple tactics to overcome the problems unique to service firms. (See Table 2.) Since intangibility is the most fundamental difference between product and service marketing (Zeithaml, Parasuraman, and Berry 1985), it is the characteristic with the most recommendations. All six Ps can be used to counteract the problems of intangibility. First, the place and the presentation components interact to offer tangible cues to the client through the actual layout, location, and decor of the office. The location and decor of the office may also help shape price perceptions of the firm (e.g., note the difference between H&R Block and the big six accounting firms). A CPA firm can make the intangible service more tangible by offering some type of written summary of the work performed (when formal reports are not a part of the specific service), as well as offering follow-up services. Although a service may be intangible, the price of a service is quite tangible. Clients can see the price and even "feel it" when they pay. Furthermore, price may be associated with quality, and firms should consider carefully the effect of pricing on the image of the firm (Ferguson and Higgins 1989). The promotion element of the positioning mix can be used in conjunction with a firm's presentation (logo, slogans) and product (CPA credential) to form a more tangible promotion before the client even enters the office. Brochures and newsletters provide an excellent source of reminders for present and/or prospective clients of the services offered by the firm. Finally, the people of the accounting firm are the most tangible cue of all. Here firms should focus on the relationship between the accountant and the client. The professionals in the firm can provide a very important tangible cue about their personality by presenting seminars and through their appearance and manner during client contact.

Usually both the accountant and client must be present at some point in time during the service process, resulting in the problem of

TABLE 2. Recommendations to Overcome Problems Unique to Service Firm

Problem	Strategy	Tactic
Intangibility (products are not physical)	Place	Location near clients
	Presentation	Decorate office with clients in mind; Provide written reports of work performed; Use logo & slogan; Use brochures & newsletters
	Prices	Set prices consistent with desired image
	Product	Display CPA credential
	People	Focus on professional/client relationships; Present seminars
Inseparability (produced and consumed at same time	Place	Select target market & then select location; Offer convenient times
	People	Develop phone relations with clients
Perishability (time cannot be saved)	People	Hire experts in different areas; Hire experienced CPAs on a temporary basis during the busy season; Adjust scheduling to meet demand
	Price	Use demand-based pricing; Pre-sell services
	Promotion	Offer small amount of free consultation to new clients
Heterogeneity (fluctuations in quality of services due to different personnel)	Product	Customize and/or standardize services
	Presentation	Display credentials on all written documents
	People	Develop and maintain quality practices in hiring and retaining employees; Maintain quality control with employees; Provide similar training to all employees

inseparability. Two positioning variables, place and people, can be utilized to counter this problem. First, accounting firms should select a location convenient for its clients. This selection requires the proper identification of a firm's target market and then, selection of a location that fits the needs of the market. Also, by offering convenient times (e.g., evenings or Saturdays) for the service, the simultaneous appearance of the client and accountant is less troublesome. Second, the people of the firm need to develop good telephone relationships with clients since much of a professional's time is spent answering specific questions that arise in the ordinary course of business.

Service firms can combat the perishability problem in several ways. The perishable nature of service firms that can result in lost time can be overcome by hiring experts in different areas to allow the firm to offer more specialized products to stay busy throughout the year. This tactic might also help to differentiate the firm from its competition. During the busy season when the majority of tax and audit services are offered, the firm can hire experienced CPAs on a temporary basis to work in the office, or out of their homes if space is a problem. In addition, different prices can be charged during different times of the year for certain services. For instance, a lower hourly rate could be used for tax planning consultation services to encourage existing tax clients to use the firm's tax planning services and to encourage clients to bring their tax information to the firm early. This use of demand-based pricing should not reduce the perceived value of the services. The discounted hourly rate should only be used during specific times of the year for certain selected services that relate to the usual service (i.e., tax return preparation) charged at the usual hourly rate. This pricing method should only be used in cases when the firm has nonbillable time to reduce lost revenue. Thus, firms would be able to charge a slightly higher price for their usual services since the client may perceive they are getting more value for their money. Accounting firms can also borrow techniques currently used by airlines and hotels and pre-sell their services to balance demand. This tactic would be particularly effective in balancing out the heavy load during tax season and the light demand that traditionally follows tax time. A combination of demand-based pricing and advance sell promotions should be used.

To identify potential new clients, the firm can offer a small amount of free consultation through various services such as "welcome wagon" or "newcomers clubs." The final tactic to combat perishability involves people and the proper scheduling of clients and employees so that work time is maximized.

The problem of heterogeneity of services can be handled through a combination of product, presentation, and people. First, by offering either customized or standardized services (depending on the target market), the professional service firm can become a more controllable factor. For instance, instead of using a standard internal control questionnaire that may have inapplicable questions for certain clients, the questionnaire can be customized for the client to provide a sense of importance to each client. The small amount of time involved in revising the questionnaire may result in obtaining an extended engagement or additional engagements with current and prospective clients. Second, by presenting the service in a consistent manner (display of credentials, written agreements), the perception of the service in the mind of the client should be less subject to variation. Third, and most important, by developing and maintaining quality practices in hiring and retaining employees, a firm can establish a more consistent position. The last factor is complex and includes recruitment, selection, training, compensation, and motivation. Simply put, quality control for a service firm is directly related to the people of the firm. To reduce the fluctuation in quality of service provided by different personnel, all employees need to be exposed to the same training programs in the respective areas which they provide service. This tactic could involve sending all professionals to the same continuing education seminars or having each professional attend different seminars and present the material received to the other professionals in the firm.

The above recommendations are contingent upon the proper identification and selection of a target market. This procedure involves segmenting the market not only by the services the firm offers, but also by the type of business (e.g., manufacturing, retailing) or the needs of the client. The firm should then emphasize this segmentation in its advertising and promotion tactics.

CONCLUSION

The common element to each of the four characteristics is the people component of the positioning mix. Thus, the people of a service firm become the "core" of a firm's position, and since the people perform the service, the people may even become the actual service itself. The people in the firm directly affect the quality of the product, its price, and the image of the firm. Furthermore, the interaction between a client and a service professional (e.g., CPA, lawyer, physician) is special because of the personal and ongoing nature of the service. When performed properly over a period of time, a unique form of loyalty–possessive loyalty–can emerge. This type of loyalty is exhibited by the use of a possessive pronoun by the client when talking about the professional (i.e., my accountant). Possessive loyalty indicates confidence and trust in the professional, and perhaps even dependency. As a result, the people of the firm have a direct effect on overcoming all the unique difficulties characteristic of service firms. Therefore, given the importance of people, much more research is needed on how the employees of a firm help establish a professional service firm's position. In particular, specific research is needed on hiring practices and standards, employee attitudes and appearance, and buyer/seller relationships for professional services.

Finally, although the people element is the core of the positioning mix, an effective strategy must contain all six elements of the mix working together in a complete and consistent manner for the firm to truly establish an easily identifiable position in the mind of the customer. This process must begin with the identification of the firm's target market and proceed through each element of the mix. Matching these tactics to client needs and perceptions reduces the magnitude of the special problems facing service firms.

REFERENCES

AICPA (1991), "A Message to All Local and Regional Firms," *The CPA Letter*, 71 (August): 4.

Corey, E. Raymond (1978), *Marketing Strategy–An Overview*, Boston, MA: Harvard Business School.

Donnelly, James H., Jr. (1980), "Intangibility and Marketing Strategy for Retail Bank Services," *Journal of Retail Banking*, (June): 39-43.

Ferguson, Jeffery M. and Lexis F. Higgins (1989), "Effects of Price of Tax Preparation Services and the CPA Credential on the Perception of Service Quality," *Journal of Professional Services Marketing*, 5:1, 87-99.

George, William R. and Kent W. Wheiler (1986), "Practice Development–A Services Marketing Perspective," *The CPA Journal*, 56 (October): 30-43.

Gray, O. Ronald (1989), "The Content of CPA Firm Advertisements in the Yellow Pages," *The Ohio CPA Journal*, (Summer): 15-19.

Hensel, Paul J. (1988), "Transferring Product Positioning Strategy to the Professional Services Market Sector," *Journal of Professional Services Marketing*, 4:1, 31-39.

Hite, Robert E. and Cynthia Fraser (1988), "Meta-Analyses of Attitudes Toward Advertising by Professionals," *Journal of Marketing*, 52 (July): 95-103.

Hodge, Thomas G., Michael H. Brown, and James R. Lumpkin (1990), "The Use of Marketing Plans and Advertising Among Accounting Firms: Is This Profession a Viable Candidate for Marketing?" *Journal of Professional Services Marketing*, 6:1, 43-52.

Honeycutt, Earl D., Jr. and John A. Marts (1990), "Marketing by Professionals as Applied to CPA Firms: Room for Improvement?" *Journal of Professional Services Marketing*, 6:1, 29-42.

Mason, J. Barry and Morris L. Mayer (1987), *Modern Retailing*, 3rd ed., Plano, TX: Business Publications, Inc.

McDougall, Gordon H. G. and Douglas W. Snetsinger (1990), "The Intangibility of Services: Measurement and Competitive Perspectives," *The Journal of Services Marketing*, 4:4, (Fall): 27-40.

O'Donohoe, Stephanie, Adamantios Diamantopoulos, and Jacqueline Lane (1989), "Advertising: Have Accountants Figured it Out?" *Accountancy*, (April): 120-123.

Regan, William J. (1963), "The Service Revolution," *Journal of Marketing*, 47 (July): 57-62.

Ries, Al and Jack Trout (1986), *Positioning: The Battle for Your Mind*, New York: McGraw-Hill Book Company.

Tootelian, Dennis H. and Ralph M. Gaedeke (1990), "Marketing of Professional Services as Applied to Tax Professionals: Representation of the Client, Public, or Profession?" *Journal of Professional Services Marketing*, 6:1, 17-28.

Van Doren, Doris C. and Louise W. Smith (1987), "Marketing in The Restructured Professional Services Field," *The Journal of Services Marketing*, 1:1, (Summer): 67-75.

Zeithaml, Valarie A., A. Parasuraman, and Leonard L. Berry (1985), "Problems and Strategies in Services Marketing," *Journal of Marketing*, 49 (Spring): 33-46.

Chapter 23

Marketing of Professional Services as Applied to Tax Professionals: Representation of the Client, Public, or Profession?

Dennis H. Tootelian
Ralph M. Gaedeke

INTRODUCTION

The marketing of services has become increasingly important as consumer and organizational buyer demand for personal and professional services has grown over the past decade. Services account for over 60 percent of the United States Gross National Product and 50 percent of consumer expenditures. Additionally, service firms comprise 30 percent of the 500 largest firms.

There are many reasons why the service sector of the economy has grown. At the consumer level, increased affluence and desires for more leisure time have significantly impacted this demand. Among organizational buyers, the complexities of regulations, competitive conditions, and other environmental conditions have made professional advice and assistance an almost essential part of doing business. The specialized expertise available from professionals often is needed to achieve the quality of management deemed essential to survival and growth.

Differences between products and services have been well docu-

This chapter was first published in *Journal of Professional Services Marketing*, Vol. 6(1) 1990.

mented in the literature. It is generally agreed that the distinguishing characteristics of services are their intangibility, perishability, inseparability of production and consumption, and heterogeneity (i.e., lack of standardization).

A unique aspect of services that often is not given sufficient attention is the issue of representation. Products are purchased to unswervingly serve the needs of the buyer and user. However, because of their intangibility and lack of standardization, some service providers have to answer to many publics. For professional services, the question of whether the provider's primary concern is the client, the public through its regulations, or the profession through its codes of ethics.

To what extent, for example, are professionals supposed to represent the interests of their clients versus those of the public at large and their profession? How far do accountants go in taking tax deductions for their clients? To what extent do attorneys defend those who are guilty of crimes and commit perjury on the witness stand? To what extent do stock brokers pass timely information to their clients to assist them in making investment decisions?

On the surface, the matter appears reasonably clear. Professionals should serve their clients interests insofar as they adhere to legal and professional codes. While there are statutes and general guidelines which address these issues, there remain "grey" areas where the borderlines between good representation, unprofessional conduct, and illegal acts are indistinct. Deductibility of certain expenses for tax purposes, defenses used in civil and criminal cases, and quality and timing of information shared with investors are not always clear.

The purpose of this study is to explore one profession to examine issues related to the extent to which the interests of the client are represented relative to those of the public and the profession, and how much variability there is in representation by service providers. For this study, issues of taxation were selected for analysis for several reasons. First, there are many "grey" areas in tax law, as evidenced by the extensive appeals processes available to tax payers and practitioners, the 1988 "Taxpayer Bill of Rights," and the rulings concerning accountant liability. Second, there are several different groups of tax practitioners that individuals and businesses can go to for advice. The extent to which these groups vary in treating the "grey" areas is a central issue in this study. Third, tax matters are a recurrent issue for clients, and variations in the service they receive can have significant economic and social implications over time.

Specific issues examined include:

1. To what extent do tax practitioners serve their clients' interests in the "grey" areas of tax law?
2. What are tax practitioner attitudes toward certain debatable practices available to members of their professions?
3. What are tax practitioner attitudes toward their responsibilities to ensure client compliance with prevailing tax law?
4. To what extent have tax practitioners disassociated themselves from clients who have made questionable requests for the treatment of their tax matters?
5. What are tax practitioners' attitudes toward certain actions available to the Internal Revenue Service (IRS) that would be detrimental to their clients?

METHODOLOGY

The population for this study was defined to be Enrolled Agents (EAs), Certified Public Accountants (CPAs), and Independent Accountants (IAs) who were registered to attend a tax conference sponsored by a professional association. These tax practitioners represent the primary groups of professionals who provide tax assistance to individuals and businesses. Differences between the groups mainly concern educational backgrounds, certification procedures, and the types of accounting activities in which they are engaged.

Mail questionnaires were sent to all of those registered to attend a large tax conference offered by a professional association. Surveys were mailed to a total of nearly 600 registrants.

The questionnaire focused on respondent characteristics with respect to their federal tax practices, their attitudes toward the value of alternative sources of information on federal tax law, their attitudes on how "grey" areas of tax law should be handled with respect to client representation, their attitudes with respect to practices available to tax practitioners and the IRS, and their attitudes toward their responsibilities to ensure client compliance with tax law. A series of 28 multiple choice and Likert-style attitudinal questions were included in the survey. Registrants were given nearly three weeks in which to respond, and did not have to identify themselves.

This group was used because by their registration they had expressed an interest in improving their skills in taxation matters, and a cross-section from all three groups of tax practitioners was available. As an exploratory study, it is not implied that this sample is representative of the entire population of EAs, CPAs, and IAs. However, aside from the fact that most respondents were EAs, and all displayed an interest in attending a tax seminar, there is little reason to believe that the sample is significantly biased otherwise.

RESULTS

Responses were received from 344 conference registrants. This represents a 57.3 percent response rate, which is considered very good for mail surveys. Of those responding, 275 categorized themselves as either EAs, CPAs, or IAs. The sample was found to be statistically adequate at the 95 percent confidence level. Results of the study are divided into five areas: respondent characteristics, sources of federal tax information used, representation in "grey" areas (including attitudes to selected tax practitioner actions), attitudes toward responsibility for client compliance, and attitudes toward actions used by the IRS. Differences between the three groups of tax practitioners were analyzed using tests of analysis of variance.

Respondent Characteristics

Of the 275 respondents, 90.2 percent were EAs, 6.2 percent were CPAs, and 3.6 percent were IAs. The high percentage from EAs reflects the fact that this group of tax practitioners are heavily involved in federal tax matters. Despite the differences in responses by professional groupings, their practice characteristics were reasonably similar.

Average years experience as a tax practitioner were 14.0 for EAs, 14.7 for CPAs, and 17.7 for IAs. The percent of their time devoted to federal tax preparation was nearly the same, with EAs indicating 80.9 percent, CPAs stating 79.1 percent, and IAs indicating 78.7 percent. The percent of their office's overall work which was devoted to federal tax matters was somewhat different, with EAs spending more of their time on this (74.4 percent) than did CPAs (61.9 percent) and IAs (63.0 percent). Finally, with respect to the number of federal tax returns they personally handled in the last tax year, averages for EAs, CPAs, and IAs were 295, 189, and 143 respectively.

Sources of Federal Tax Information Used

Sources of information commonly used by tax practitioners are shown in Table 1. Respondents were asked to rate each of these from "very valuable" (1) to "of no value" (5). As is evident, the most valuable source was considered to be seminars, programs, and classes by all three groups of tax practitioners. This may be expected given the population for the study. The other valuable source of information to all three groups was subscription research services.

There were four statistically significant differences between the groups of tax practitioners. CPAs found seminars, programs, and classes to be of less value than did EAs and IAs. Furthermore, IAs found IRS Bulletins/Announcements, the IRS Manual, and IRS Publication 17 to be of more value than did either EAs or CPAs.

Representation in "Grey" Areas

With respect to representing their clients in the "grey" areas of tax law, all three groups of practitioners indicated that their loyalties were more toward their clients than to the tax authorities. Furthermore, they "somewhat approved" to "completely approved" of resolving all questionable items that have a reasonable basis in favor of their clients. As shown in Table 2, there were no differences between the three groups on either of these issues.

In terms of specific actions, the respondents "somewhat" approved of filing Tax Court petitions as a means of strengthening their negotiating positions, and advising clients to show deductions in ways to minimize the chances of being audited. CPAs strongly

TABLE 1. Sources of Information Used*

Information Source:	EA	CPA	IA	Signif. Diff.
Seminars, Programs, Classes	1.15	1.50	1.20	0.01
Correspondence Courses	2.98	2.92	2.50	
Subscription Research Services	1.56	1.65	1.67	
IRS Bulletins/Announcements	2.09	2.69	1.62	0.01
IRS Manual	2.65	3.00	1.67	0.02
IRS Letter Rulings	2.42	2.83	2.33	
IRS District Director Newsletter	2.34	2.86	2.11	
IRS Publication 17	2.04	2.86	1.44	0.00
Fellow Practitioners	1.97	2.19	1.89	
Tax Journals	2.06	2.40	2.20	
Audio-Visual Tapes	3.19	3.00	2.67	

Mean scores: 1= very valuable, 5 = of no value.

TABLE 2. Representation of Client*

Issue:	EA	CPA	IA	Signif. Diff.
Overall loyalty in "grey" areas**	3.54	4.06	3.40	
Resolve all in favor of client	1.79	2.12	1.40	
Advise not to take a deduction	3.64	3.69	4.00	
Fail to advise to amend return	4.59	4.73	5.00	
Advise to show deduction differ.	2.31	2.44	2.70	
Sign without full documentation	3.25	2.60	4.22	0.01
File Tax Court petition for negot.	2.58	1.87	2.22	0.03
Fail to probe for other income	3.96	2.79	4.50	0.00
Sign when suspect underreporting	4.60	4.53	4.60	

*Mean scores: 1 = completely approve, 5 = completely disapprove
**Mean cores: 1 = completely loyal to tax authorities, 5 = completely loyal to client.

319

approved the use of Tax Court petitions to enhance negotiating positions, while there was no statistically significant difference between the tax practitioners concerning the showing of deductions.

Respondents "somewhat" to "completely" disapproved of failing to advise a client to file an amended return that could increase the client's tax liability, and signing a tax return when there is a strong suspicion that income had been understated. They also disapproved of advising clients to not take deductions in order to reduce the possibility of an audit, failing to probe for other income, and signing tax returns without full documentation that may be available later.

There were some differences in these responses between the groups of tax practitioners. CPAs indicated slight approval to signing a return without full documentation and not probing for other income. EAs and IAs tended to disapprove of these practices.

Attitudes Toward Responsibility for Client Compliance

Respondents were asked what responsibilities they felt they had to ensure their client's compliance with tax law. The results are shown in Table 3. Generally, EAs and CPAs were neutral on how much responsibility they had to ensure that their clients paid estimated taxes and filed completion of payment agreements. Furthermore, they felt only slightly responsible for ensuring that their clients paid federal tax deposits and filed required returns.

The major differences in these attitudes were between IAs and the other two groups. IAs felt they had more responsibility to ensure payment of estimated taxes, make federal tax deposits, and file required returns.

Attitudes Toward Actions Used by the IRS

Finally, respondents were asked whether they approved or disapproved of selected actions available to the IRS in tax matters. These results are shown in Table 4.

While respondents disapproved of nearly all actions cited in this study, they disapproved most of the IRS taking preemptive collection action before a case was fully litigated, and to disallowing

TABLE 3. Responsibility of Tax Practitioner to Ensure Compliance*

Compliance Issue:	EA	CPA	IA	Signif. Diff.
To pay estimated taxes	3.23	3.31	1.89	0.02
To pay federal tax deposit	2.98	2.62	1.44	0.00
To file required returns	2.41	3.00	1.56	0.02
To file completion of pay. agree.	3.53	3.75	2.67	

*Mean scores: 1 = complete responsibility; 5 = no responsibility

TABLE 4. IRS Actions*

Possible IRS Action:	EA	CPA	IA	Signif. Diff.
Disallow estimated expenses	4.17	4.19	4.30	
Seize business	3.19	2.67	3.10	
Preemptive collection	4.48	4.20	4.89	
Initiate prior collection procedure	4.14	3.47	4.20	0.05
Attach bank account	3.53	3.31	4.00	

*Mean scores: 1 = completely approve; 5 = completely disapprove

expenses which are subject to estimation. They objected least to seizing a business to stop the accumulation of unpaid withholding tax liabilities.

The three groups of tax practitioners held similar attitudes with respect to possible IRS actions. The only difference between the groups of tax practitioners was that CPAs disapproved less of IRS actions to initiate collection procedures based solely on written correspondence.

CONCLUSIONS

Based on the data obtained from this survey, it appears that there are relatively few differences between EAs, CPAs, and IAs with respect to their treatment of client tax matters. Although the sample is not portrayed as being representative of the larger population, tax practitioners tend to view themselves as primarily representing their clients.

Importantly, however, the loyalty is not absolute. Respondents consistently indicated misgivings about actions that were questionable from a tax law standpoint. They opposed not advising clients to file amended returns which could lead to higher tax liabilities, and disapproved of signing tax returns in situations where there were suspicions that income was being underreported.

From a marketing perspective, therefore, this issue of representation is highly significant. Users of professional services cannot be assured that providers will side with them where there may be concerns about practices that are in the "grey" area of legality and propriety. Assuming that representation is absolute appears to be erroneous.

Further research is needed in this area to more fully examine different groups of professionals. Additionally, consideration should be made of possible variations in representation among various types of clients.

BIBLIOGRAPHY

Boone, Louis E., and David L. Kurtz. *Contemporary Marketing*, Chicago: The Dryden Press, 1988, pp. 677-680.

"CPAs Not Liable For Third-Party Loss In Review Engagement," *Journal of Accountancy*, June, 1988, p. 14.

"The Fortune 500," *Fortune*, Volume 117, No. 9 (April 25, 1988), pp. D11-D59.

"N.Y. Ruling Reaffirms Limits On Accountants' Liability," *Business Insurance*, April 18, 1988, p. 182.

Pride, William M., and O. C. Ferrell. *Marketing Concepts and Strategies*, Boston: Houghton Mifflin Company, 1988, p. 743.

Tan, Amy. "Legal Liability and Professional Responsibility: A Precarious Balance," *Outlook*, Summer, 1987, pp. 9-16.

"Taxpayers Are Finally Getting Rights in the IRS Rule Book," *Insight*, November 21, 1988, pp. 24-25.

Chapter 24

Practical Approaches
for Evaluating the Quality Dimensions
of Professional Accounting Services

Lexis F. Higgins
Jeffery M. Ferguson

INTRODUCTION

In the last few years marketing has been recognized as an important element in the delivery of professional accounting services (Denney 1983; Mahon 1982; George and Wheiler 1986). Increasingly, providers of accounting services have begun to realize the importance of evaluating the quality of their services and making appropriate adjustments to their marketing programs (Ferguson and Higgins 1989). This renewed focus on service quality is inspired in part by the evidence that service quality correlates with profits and market share (Zeithaml, Berry, and Parasuraman 1988; Sellers 1988). In the highly competitive market for accounting services, understanding how customers perceive service quality is of critical importance. We use service quality dimensions reported by Parasuraman, Zeithaml, and Berry (1985) to describe some practical approaches to evaluating service quality for accounting firms. We also discuss how accountants can make adjustments to their service offering in order to serve more effectively their chosen target markets.

Professionals in the field of accounting are familiar with the

This chapter was first published in *Journal of Professional Services Marketing*, Vol. 7(1) 1991.

concept of auditing as it applies to accounting programs. A similar approach, called the marketing audit, can be used for evaluating marketing programs. A recent article by Crane (1989), discusses the marketing audit as it relates to services marketers. We describe this concept and show how such an audit can help an accounting firm evaluate the quality of its marketing program and begin to create an effective, integrated marketing effort for the organization. This requires the firm to establish a marketing information system for evaluating the quality of its services and marketing efforts, and identifying business opportunities. The firm must also develop methods to constantly monitor selected elements of service quality.

We begin this chapter with a discussion of the marketing audit: how the firm can approach a total evaluation of its firm's marketing effort. With the marketing audit as a framework we then examine the key dimensions of service quality as well as practical approaches for evaluating and measuring these dimensions. The chapter concludes with an examination of the managerial implications of evaluating service quality and completing a marketing audit.

THE MARKETING AUDIT
FOR ACCOUNTING SERVICES

Virtually all accountants are familiar with the concept of an audit. In the accounting field the auditing process can be defined as:

> The process by which a competent, independent person accumulates and evaluates evidence about quantifiable information related to a specific economic entity for the purpose of determining and reporting on the degree of correspondence between the quantifiable information and established criteria. (Arens and Loebbecke 1988)

There are three key components in this definition that are central to the concept of an audit: (1) the audit is performed by a competent and independent person, (2) who accumulates and evaluates information, (3) for the purpose of determining the correspondence between that information and pre-existing evaluation criteria.

The accounting audit is highly related to the concept of a marketing audit. A marketing audit can be defined as:

A comprehensive, systematic, independent, and periodic examination of a company's–or business unit's–marketing environment, objectives, strategies, and activities with a view to determining problem areas and opportunities and recommending a plan of action to improve the company's marketing performance. (Kotler 1988)

As in the case of an accounting audit this definition includes some key concepts. The marketing audit is comprehensive in that it reviews the total marketing effort of the organization including the marketing strategy objectives and all elements of the marketing mix (product/service, price, distribution, promotion). Accountants will be quite familiar with the systematic nature of the audit because most accounting audit procedures also include a specific order of procedures. Accountants are also acquainted with the requirement that the person or group of persons performing the audit must be independent and unbiased and that the audit be performed periodically.

Many organizations often ignore assessment of their marketing effort until serious problems arise. They then react by searching for an independent marketing professional to do the assessment and solve some specific marketing dilemma. Unfortunately, it is often quite expensive to repair the damage done to the organization and recover from marketing setbacks already suffered as a result of this marketing problem (such as loss of market share or image in the marketplace).

While the marketing audit is performed by an independent, external organization, the firm can initially evaluate its operation from an internal perspective by using the dimensions of service quality given in Table 1. Table 1 and the directions we give based on the table are not meant to be a replacement for the marketing audit but can serve as an initial internal step toward an overall evaluation of the organization's marketing program.

Some practical approaches for making this evaluation are discussed below. The marketing audit usually begins with a meeting of the organization that will perform the audit and the firm to be audited. The purpose of this meeting is to draft an agreement on the objectives and time period for the audit (Kotler 1988). Close atten-

TABLE 1. Dimensions of Service Quality

ility

Is the quality of your accounting service consistent across clients, services, and time?

Can your clients have confidence that their taxes/audit will be done correctly the first time?

Responsiveness

Do your employees act promptly in returning calls and setting appointments?

Can your firm meet unique requests from clients?

Does your firm meet promised deadlines for delivery of services?

Competence

Is the knowledge and skill of all personnel that interact with the client appropriate for that interaction?

Is tax research in your firm managed effectively?

Are all employees trained in their particular functions?

Are all employees trained in customer service?

Access

Can clients easily talk to an appropriate person in your firm? (For example, do clients often get a busy signal or are they put on hold when telephoning your office?)

Do your hours of operation and location match the needs of present and potential clients?

Courtesy

Are your clients always treated politely and considerately both on the telephone and in person by all contact personnel?

Has your firm developed the ability to deal with customer problems and concerns?

Communication

Do your tax preparation personnel consider the knowledge level of each customer when writing them or talking to them? (For example, the same statement might seem confusing to one client and condescending to another.)

Do your tax preparation personnel effectively explain the approximate cost of your service and the expected time for completion of tax returns?

Do you provide information to give your clients the maximum service?

How well do you listen to your clients to assess their particular needs/wants?

Credibility

Does your organization make it clear to your clients that the organization exists to effectively meet their needs and your reputation is partially a function of how well this is done?

Does all your market communication instill present and potential clients with confidence in the integrity of your firm?

Do you stand by what you say?

Does your promotional material accurately reflect the services offered?

Security

Does your firm attempt to free each client of risk or doubt in the preparation of his/her taxes? (For example, is there ever any question in the client's mind regarding confidentiality?) Do you actively try to reduce risks perceived by your clients?

Understanding/Knowing the Customer

Do you have a system by which the individual needs of each client are determined?

Do you provide personal, individualized attention to each client or are they made to feel "like a number"?

Do you take the opportunity to recognize your long-time clients or do you ignore them in favor of seeking new clients?

Do you regularly measure your performance in the eyes of your clients?

Do you actively assess each client's needs?

Tangibles

Do your offices and the appearance of your personnel project the image that your firm is seeking?

Are your written communications (letters, brochures, reports, business cards, etc.) projecting a feeling of quality?

Adapted from Parasuraman, Zeithaml, and Berry (1985).

---

tion to Table 1 can be helpful in preparing for this first meeting or for assessing the firm's most pressing areas of marketing need. Table 1 and the methods of evaluating service quality that we describe can be particularly useful for the accounting firm that has recently implemented a marketing program or is attempting to improve its marketing management effort. Because this is an internal evaluation it need not be performed independently. However, it should be evaluated objectively by a designated individual or group within the accounting firm.

Before one can effectively evaluate the marketing program, it is necessary to understand the basic concepts of service quality as well as identify the specific dimensions clients use in assessing the quality of accounting services. The next section reviews these basic concepts.

OVERVIEW OF SERVICE QUALITY

Service quality is the cornerstone of the marketing program, and the most important aspect of service quality is understanding how it is defined in the mind of the firm's clients. Very often professionals feel highly confident in their understanding of what makes a good audit or tax return. Both training and experience suggest that a professional accountant is in an excellent position to assess the quality of his/her own work. Clients, unfortunately do not always share the same perceptions or utilize the same evaluation criteria as the accountant does. The services marketing literature explains why this is the case. There are two facets to a service transaction: process and outcome. *Process* deals with the manner in which the service is performed while *outcome* involves the result of a service. In the case of a tax return, process would include how the client was treated, including courtesy, responsiveness to questions, prompt scheduling, and returning of phone calls, among other things. Outcome, on the other hand, would be the technical quality of the return including accurate completion of forms, taking all allowable deductions, counseling on tax savings steps, and other activities.

Many accountants look at outcome as the most important facet of service quality. There are two main reasons for this view. First, an accountant's training is in the technical areas of delivering the service; and second, the outcome is presumably what the customer is buying.

Unfortunately, the client comes to the service encounter with a different set of perceptions and mind-set. Because of the intangible nature of the service, it is often difficult for the clients to evaluate the technical quality or outcome of the service provided. As a result, other aspects of the service encounter are included in the evaluation process. For most clients determining whether or not they are treated with courtesy, respect, and consideration is an easy task. Consequently, these process dimensions may carry an inordinate amount of weight in the client's calculation of service quality. In fact, studies (Swan and Comb 1979) have shown that customers become dissatisfied with service when technical quality is satisfactory but process is handled poorly. This statement does not suggest that technically accurate accounting is unimportant. To the contrary, *both* the outcome and the process of receiving accounting services are contributors to service quality from the perspective of the client.

For professional accounting firms the message is clear: both service outcome and process must meet clients' expectations if the service is to be evaluated as being of high quality. While attending to both facets of service quality is necessary for delivering quality service to the client, knowledge of the specific dimensions used by clients in service evaluation is also required. The next section outlines these service dimensions and explains specific ways they can be used by accountants.

PRACTICAL APPROACHES TO EVALUATING SERVICE QUALITY

Table 1 illustrates ten service quality dimensions and gives examples of specific applications for accounting firms. The ten dimensions evolved from the research program of Parasuraman, Zeithaml, and Berry (1985) and were developed from a series of focus groups with service customers and in-depth interviews with executives in service firms. Notice that some of the dimensions–reliability, competence, and security–are clearly related to outcome or technical quality facets of the service transaction, while other dimensions–responsiveness, access, and courtesy–are more closely related to process facets of service quality. The remaining dimensions–communication, credibility, knowing the customer, and tangibles–impact both process and outcome. Our objective is not to categorize the dimensions but to suggest that they address both process and outcome facets of service quality.

The example questions in the table demonstrate specific inquiries an accounting firm might want to make concerning the services they offer. Careful consideration must be given to question development since the items which are measured will become the focus of attention and management action. In other words, a firm should measure those things which are most important for their success.

It is virtually impossible to develop a generic checklist which contains all the questions which might be relevant to a given firm. However, these examples will stimulate discussion of what are the most important questions in a given situation.

An example will help demonstrate the use of the table. A CPA firm was seriously concerned about the attention being paid to the process aspects of client interactions. One of the partners expressed particular concern that they had established no written standards or guidelines in the areas of responsiveness. Using the questions in Table 1 as a catalyst, members of the firm brain-stormed various elements of responsiveness that might be important to their clients. From this list they selected (1) time taken to return calls, (2) time taken to schedule appointments, and (3) specific responses to client requests as three areas to target for improvement. At this point they established ways to measure, evaluate, and adjust their approaches for dealing with these issues. For example, clerical personnel were given the assignment to keep a log recording when calls were received from customers and how much time elapsed before the calls were returned (measure for (1)). Members of the staff were asked to keep notes and estimate how much time usually elapsed before their appointments were rescheduled by picking a two-week period for this measure (2). A telephone survey was done with forty clients who were randomly selected from the client list to measure (1), (2), and (3) above. The measures above served several purposes. The firm established a base line performance level, and also learned more about their clients' expectations in these areas. The firm was able to modify its handling of special requests from clients and increase overall client satisfaction.

These activities focused the partners' attention and reaffirmed the whole organization's commitment to being responsive to client needs.

APPROACHES FOR MEASURING SERVICE QUALITY

After selecting the right questions to ask, the accounting services provider needs to develop an appropriate data collection approach. There are several different approaches accounting firms can use for assessing their effectiveness at satisfying the requirements of the various service quality dimensions. This section reviews several approaches for evaluating service delivery performance.

Process and outcome facets of service quality require different measurement approaches. Process dimensions like courtesy, convenience, or caring do not lend themselves well to quantification. Qualitative approaches such as focus groups or informal interviews are more effective for these dimensions. The outcome dimensions, on the other hand, can be assessed nicely through more quantitative approaches like surveys or performance logs.

A firm need not attempt to implement all of these approaches at one time. While it would be valuable to continually obtain measures of all service quality dimensions, it is more feasible to implement measurement approaches on an incremental basis. The idea is for measurement to become an integral part of the company culture. As a result, any changes should be implemented in a manner which can be accepted by the organization.

Performance Logs

Two excellent approaches for assessing outcome quality are performance logs and surveys. Both of these techniques are highly versatile in their applications and well suited for providing quantifiable results. A straightforward, easily implemented approach is to keep a log of the performance of activities necessary for delivering service quality. American Airlines, for example, logs the number of rings before a reservation phone is answered, the number of minutes between touchdown and the opening of the door for deplanement, and the percent of on-time departures and arrivals. An accounting firm might decide that promptly returning clients' phone messages is an effective way to communicate "responsiveness" to their clients. It is a relatively simple task to compute the elapsed time between receipt of the message and when the call is returned. There may even be a report published which tracks the mean time to return a call so that management can take some corrective action in the event of a highly unfavorable variance. Often merely reporting results will favorably alter the behavior of service personnel. The very act of measuring an activity will call attention to it and change the way it is performed.

There are innumerable activities which may be logged such as number of complaints received, number of jobs returned because of mistakes, and time to complete certain tasks. Our purpose is not to list all possibilities, but to encourage firms to find appropriate activities to measure and track–activities which are important to clients and to the success of the firm.

Surveys

Because of their great flexibility and adaptability to a variety of situations, surveys are a commonly used data collection approach. Customer surveys are one of the most valuable assessment devices because they measure the customers' perception of service quality. Customer surveys not only allow you to evaluate any or all of the service quality dimensions, but also communicate to your clients a commitment to service quality.

Another type of survey that can be completed more quickly and less expensively is a survey of service delivery personnel. These front line people may experience hundreds or even thousands of customer interactions. From this broad base of experience they can become well aware of problems clients face when dealing with your firm. While the possibility exists that employees might shade their answers in order to look good, past research (Schneider, Parkington, and Burton 1980) has demonstrated that front-line employees and their customers share similar views of service quality. Branch managers, on the other hand, were unable to accurately identify customer preferences. Service delivery personnel possess a potential wealth of customer information if one makes the effort to tap into it.

An example of the use of both types of surveys is a CPA firm that wanted to assess service quality from the perspectives of both the client and the service delivery personnel. This study asked clients to evaluate the firm on the ten service dimensions listed in Table 1, as well as indicate the service dimensions which were most important to them. These same questions were also asked of the service personnel. As anticipated, the survey results showed close agreement. However, differences in a couple of quality dimensions required a reformulation of the way service was being provided.

In addition, analysis of the data revealed that not all customers had the same service needs and expectations. Indeed, there is the opportunity for categorizing clients into segments based on profitability and service requirements. Specific services programs can then be targeted to each client group. This example shows but one application of client and service provider surveys.

Focus Groups

While surveys allow for the collection of large amounts of information on a variety of topics, they are not as well suited for assessing process dimensions which require probing and deeper thought by the respondent. A common way of getting a more thoughtful, comprehensive evaluation is through focus groups. These sessions allow interaction with a small number of clients (usually eight to twelve) in a conversational setting. The idea is to "focus" the discussion on topics pertinent to the firm while taking advantage of the synergy of ideas generated by the discussion among participants. Subjects are allowed to express their opinions and evaluations in their own words as well as comment on the responses of others.

For example, a firm may want to assess the quality of a new service it has offered to its clients (a personal computer link between the firm and its tax clients). A focus group of recent users of the service examined the advantages and problems involved with using the service, their applications of the service, and ways of making it more valuable and easier to use. Participants were even asked for suggestions on how to promote the new service most effectively to other clients. Research of this kind can provide a wealth of information on how to improve the service offering.

The two main drawbacks to focus groups are the cost and representativeness of the results due to small sample size. The small sample size can be addressed by doing multiple groups or conducting a follow-up survey of a representative sample of clients.

Personal Interviews

Interviews can be conducted either formally or informally. With a little training, service personnel can collect information effectively during the normal course of interacting with clients. This kind of informal feedback can become a regular part of doing business. The main benefits of this approach are that information on service quality is routinely collected, corrective action can be taken on a timely basis, and concern for the satisfaction of the client is actively communicated.

Formal interviews combine many of the strengths of focus groups and mail surveys. Both quantitative and qualitative information can be collected efficiently. Information can be collected on a wide variety of subjects and follow-up questions can be asked to probe for clarification or additional information. The main drawback to formal personal interviews is the expense.

Mystery Shoppers

One of the most effective ways of evaluating service is to experience it from the perspective of clients. The partners in one accounting firm asked business associates to pose as clients and call the accounting office and request some type of service. The business associates recorded how long it took to get a response, and commented on how well they were treated. A partner or manager can also have a friend or family member sample several of the firm's services and report back on the quality of service received. If the firm wants a more objective evaluation of its operation, it can hire a research firm to conduct the mystery shopper study. Many firms have found this to be a very useful way of keeping their service offerings on target with customers' needs and expectations.

MANAGERIAL IMPLICATIONS

Creating and keeping a sustainable competitive advantage is critical for any accounting firm in today's fiercely competitive environment. In order to position its accounting services successfully the firm must know what its customers value. We have pointed out that customers often value *process* dimensions of service quality as much or even more than *outcome* dimensions. The application of the questions in Table 1 can help the accounting services provider establish a better understanding of customers' value judgments for both process and outcome dimensions and improve the areas most important to success. Through this activity, the firm takes a critical step in creating its own sustainable competitive advantage. This practical application of Table 1 can serve as an initial step in the evaluation of the firm's total marketing effort–a marketing audit. Any accounting firm can begin by addressing only a few of the service quality dimensions. It is not necessary or even advisable for most firms to attempt to completely evaluate *all* of the dimensions initially. The partners in the firm may select a few dimensions to evaluate first and apply this experience toward each subsequent evaluation effort as our examples above point out.

After the firm becomes comfortable with monitoring the dimensions of service quality, it may decide to contract to have a marketing audit performed. The marketing audit, as described earlier in this paper, provides an assessment of all of the firm's marketing activities including communications programs (promotion), pricing policies, service "bundling," competitive analysis, and marketing planning to name a few of the areas. Today's environment for accounting service providers is becoming more competitive all the time. As the profession enters the 1990s, expenditure of funds for any purpose must be cost-effective and return increased productivity and profitability. We believe the work necessary to assess the firm's performance on the dimensions of service quality is such a practical resource allocation. This assessment can help the firm better understand its customers, deliver more value to each customer, and create a strong competitive position in the marketplace for accounting services.

REFERENCES

Arens, Alvin A., and James K. Loebbecke (1988), *Auditing: An Integrated Approach*, Fourth Edition, Englewood Cliffs, NJ: Prentice Hall.

Crane, F.G. (1989), "A Practical Guide to Professional Services Marketing," *Journal of Professional Services Marketing*, Vol. 5. No. 1 (Fall/Winter).

Denney, Robert W. (1983), *Marketing Accounting Services*, New York: Van Nostrand Reinhold Company.

Ferguson, Jeffery M., and Lexis F. Higgins (1989), "Effects of Price of Tax Preparation Services and the C.P.A. Credential on the Perception of Service Quality," *Journal of Professional Services Marketing*, Vol. 5, No. 1 (Fall/Winter).

George, William R., and Kent W. Wheiler (1986), "Practice Development–A Services Marketing Perspective," *The CPA Journal*, (October), pp. 30-43.

Kotler, Philip (1988), *Marketing Management: Analysis, Planning, Implementation, and Control*, Sixth Edition, Englewood Cliffs, NJ: Prentice Hall.

Mahon, James J. (1982), *The Marketing of Professional Accounting Services*, Second Edition, New York: Ronald Press/John Wiley & Sons.

Parasuraman, A., Valerie A. Zeithaml, and Leonard L. Berry (1985), "A Conceptual Model of Service Quality and Its Implications for Future Research," *Journal of Marketing*, Vol. 49 (Fall), pp. 41-50.

Schneider, B., J.J. Parkington, and V.M. Burton (1980), "Employee and Customer Perceptions of Service in Banks," *Administrative Science Quarterly*, Vol. 25, pp. 252-267.

Sellers, Patricia (1988), "How to Handle Customers' Gripes," *Fortune*, (October 24), p. 88.

Swan, J.E., and L.J. Comb (1979), "Product Performance and Customer Satisfaction: A New Concept," *Journal of Marketing*, Vol. 40 (April), pp. 25-33.

Zeithaml, Valerie A., Leonard L. Berry, and A. Parasuraman (1988), "Communications and Control Processes in the Delivery of Service Quality," *Journal of Marketing*, Vol. 52 (April), pp. 34-48.

Chapter 25

An Empirical Investigation of the Pricing of Professional Services (As Applied to Public Accounting)

Madhav N. Segal

INTRODUCTION

Services Marketing

During the past few years, there has been an increasing focus on service marketing in the marketing literature. This is partially due to the movement in the United States toward a service economy. Services, defined by the U.S. Department of Commerce as transportation, communication, utilities, retail and wholesale trade, finance, government, law, medicine, education, and entertainment now account for almost 70 percent of the GNP. A particular growth explosion has occurred in the area of information, with information related jobs such as programming and accounting having grown to nearly 50 percent of the U.S. jobs. The rapid pace of technological development has also influenced the number of service jobs, since an increasing number of goods must be co-marketed with an accompanying package of services.

A review of the literature on service marketing provides some insight into unique problems faced by services and identifies some strategies that can be used to solve these problems. In an attempt to determine how the theories on service marketing relate to practices and perceptions of service professionals, Zeithaml, Parasuraman,

This chapter was first published in *Journal of Professional Services Marketing*, Vol. 7(1) 1991.

and Berry (1985) reviewed the literature and identified a series of commonly stated marketing problems and a group of strategies generally thought to be effective in resolving them. Members of a group of service firms generally felt that, with the exception of a concern over the fluctuation in demand for services, the problems indicated were not significant. The marketing strategies specified were widely used, however, and there was considerable variety within the service sector. Specific differences in approach were noted between local and non-local firms and between firms serving chiefly institutional customers and those serving individual clients. Since the service segment is so diverse, it is quite likely that marketing approaches to professional services within the service sector deserve special attention. The legal sanctions, intense competition, and a declining public image are key developments which are pushing numerous professional service firms into the marketing arena (Bloom 1984).

Professional Service Marketing and Pricing Issues

Professionals are facing increased marketing challenges as they now have both an increasing need and increasing ability to market their services. Bloom (1984) has outlined specific marketing strategies for use by professionals in developing a marketing orientation for their firms. Perhaps, pricing of professional services offer the greatest challenge to marketers in this arena.

Pricing of professional services has been studied both from the aspect of the person providing the service (Arnould and Friedland 1981) and that of the consumer of the service (Miller 1982), but this area has not been adequately researched. Because of the differences within service firms, it was suggested that future studies should focus on one particular service area (Zeithaml, Parasuraman, and Berry 1985). Therefore, this study focuses on pricing issues in the context of public accounting firms.

The fees for public accounting services, as well as other professional services, are undergoing constant scrutiny by clients and customers. Recent studies highlight the importance of public accounting fees and indicate that these fees are extremely influential in the selection of a firm by a client (Larkin and Sherwood 1981, George and Solomon 1980, Wood and Ball 1978).

Public accounting fees are based on a time and expense accrual system. That is, fees are based upon the number of hours worked, plus out-of-pocket expenses (Paneth, Haber, and Zimmerman 1984). Billing rates vary according to the person performing the service and the amount of chargeable time reported for that service. Further, some CPA firms avoid the hourly billing method by charging a fee based on the complexity of the service, a practice known as value-based billing (Becker 1984).

Even in situations where hourly rate is the common unit of billing, pricing approaches to set the hourly rate vary greatly. While there is agreement that rates should be set to cover direct salaries and overheads (Bremen 1984, Myers 1981), methods for determination of profit margins differ. The most common factor used in setting the final price is likely to be the prices charged by competitors, as determined from word-of-mouth, and the income tax returns of new clients (Bremen 1984). In addition, the method of fee assessment is undergoing a transitory phase within the public accounting profession with the increased use of commissions and contingency fees (Becker 1984).

PURPOSE OF THE STUDY

Given these problems and inconsistencies, it is not surprising that the pricing of public accounting services is relatively subjective and nonstandardized. Most research investigation in this area has taken a qualitative and descriptive approach. The extent of any quantitative research has been limited to an analysis of the hourly billing structure based on salaries and other operating expenses of the firm. This chapter proposes a quantitative multivariate approach to the pricing of public accounting services. The study attempts to investigate the relationship between accounting fees and some client-related factors along with the complexity of services rendered.

RESEARCH METHODOLOGY

Sample

Data on a sample of 103 individual tax clients were collected from a certified public accounting firm located in a large metropolitan area of the midwestern region of the country.

Individuals served by the firm who were owners, partners, or employees of a business were excluded from the study in order to ensure that only individual tax work charges were accrued on the client's account receivable. Data were collected from each client's yearly federal income tax return and pertained to the following variables included in the analysis.

Dependent Variable

The dependent variable (Y) chosen was the yearly billing and was the amount billed to the client for his yearly professional accounting work. This fee was for the preparation of the tax return and any other accounting work done during the taxable year, such as the revision of estimates, research, and planning.

Independent Variables

As discussed earlier, it was hypothesized that the fee charged is positively correlated with two sets of factors—relating to client income and those relating to the complexity of the service required. The following independent variables were chosen with this hypothesis in mind:

a. *Number of indexes* (X_1). This number is analogous to the number of computations performed in preparing client tax returns. Bremen (1984) suggests that the bulk of a client billing will be the result of charges for time and service through the time management system which is computerized in the firm.

b. *Rents, Royalties, Partnerships, Estates, and Trusts Income* (X_2). These are additions to the total income from passive sources.

c. *Exemptions* (X_3). These constitute the total number of exemptions claimed by the client.

d. *Interest and Dividend Income* (X_4). This is the sum of interest and dividend income reported, which in turn affects the total income.

e. *Capital Gains Income* (X_5). This is the amount of capital gain/loss reported for the year.

f. *Total Tax* (X_6). This figure represents the tax liability assessed to the individual, net of most normal credits.

g. *Number of Pages* (X_7). This is the length of the client's federal tax return including Form 1040 and any attached schedules. This variable was chosen to reflect the possible complexity of service.

h. *Adjustments to Income* (X_8). The total adjustments to gross income is a factor involved in both the income and complexity issues.

i. *Total Income* (X_9). The total yearly income was chosen as the leading indicator of the income factors, with the others (numbers 4, 5, and 6) that serve as individual components.

A summary of these variables and their mean values is presented in Table 1.

RESULTS AND DISCUSSION

A linear regression model was hypothesized with yearly billing as the dependent variable. The initial results of the regression analysis and related data are displayed in Table 2.

The table shows that the final equation contains nine predictor variables and, taken as a group, these variables explain 68 percent of the variance in the billing fees (64 percent when adjusted for degrees of freedom). The F-ratio for the analysis of variance is 21.74, significant at the 0.00 level. The three-factor solution preserved 80.9 percent of the variance in the original data matrix and, therefore, was considered an acceptable outcome. The use of varimax rotation improved the interpretation of these factors.

Table 3 shows the varimax rotated solution.

It is possible to provide the following interpretation of the three factors by considering the variables with largest factor loadings. The factors are labelled and interpreted as follows:

- *Factor 1–The Complexity Factor.* Variables which loaded highly on factor 1 were X_2 (rents, royalties, and other income), X_6 (total tax), and X_8 (adjustments to income). It was felt that this factor reflected the depth of involvement which was required in client affairs and was a fair measure of complexity.

- *Factor 2–The Income Factor.* Three variables directly related to income loaded highly on factor 2. They were X_4 (interest and dividend income), X_5 (capital gains income), and X_9 (total income).
- *Factor 3–The Physical Labor Factor.* This final factor had high loadings for X_1 (number of computer indexes), X_3 (number of exemptions claimed), and X_7 (number of pages). It was felt to be representative of another aspect of the complexity issue, that of actual physical work done.

A new linear regression model is hypothesized with yearly billings as the dependent and three identified factors as the independent variables. The regression analysis results and related data are displayed in Table 4.

Taken as a group, the three independent variables (factors) jointly explain 68 percent of the fee variation (66 percent when adjusted for degrees of freedom). The F-ratio for the analysis of variance is 66.37, significant at the 0.00 level. An examination of regression

TABLE 1.Variables Used in the Study

SYMBOL	VARIABLE NAME	MEAN VALUE*
Y	Yearly Billing	$ 319.54
X_1	Number of Computer Indexes	60.95
X_2	Rents, Royalties, and Other Income	$ 5,796.22
X_3	Number of Exemptions Claimed	2.82
X_4	Interest and Dividend Income	$18,533.92
X_5	Capital Gains Income	$ 4,087.73
X_6	Total Tax	$10,236.30
X_7	Number of Pages on 1040 Form	11.04
X_8	Adjustments to Income	$ 1,355.12
X_9	Total income	$47,720.91

*Because of client confidentiality, all financial figures have been rescaled by a constant discount factor.

TABLE 2. Initial Regression Results

$R^2 = 0.68$	F = 21.74 (Sig < .00)			
$Ra^2 = 0.64$	Dependent Variable = Yearly Billing (Y)			

INDEPENDENT VARIABLES	B	β	Sig
X_1	1.81	0.24	0.05
X_2	0.0015	0.20	0.03
X_3	13.82	0.09	0.20
X_4	0.0002	0.03	0.74
X_5	0.0016	0.10	0.27
X_6	0.0028	0.18	0.49
X_7	8.00	0.22	0.50
X_8	0.23	0.003	0.98
X_9	0.69	0.13	0.64
(constant)	−0.96		

coefficients shows labor-related factor 3 to be the most important indicator in setting the client fee. This finding is consistent with the two commonly used methods of fee determination reported in the literature (Bremen 1984). Table 4 also indicates the complexity factor (factor 1) is the next most important variable influencing the dependent variable and is followed by the income factor (factor 2). All three independent variables are statistically significant ($p < 0.00$). These results clearly indicate that labor, complexity involved in providing accounting services, and the client's income exert the greatest influence on the pricing of accounting services. Since these dimensions are so broad, a final regression analysis was performed to provide specificity to the empirical investigation. The factor analysis also identified three variables (one from each factor) which load the highest and, therefore, can be used as "representative" independent variables. They are: X_7 (no. of pages), X_8 (adjustments to income),

TABLE 3. Varimax Rotated Factor Matrix

VARIABLE	FACTOR 1	FACTOR 2	FACTOR 3	COMMUNALITIES
X_1	0.07844	0.39317	**0.83888**	0.86445
X_7	0.23129	0.11916	**0.84146**	0.77575
X_3	0.00222	0.06676	**0.43822**	0.19650
X_4	-0.09532	**0.73606**	0.17612	0.58189
X_5	-0.07877	**0.78541**	0.14603	0.54440
X_9	0.62141	**0.67930**	0.31414	0.94628
X_2	**0.77273**	-0.09077	0.00637	0.60540
X_8	**0.95801**	-0.06071	0.13494	0.93968
X_6	**0.66375**	0.66001	0.24647	0.93693
% of Variance	58.7	27.0	14.3	
Cumulative Variance	58.7	85.7	100.0	
Eigen Value	3.80	1.75	0.92	

TABLE 4. Final Regression Results

$R^2 = 0.68$	F = 66.37 (Sig < 0.00)		
$Ra^2 = 0.66$	Dependent Variable = Yearly Billing (Y)		

INDEPENDENT VARIABLES	B	β	Sig
F_1	78.54	0.39	0.00
F_2	74.75	0.36	0.00
F_3	121.78	0.58	0.00
(constant)	319.53		

and X_5 (capital gains income). The final regression results and related data are displayed in Table 5.

Overall, these independent variables collectively explain 59 percent of the variation in the accounting fees charged (58 percent when adjusted for degrees of freedom). The F-ratio for the analysis of variance is 47.03, significant at the 0.00 level. The independent variables in order of importance are: X_7, X_8, and X_5. This again reinforces an earlier observation by Bremen (1984) who suggested that the majority of client billing is a function of charges for time and services provided. All three independent variables are positively correlated with the fees charged and are statistically significant.

IMPLICATIONS AND CONCLUSIONS

The pricing of professional services in general, and public accounting services in particular, is a relatively complex, ambiguous, and subjective undertaking. With an increased emphasis on services marketing, the managerial importance of research in this area cannot be overstressed. This research examined the viability of a quantitative multivariate approach to the pricing of accounting services. The results indicate that a number of factors influence the fees charged to clients. Even though causality cannot be demon-

TABLE 5. Regression Results–Final Analysis

$R_2 = 0.59$	$F = 47.03$
$Ra_2 = 0.58$	Sig 0.00
Dependent Variable = Yearly Billing (Y)	

INDEPENDENT VARIABLES	B	β	Sig
X7	17.13	0.46	0.00
X8	0.0057	0.34	0.00
X5	0.02	0.33	0.00
(constant)	79.25	—	—

strated, certain inferences can be made and the quantification of certain relationships is now possible. The overall results demonstrate that client income and complexity of services provided exert a great influence in the determination of client fees and charges. Depending on the nature of competition, the management may elect to improve profitability by raising fees or minimizing costs associated with labor and with the number of services performed. Any managerial efforts toward simplifying the complexity associated with the services rendered and computerization/automation of services provided should help in improving profit margins. From a marketing perspective, as Bloom (1984) suggested, marketing research undertaken to understand client problems and needs should help in making services more effective and efficient.

Though the assumptions that public accounting fees are related to both client income and complexity of client services are supported in this investigation, caution should be exercised in generalizing the findings to other public accounting firms, to different geographical areas, or to different years. In addition, in view of the differences found for service marketing between institution and individual customers (Zeithaml, Parasuraman, and Berry 1985), a similar research investigation involving different business clients could be helpful to the practitioner. As an alternative approach, Brown and Swartz's

(1989) model for evaluating professional services can also be used to assess gaps between client expectations and experiences pertaining to prices charged. Furthermore, any pricing approach must also incorporate competitive factors and demand-related variables. Since the fluctuations in demand for services is a major area of concern, an expanded study attempting to integrate some demand variables into the model would provide improvement to our approach. These suggested improvements are anticipated to help develop and better market professional accounting services for a market which is expected to grow increasingly more competitive in the 1990s (Berton 1989).

REFERENCES

"A Glut of Lawyers–Impact on U.S." *U.S. News and World Report*, December 19, 1983, p. 61.

Arnould, Richard and Thomas Friedland (1981). "The Effect of Fee Schedules on the Legal Services Industry," *The Journal of Human Resources*, pp. 82-89.

Becker, C. (1984). "CPAs Weigh the Ethics of Billing Like Brokers," *Business Week*, (November 12), pp. 146-148.

Berton, Lee (1989). "Accountants Struggle as Marketers," *The Wall Street Journal*, (July 10), pp. 81-82.

Bloom, Paul N. (1984). "Effective Marketing for Professional Services," *Harvard Business Review*, (September-October), pp. 102-110.

Bremen, Sidney (1984). "Determining Fees: How Much Should You Bill?" *Practical Accountant*, (April), pp. 56-66.

Brown, Stephen W., and Teresa A. Swartz (1989). "A Gap Analysis of Professional Service Quality," *Journal of Marketing*, Volume 53, (April), pp. 92-98.

Cottle, D.W. (1984). "Use Staff Input when Billing," *Journal of Accountancy*, Volume 157, (March), pp. 112-113.

Eder, Bernard (1985). "Fee Increases: When, How Much, and How?" *Practical Accountant*, (February), pp. 54-58.

George, W.R., and P.J. Solomon (1980). "Marketing Strategies for Improving Practice Development," *Journal of Accountancy*, Volume 149, (February), pp. 79-84.

Goldfarb v. Virginia State Bar (1974). 95 S. Ct. 2004, *Trade Cases* (1975), 60, 355.

Heinemann, H. Erich (1985). "Why Not Have a Service Economy?" *Dun's Business Month*, (April), pp. 64-68.

Larkin, J.J., and M.B. Sherwood (1981). "Strategic Marketing of Public Accounting Services," *CPA Journal*, Volume 51, (September), pp. 46-51.

Lightner, S.M., J.J. Leisenring, and A.J. Winters (1983). "Underreporting Chargeable Time," *Journal of Accountancy*, Volume 155, (January), pp. 52-57.

Lore, M.M., and L. Goldfein (1982). "Accountants' Fees for Tax Work Disclosed by Survey," *Journal of Taxation*, Volume 57, (July), p. 55.

Miller, Girard (1982). "Providing Public-Sector Financial Information," *Governmental Finance*, (June), pp. 27-35.

Myers, Tony. (1981). "How Does a Practitioner Set and Collect a Fair Fee?" *Accountancy*, Volume 92, (September), pp. 136-138.

Paneth, Haber, and Zimmerman (1984). "Controlling Accounting Fees," *CPA Journal*, Volume 54, (April), pp. 78-79.

Sammons, Donna (1982). "Accounting for Growth," *Inc*, (January), p. 75.

Shaked, Avner, and John Sutton (1981). "Heterogeneous Consumers and Product Differentiation in a Market for Professional Services," *European Economic Review*, Volume 15, pp. 159-177.

Simunic, Dan A. (1980). "The Pricing of Audit Services: Theory and Evidence," *Journal of Accountancy Research*, (Spring), pp. 161-190.

Werner, Ray O. (1982). "Marketing and the United States Supreme Court, 1975-1981," *Journal of Marketing*, (Spring), pp. 73-81.

Wood, T.D., and D.A. Ball (1978). "New Rule 502 and Effective Advertising by CPAs," *Journal of Accountancy*, Volume 145, (June), pp. 65-70.

Zeithaml, Valarie A., A. Parasuraman, and L. Berry (1985). "Problems and Strategies in Service Marketing," *Journal of Marketing*, (Spring), pp. 33-46.

Chapter 26

Persuasion Timing and Content in Public Accounting Practice

Eric Panitz
Mohamed E. Bayou

INTRODUCTION

Marketing of professional accounting services has only recently been allowed by the professional organization (AICPA) to include all aspects of the promotional mix (Ostlund, 1978). Promotion consists of four elements: advertising, publicity (including public relations), sales promotion, and personal selling. Each of the component parts of promotion consists of sets of activities involving persuasion. Persuasion involves convincing a service recipient that specific service activities are necessary to the recipient's well-being. Sucessful persuasion also benefits the service provider, usually financially (Bayou and Panitz, 1991).

PURPOSE OF THIS STUDY

This chapter presents results of a study examining when accountants use persuasion. The importance of using persuasion relative to various types of competition is reported. Client retention and increased use of services by current clients is generally regarded as more cost effective and profitable than new client acquisition. Thus

This chapter was first published in *Journal of Professional Services Marketing*, Vol. 10(1) 1993.

data determining when CPAs feel the use of persuasion is important during the client acquisition, service delivery, and retention processes were collected. Further, the importance of selected promotion activities by CPAs in the marketing of their firm are examined.

PRIOR RESEARCH

Advertising of CPA services has been examined by viewing its economic impact (Novin and Motameni, 1990) and content (Hite, Schultz and Weaver, 1988). Pincus and Pincus (1988) examined accountants' impressions of public relations and its impact upon their firm. Recently Bayou and Panitz (1991) reported that CPAs (primarily in audit or tax practice) used six kinds of content tools when implementing persuasion to expand their revenue-generating practice activities. These were identified as: tax regulations, accounting authority and standards, presentation characteristics, novelty of accounting information, the accountants and firms providing the services, and qualitative characteristics of accounting information.

Persuasion Described

Persuasion has been described as an interactive process that attempts to satisfy the needs of both the persuader and the persuadee (Jowett and O'Donnell, 1986, p.13). Persuasion may be viewed as a two-component activity. The first element is the *process* of persuasion, which includes the modes of expression and the effort, creativity, or special talents used by the CPA engaging in persuasion. The quality with which this process is implemented often determines the sucessful outcome of the persuasion act.

The second element is the *content* of persuasion. Content of persuasion includes the words used in this communication act, the information pieces, reports, and in the case of CPAs, financial statements, authoritative support (tax regulations or SEC requirements), and the qualitative content characteristics of the information developed. Further, the promotion (advertising, personal selling, sales promotion, and publicity) activities implemented by the firm are content components of persuasion.

METHODOLOGY

A mail survey was sent to a national sample of 1,187 members of the AICPA with a repeat mailing to increase the response rate. A total of 287 useable responses were received for a response rate of 24.3 percent.

Respondents were asked to rate the importance of using persuasion relative to various types of competitors and when using persuasion was important in the obtaining/retaining of clients and in performance of accounting services. Respondents were also asked to rank the importance of selected types of information which might be presented in advertising. They were asked to rate selected publicity activities' importance to the growth of the firm. Demographic data consisting of age, experience, education, gender, area of specialization, and title were also requested.

Each respondent rated each variable examined on a scale of 1 to 5 (1 = very important to 5 = very unimportant). Ten advertising content issues were presented for respondents to rank from most (1) to least (10) important. The "other" category did not reveal any interesting information and is omitted from further consideration.

Each set of variables was subjected to factor analysis with varimax rotation to determine any common underlying elements. Eigenvalues of 1.0 and the scree test were used to determine numbers of factors present in each variable set. A factor loading of 0.5 was used as the cutoff with a maximum of 0.05 difference required to claim multiple loadings for purposes of interpretation. In addition, mean rating or ranking values for each question are presented.

RESULTS

Using persuasion was regarded as most important by respondents when faced with increased competition from other CPA firms (Table 1). Competition from the legal and financial planning professions was not regarded as important as that from other CPA firms. All three professions fit into a single factor which we call "competition."

Further, persuasion was rated more important by respondents

when approaching potential clients and progressively less important in other aspects of the service provision cycle (Table 2). Persuasion was not regarded as important in client retention as it was in gaining new clients.

The two factors identified as associated with the accounting process suggest that accountants view persuasion as most important

TABLE 1. CPA's evaluation of persuasion importance in comparison to various competitors.

Competitor	rating	Factor 1
when competition from other CPA firms increases	1.878 +− .768	.67
when competition from Lawyers increases	3.010 +−1.013	.89
when competition from Financial Planners increases	2.738+−1.166	.88
Variance accounted for (percentage)		100

TABLE 2. CPA's rating of persuasion importance in the stages of service provision.

Service provision stage	Rating	Factor 1	2
when approaching a potential client	1.699 +− .790		.81
before providing services to a client	2.108 +− .863		.77
during performance of accounting services	2.293 +− .952	.87	
after the services are performed	2.294 +−1.066	.81	
keeping a current client	2.028 +− .763	.66	
variance accounted for (percentage)		43.3	2.1

during and after the provision of service and for client retention and somewhat less important before and when approaching a potential client (Table 2). This apparent anomaly may be resolved when one realizes that CPAs may often be the bearer of bad news (especially in conducting tax and audit activities) so client retention (and the associated revenues) may take on a high priority. Alternatively, the difference between the factor rankings and the mean question ratings may reflect the intensity of the persuasion effort required to obtain a new client at one point in time as much greater than the continuing effort to retain a client during and after provision of service.

Examination of items that should comprise the contents of the firms' advertising resulted in the firms' talents and expertise and services offered as most highly ranked, followed by additional services offered (management consulting) and location (Table 3). While recommendations by other clients and third-party referrals have been indicated as major factors influencing client's CPA firm selection (Day, Denton, and Hickmer, 1988; George and Solomon, 1980), the use of case histories (including endorsements), which may be regarded as the advertising equivalent of word-of-mouth, was not highly ranked. Among the publicity activities, social contacts, presenting seminars and speeches, and civic contacts were

TABLE 3. Mean rankings of content elements that CPAs feel should be presented in advertising.

talents/expertise	1.986	1.442
services offered	2.318	1.479
non-accounting services (business consulting)	3.552	1.859
location	4.703	2.405
accountants' names	5.091	2.874
firm size	5.227	2.196
service fees	5.787	2.681
case histories	7.085	2.929
college degrees	7.996	3.075

highly rated as mechanisms for marketing the firm. Yet public relations itself was not highly rated (Table 4).

Demographic data indicated that most of the respondents were in their forties with approximately ten to 20 years experience. Primary business emphasis was on Auditing and Taxation. Most indicated post-graduate education and 286 of the respondents were CPAs (Table 5).

DISCUSSION

The demographics presented above suggest that the responses should be interpreted in terms of auditing and tax practice. Apparently while CPAs claim increased competition from financial planners and lawyers, they view them as a different form of competition than other CPA firms. Further, persuasion is thought to be more important while services are being provided and after the provision of services. Presumably many of these respondents act to increase the demand for their services and to retain existing clients while service is being provided. Since the tax needs and auditing needs of many of the clients are similar and could be provided by any CPA firm, and most of the respondents were engaged in tax and audit work, this may explain the importance placed on other CPA firms as significant competitors and the importance of client retention. These respondents felt that persuasion was different in the activity of approaching potential clients or before service is provided than while services are performed. It is well understood by most mar-

TABLE 4. CPA's evaluations of public relations and related activities in improving accountant's persuasion effectiveness.

social contacts	2.024	1.108
seminars	2.123	1.159
speeches	2.188	1.214
civic contacts	2.297	1.164
public relations	3.371	1.142
direct mail	3.567	1.201

TABLE 5. Demographic pattern of CPA respondents.

Age Distribution*		Education level*	
<29	1	some college	4
30-39	7	Baccalaureate	162
40-44	174	Master's	51
45-49	86	Doctorate	58
50-59	24	Other	11
60-69	12		
>70	7		
Gender*		**Number with CPA certificate***	
Female	11	Yes	285
Male	272	No	1
No response	3		
Area of Specialization*		**Title***	
auditing	71	senior accountant	4
taxation	117	manager	10
management		partner	214
advisory	35	other	58
management			
accounting	18		
administration	20		
other	25		
Years of experience*			
<10	7		
10-14	11		
15-20	167		
21-25	71		
26-30	18		
>30	12		

*figures indicate numbers of respondents in category

keters that a significant part of any salesperson's job is to retain existing customers as well as develop and expand the client base in both numbers and use of a variety of the firm's services. Consistent with studies of salesperson activity (Dixon, 1962), CPAs view customer retention as important as customer acquisition. The greater overt importance attached to the function of obtaining new clients may reflect the intensity of effort required at one point in time while the retention activity is less intense but a continuing and more important effort as reflected by the factor analysis.

While most accountants would not consider themselves salespersons, most of these CPAs recognize that persuasion is important in the retention of existing clients and gaining new clients, as the mean ratings generally fell in the "important" and "very important" categories. Surprisingly, expanding clients' use of other services offered by the CPA firm (beyond tax and audit services) such as management consulting was not regarded as important as the accounting services despite their higher profitability (Scherschek, 1982). With the recognized importance of personal selling of complex services, it is surprising that CPAs do not recognize the importance of persuasion in cross-selling other (non-accounting) services to existing clients. Non-accounting services might be provided by accounting firms to their clients by careful use of subcontract specialists. Further, the benefit of other activities which may give a client a competitive advantage without the added expense of permanent employees might be very welcome in a time when competition is expanding to global dimensions and increasing in intensity (Festervand, Vitell, and Reidenbach, 1988).

REFERENCES

Bayou, M., and E. Panitz "Persuasion: Definitional Issues and Content Analysis In Accounting," Paper presented at the *Thirty-Second Atlantic Economic Conference*, Washington D.C., October 5, 1991.

Day, Ellen, L.L. Denton, and J.A. Hickmer "Clients Selection and Retention Criteria: Some Implications for the Small C.P.A. Firm," *Journal of Professional Services Marketing* 3(3/4):283-295, 1988.

Dixon, William R. "Redetermining the Size of the Salesforce: A Case Study" in *Changing Perspectives in Marketing Management* ed. Martin R. Warshaw (Ann Arbor: University of Michigan, Michigan Business Reports 1962) no. 37, p. 58.

Festervand, T.A., S.J. Vitell, and R.E. Reidenbach "Strategic Marketing Planning for the Development of the Small Accounting Practice," *Journal of Professional Services Marketing* 3(3/4):59-69, 1988.

George, W. R., and Paul J. Solomon "Marketing Strategies for Improving Practice Development," *The Journal of Accounting* Vol 149(2):79-84, 1980.

Hite, Robert E., N. O. Schultz, and Judith A. Weaver "A Content Analysis of CPA Advertising in National Print Media from 1979 to 1984," *Journal of the Academy of Marketing Sciences* 16(3/4):1-15, 1988.

Jowett, G. S., and V. O'Donnell, *Propaganda and Persuasion,* Newbury Park, CA, U.S.A., Sage Publications, 1986.

Novin, Adel M., and R. Motameni "Advertising and Direct Solicitation By CPA Firms: A Survey," Paper presented at *Western Decision Sciences Institute,* Meeting 1990.

Ostlund, A. C. "Advertising–In The Public Interest?" *Journal of Accountancy* 145(January):59-63, 1978.

Pincus, J. David, and Karen V. Pincus "Public Relations in Accounting: A Benchmark Study," *Public Relations Review* 14:39-52, 1988.

Scherschek, P.M. "The Powerful Unseen Hand of the Accountant," *U.S. News and World Report* (April 19):50-52, 1982.

Chapter 27

Marketing Financial Planning Services: Highlights of a Survey of CPAs

Ralph A. Pope

The deregulation of financial markets and institutions, long-run inflation, the introduction of new financial instruments, and a continuously changing tax code have ushered in a new era of financial planning for individuals and businesses. The increase in demand for financial planning services has brought about an increase in the supply of practitioners. Banks, insurance companies, brokerage houses, and independent financial planners have all entered this market.

Since comprehensive financial planning includes several areas of expertise (tax planning, estate planning, retirement planning, insurance and investment planning), it has been suggested that CPA firms are a natural participant in this market, already possessing training in several key areas. The American Institute of Certified Public Accountants (AICPA) and several state CPA societies have been encouraging CPAs to enter the financial planning market by offering programs of study in financial planning.

The purpose of this chapter is to present the findings of a study examining the participation of CPA firms in the emerging financial planning market and investigate the reasons why CPAs are in this market. The chapter also queries CPAs with respect to their financial planning training and discusses the perception CPAs have with respect to the competitiveness and quality of others in the market.

The study was conducted by sending a questionnaire to 500 CPA

This chapter was first published in *Journal of Professional Services Marketing*, Vol. 3(3/4) 1988.

firms that were listed in the *1985 Accounting Firms and Practitioners Directory* published by the AICPA. This publication lists practitioners, accounting firms, and professional corporations whose partners or shareholders are members of the AICPA. The data presented are based on the 174 usable responses that were returned.

PENETRATING THE FINANCIAL PLANNING MARKET

Almost all CPA firms are engaged in some aspect of financial planning. This is shown in Table 1. Forty-three percent of the firms are engaged in comprehensive financial planning with the purpose of coordinating and guiding the individual's financial planning. Fully 64 percent stated that they were involved with investment planning, while 80 percent are engaged in estate planning. Only 44 percent of the respondents stated that they were engaged in risk and insurance management for their clients.

For all the fanfare given to personal financial planning in the last few years, and considering the fact that most CPA firms are engaged in some aspect of financial planning, CPA firms do not appear to have entered the market enthusiastically. CPA firms have increased the percentage of total billings derived from providing financial planning services, but these gains appear to be modest.

Table 2 shows that in 1980, 62 percent of the respondents derived

TABLE 1. Percent of CPA Firms Engaged in Each Activity

ACTIVITY	PERCENT OF FIRMS
Income Tax Planning	99%
Investment Planning	64
Estate Planning	80
Risk/Insurance Management	44
Retirement Planning	72
Financial Needs Planning (e.g., education planning)	66
Comprehensive Financial Planning	43

from 1 to 10 percent of billable hours from providing financial planning services. In 1986, this had increased to 69 percent. In 1980, 11 percent of the firms reported deriving over 10 percent of billings from financial planning services. By 1986, this had increased modestly to 13 percent of the firms.

Eighty-three percent of the financial planning clients of CPA firms are individuals who pay their own fees for the services provided. This is indicated in Table 3. Fourteen percent of clients are company executives. The fees for this group of clients are paid by the executive's company as a perquisite.

WHY CPAs MARKET FINANCIAL PLANNING SERVICES

CPA firms offer financial planning services for a variety of reasons. Although all the reasons in Table 4 were deemed to contain some measure of importance, the most important reason why firms provide financial planning services is to meet the needs and demands of existing clients. The reason that was ranked second is to

TABLE 2. Percent of Firms Deriving Billable Hours from Financial Planning Services Other than Tax Planning

PERCENT OF BILLABLE HOURS DERIVED FROM FINANCIAL PLANNING SERVICES	PERCENT OF FIRMS 1980	1986
0%	27%	18%
1-5%	41	42
6-10%	21	27
>10%	11	13

TABLE 3. Financial Planning Clients

TYPE OF CLIENT	PERCENT
Individuals	83%
Company Executive	14
Other	3

compete for new clients. Firms providing comprehensive financial planning, as well as those that are not engaged in comprehensive financial planning, rank these two reasons in the same order.

Although financial planning has become popular in the press in recent years, providing financial planning services is not the most lucrative service that can be offered by CPAs. Table 4 shows that the reason "it is a lucrative market" was rated fourth out of four reasons by all firms in the survey, and third out of the four reasons by firms providing comprehensive financial planning.

This is corroborated in Table 5. When CPAs were asked to rank the marginal profitability to the firm of an expansion in tax, managerial advisory and accounting services, personal financial planning services, and auditing, the marketing of personal financial planning services ranked third. Firms providing comprehensive financial planning services also ranked these services third out of the four broad areas listed.

CPAs were also queried as to why they did not engage in specific personal financial planning activities. Each reason was evaluated on a basis of one to five (1 = very important reason to not engage; 2 = important reason not to engage; 3 = neither important nor unimportant reason; 4 = unimportant reason; 5 = very unimportant reason). Table 6 illustrates the results.

CPAs feel that a lack of expertise is the biggest obstacle to engaging in financial planning activities. The results also suggest that CPAs find all of the traditional financial planning areas to be more or less appropriate activities for CPA involvement. The area with the least support among CPAs is investment management. However this is also the activity where respondents indicated the greatest lack of expertise.

FORMAL FINANCIAL PLANNING TRAINING OF CPAs

As financial planning has become more important in society, formal programs of training and preparation have been introduced at several universities across the country. These degree programs and areas of specialization have supplemented the two existing home study programs that have been in existence for several years.

Furthermore, the AICPA as well as state CPA societies have developed courses in order for practicing CPAs to have the opportunity to gain expertise in financial planning.

Respondents were asked to indicate if members of their firm engaging in financial planning activities had formal financial planning training in the following areas: courses offered by the AICPA; programs offered by a state society; courses offered by a university; a degree in financial planning; a financial planning certificate.

TABLE 4. Reasons for Providing Financial Planning Services

	All Firms	Firms providing comprehensive financial planning	Firms not providing comprehensive financial planning
Financial Planning services are in great demand by clients	1.88	1.80	2.06
To compete for new clients	2.32	2.17	2.48
Would lose clients to competition if services were not provided	2.56	2.50	2.58
It is a lucrative market	2.57	2.37	2.73

(1=very important reason; 2=important reason; 3=neither important nor unimportant reason; 4=unimportant reason; 5=very unimportant reason).

TABLE 5. Profitability of Activities

	Rank	All Firms	Firms providing comprehensive financial planning	Firms not providing comprehensive financial planning
Tax	1	1.65	1.40	1.88
MAS and General Accounting Services	2	2.28	2.34	2.24
Personal Financial Planning Services	3	2.45	2.45	2.45
Auditing	4	3.13	3.17	3.10

(1=highest additional profitability; 4=lowest additional profitability)

The most prevalent financial planning training for members of CPA firms involved courses offered by the AICPA with 56 percent of the respondents indicating that at least one member of the firm had undertaken such courses. This is shown in Table 7. Programs offered by state CPA societies are the second most important method of financial planning preparation for CPAs. Forty-eight percent of the respondents indicated that at least one professional engaged in financial planning activity had undertaken such a program.

Respondents indicated that a degree in financial planning and

TABLE 6. Reasons Why CPAs Do Not Engage in Financial Planning Activities

	Investment Management	Estates Management	Risk Management	Retirement Planning	Compre-hensive Financial Planning
Lack of client interest	2.90	2.69	2.37	2.50	2.45
Firms too small or practitioners do not have time	2.45	2.25	2.41	2.60	2.51
Lack of expertise	1.61	1.75	1.69	2.24	2.00
Not an appropriate activity of a CPA	2.71	4.38	3.05	3.85	3.27

TABLE 7. Percent of Firms Engaged in Financial Planning Activities with Professionals that Have Undertaken Financial Planning Training

Financial Planning Preparation	Percent of Firms with Professionals that Have Undertaken Activities
Course offered by AICPA	56%
Programs offered by state society	48%
Courses offered by a university	19%
A degree in Financial Planning	5%
Percent of firms with one or more CPAs holding the CFP or ChFC*	10%

*Only three responses indicated that more than one member had earned a certificate. In each case, certificates were held by two members.

formal financial planning certificates are the least popular methods of financial planning preparation for CPAs. Only 5 percent of the firms indicated that a member had a degree in financial planning. Ten percent of the respondents indicated that one or more members had obtained a financial planning certificate.

COMPETITION AND QUALITY OF SERVICE

The 1980s have become the decade of deregulation, with federal legislation permitting an environment of increased competition in the financial services market. Traditional financial institutions that have previously been limited by law as to the services they could provide are now able to market a variety of services. Along with deregulation of the financial services market has come an emerging financial planning sector. These developments have resulted in enhanced competition in the financial planning market.

The survey queried CPA firms as to which provider of financial planning services was the most competitive and aggressive with respect to attracting the existing clients of CPA firms in providing financial planning services. A scale of 1 to 5 was used with a one indicating the highest level of aggressive behavior and a five representing the least competitive behavior. Table 8 indicates that CPAs view the insurance industry as being the most aggressive element in the financial planning industry. Following insurance agents companies in order of ranking are stockbrokers, independent financial planners, and banks. CPAs view CPA firms as being the least competitive element in the financial planning market.

Although insurance agents and companies are viewed by CPAs as being the most aggressive in trying to attract the clients of CPAs, they are also ranked last in terms of providing quality service. The weighted average of the insurance sector is 3.22. This is followed by banks, independent financial planners, and stockbrokers, all with weighted averages of about three. As expected, CPAs perceive themselves as providing the highest quality service with a weighted average of 1.41.

TABLE 8. Views of CPAs with Respect to Competitive Behavior and Quality of Service

Sector	Competitive Behavior Rank	Wgt. Avg.	Quality of Service Rank	Wgt. Avg.
Insurance Agents and Companies	1	(1.66)	5	(3.22)
Stock Brokers	2	(2.00)	3	(3.07)
Independent Financial Planners	3	(2.48)	2	(3.04)
Banks	4	(3.25)	4	(3.09)
CPA Firms	5	(3.47)	1	(1.41)

CONCLUSION

Although the great majority of CPA firms derive 10 percent or less of revenue from financial planning, the percent of total billings attributable to providing financial planning services has increased over the first half of this decade.

It appears that CPA firms are offering financial planning services in order to satisfy a growing demand by clients. Furthermore, financial planning is also being used as a marketing tool whereby CPAs can attract new clients. The data also presents some evidence that suggests that there is a fear of losing existing clients if financial planning services were not offered. Regardless of the reason, CPA firms have exhibited some deviation from their traditional product mix.

Satisfying this demand has not, as of yet, been as profitable as the tax area and management advisory services. However, financial planning does appear to be more lucrative than auditing.

If demand for these services continues to increase, scale economies and increased efficiencies could possibly increase the profitability of supplying these services. Given the liability associated with auditing public corporations, perhaps financial planning will replace this activity for some of the CPA firms providing this service.

Index

Page numbers in italics indicate figures; page numbers followed by t indicate tables.

DATE DUE			